No Matter How I Look at It, It's You Guys' Fault I'm Not Popular

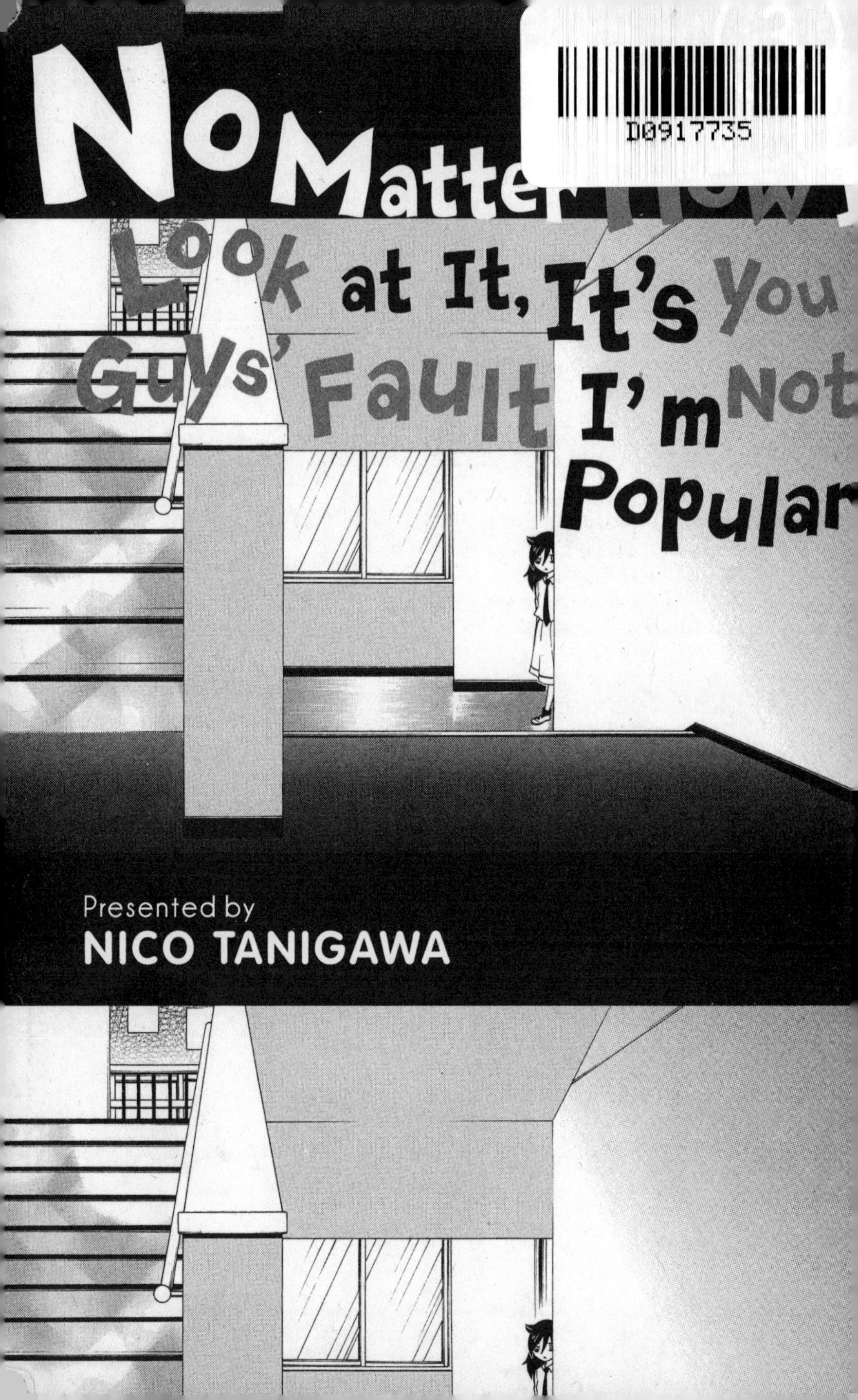

Presented by

NICO TANIGAWA

FAIL 19 I'M NOT POPULAR, SO ▸ *SECOND TERM IS STARTING.* 003

FAIL 20 I'M NOT POPULAR, SO ▸ *I'LL MAKE PREPARATIONS.* 019

FAIL 21 I'M NOT POPULAR, SO ▸ *I'LL BE IN THE CULTURE FEST.* 036

FAIL 22 I'M NOT POPULAR, SO ▸ *I'LL GET MY PICTURE TAKEN.* 055

FAIL 23 I'M NOT POPULAR, SO ▸ *THE WEATHER'S LOUSY.* 067

FAIL 24 I'M NOT POPULAR, SO ▸ *I'LL GET GROPED.* 081

FAIL 25 I'M NOT POPULAR, SO ▸ *I'LL NURSE THE SICK.* 097

FAIL 26 I'M NOT POPULAR, SO ▸ *I'LL START MY OWN CLUB.* 113

FAIL 27 I'M NOT POPULAR, SO ▸ *I'LL HAVE A NICE DREAM.* 129

...AWW, IF I'D BEEN A WORM, I WOULD'VE HAD A MAN FROM THE GET-GO AND DEFINITELY HAVE HAD S●X, NOT TO MENTION KIDS...

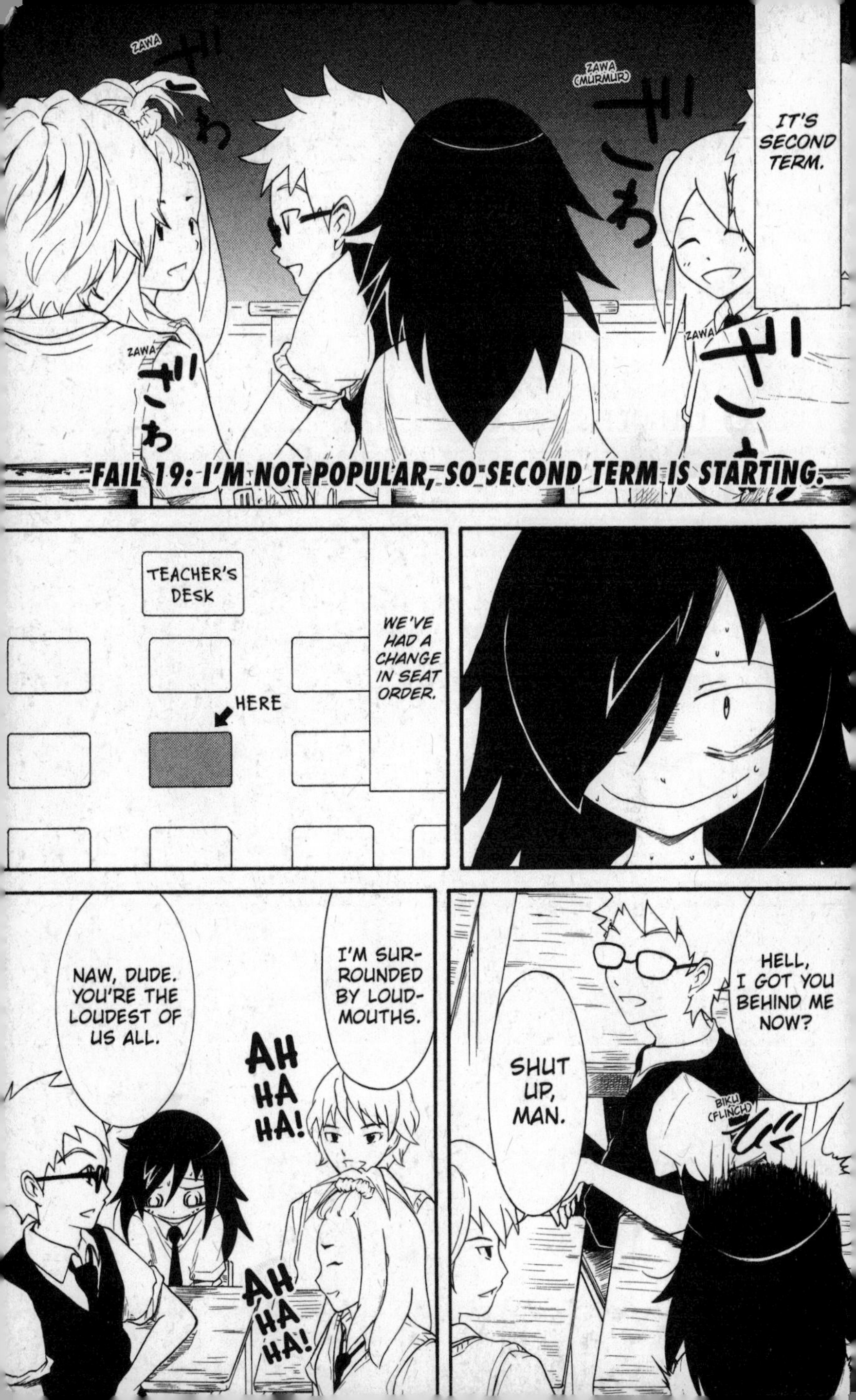
IT'S SECOND TERM.
ZAWA (MURMUR)
ZAWA
ZAWA
ZAWA
FAIL 19: I'M NOT POPULAR, SO SECOND TERM IS STARTING.
WE'VE HAD A CHANGE IN SEAT ORDER.
TEACHER'S DESK
HERE
HELL, I GOT YOU BEHIND ME NOW?
SHUT UP, MAN.
BIKU (FLINCH)
I'M SURROUNDED BY LOUDMOUTHS.
NAW, DUDE. YOU'RE THE LOUDEST OF US ALL.
AH HA HA!
AH HA HA!

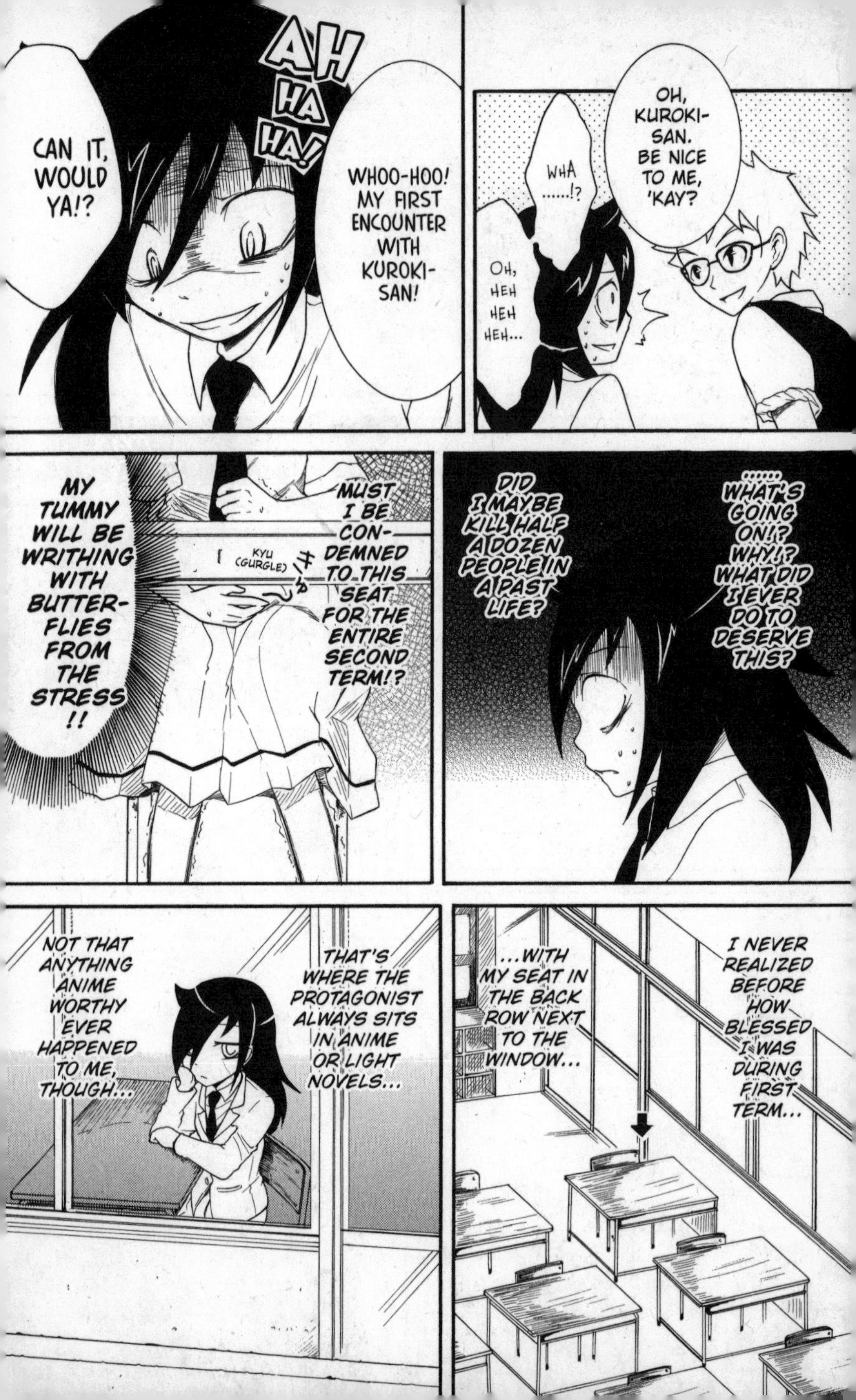
OH, KUROKI-SAN. BE NICE TO ME, 'KAY?
WHA ......!?
OH, HEH HEH HEH...
WHOO-HOO! MY FIRST ENCOUNTER WITH KUROKI-SAN!
AH HA HA!
CAN IT, WOULD YA!?
......WHAT'S GOING ON!? WHY!? WHAT DID I EVER DO TO DESERVE THIS?
DID I MAYBE KILL HALF A DOZEN PEOPLE IN A PAST LIFE?
MUST I BE CON-DEMNED TO THIS SEAT FOR THE ENTIRE SECOND TERM!?
KYU (GURGLE)
MY TUMMY WILL BE WRITHING WITH BUTTER-FLIES FROM THE STRESS !!
I NEVER REALIZED BEFORE HOW BLESSED I WAS DURING FIRST TERM...
...WITH MY SEAT IN THE BACK ROW NEXT TO THE WINDOW...
THAT'S WHERE THE PROTAGONIST ALWAYS SITS IN ANIME OR LIGHT NOVELS...
NOT THAT ANYTHING ANIME WORTHY EVER HAPPENED TO ME, THOUGH...

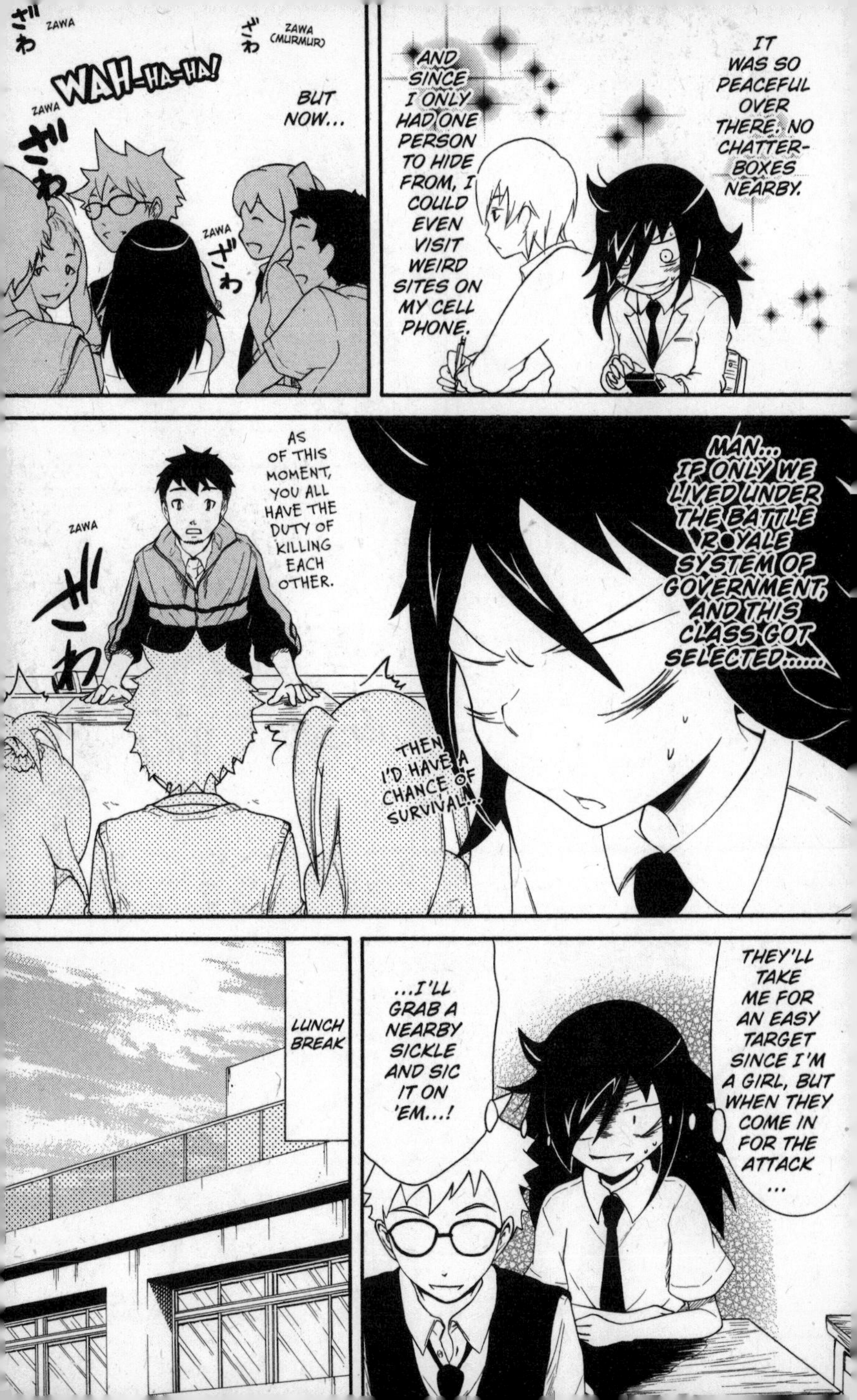
IT WAS SO PEACEFUL OVER THERE. NO CHATTER-BOXES NEARBY.
AND SINCE I ONLY HAD ONE PERSON TO HIDE FROM, I COULD EVEN VISIT WEIRD SITES ON MY CELL PHONE.
ざわ ZAWA (MURMUR)
ざわ ZAWA
BUT NOW...
WAH-HA-HA!
ZAWA ざわ
ZAWA ざわ
MAN... IF ONLY WE LIVED UNDER THE BATTLE ROYALE SYSTEM OF GOVERNMENT, AND THIS CLASS GOT SELECTED......
AS OF THIS MOMENT, YOU ALL HAVE THE DUTY OF KILLING EACH OTHER.
ZAWA ざわ
THEN I'D HAVE A CHANCE OF SURVIVAL...
THEY'LL TAKE ME FOR AN EASY TARGET SINCE I'M A GIRL, BUT WHEN THEY COME IN FOR THE ATTACK...
...I'LL GRAB A NEARBY SICKLE AND SIC IT ON 'EM...!
LUNCH BREAK

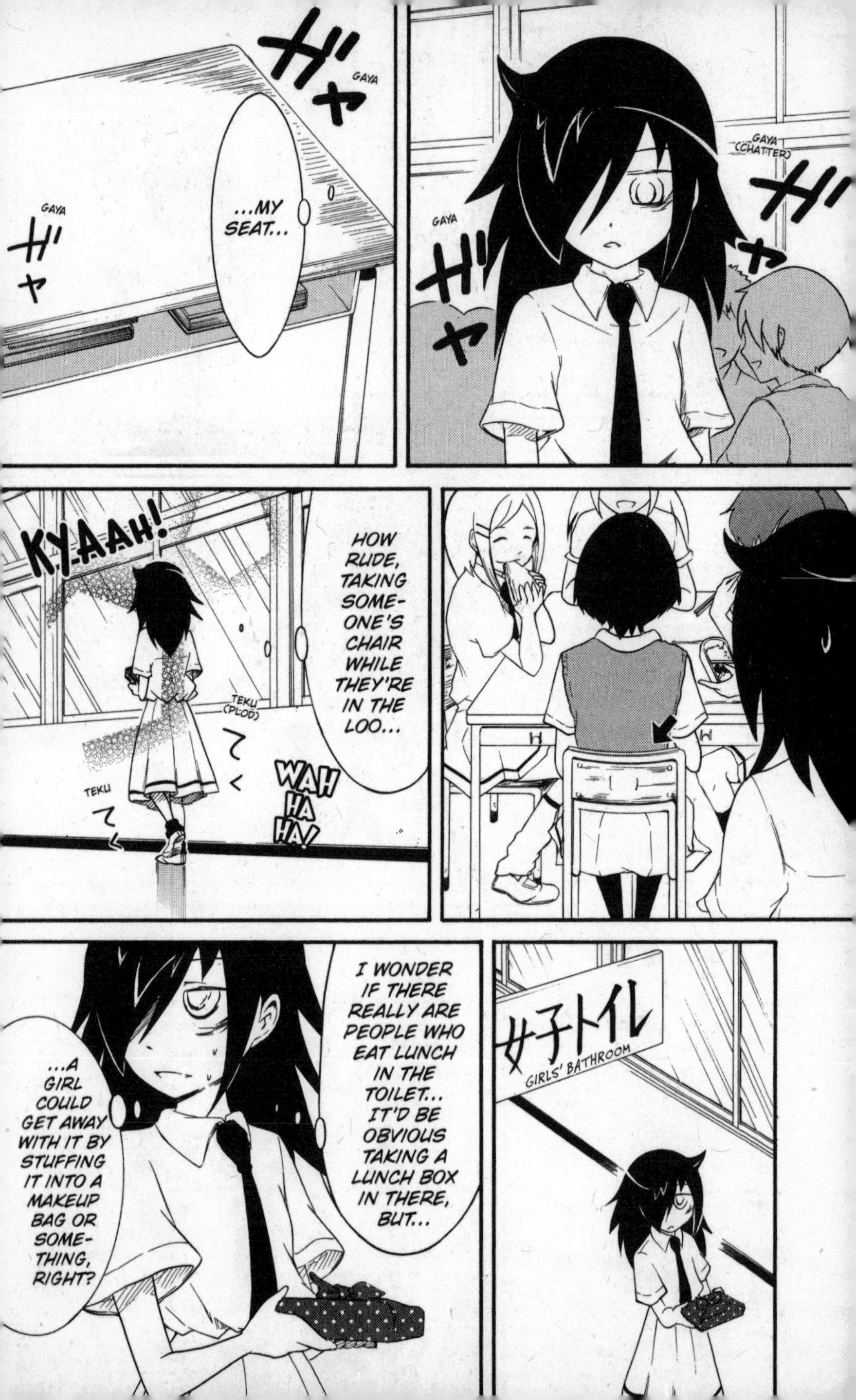
GAYA (CHATTER)
ガヤ
GAYA
ガヤ
...MY SEAT...
GAYA
ガヤ
GAYA
ガヤ
HOW RUDE, TAKING SOMEONE'S CHAIR WHILE THEY'RE IN THE LOO...
KYAAAH!
WAH HA HA!
TEKU (PLOD)
てく
TEKU
てく
女子トイレ
GIRLS' BATHROOM
I WONDER IF THERE REALLY ARE PEOPLE WHO EAT LUNCH IN THE TOILET... IT'D BE OBVIOUS TAKING A LUNCH BOX IN THERE, BUT...
...A GIRL COULD GET AWAY WITH IT BY STUFFING IT INTO A MAKEUP BAG OR SOMETHING, RIGHT?

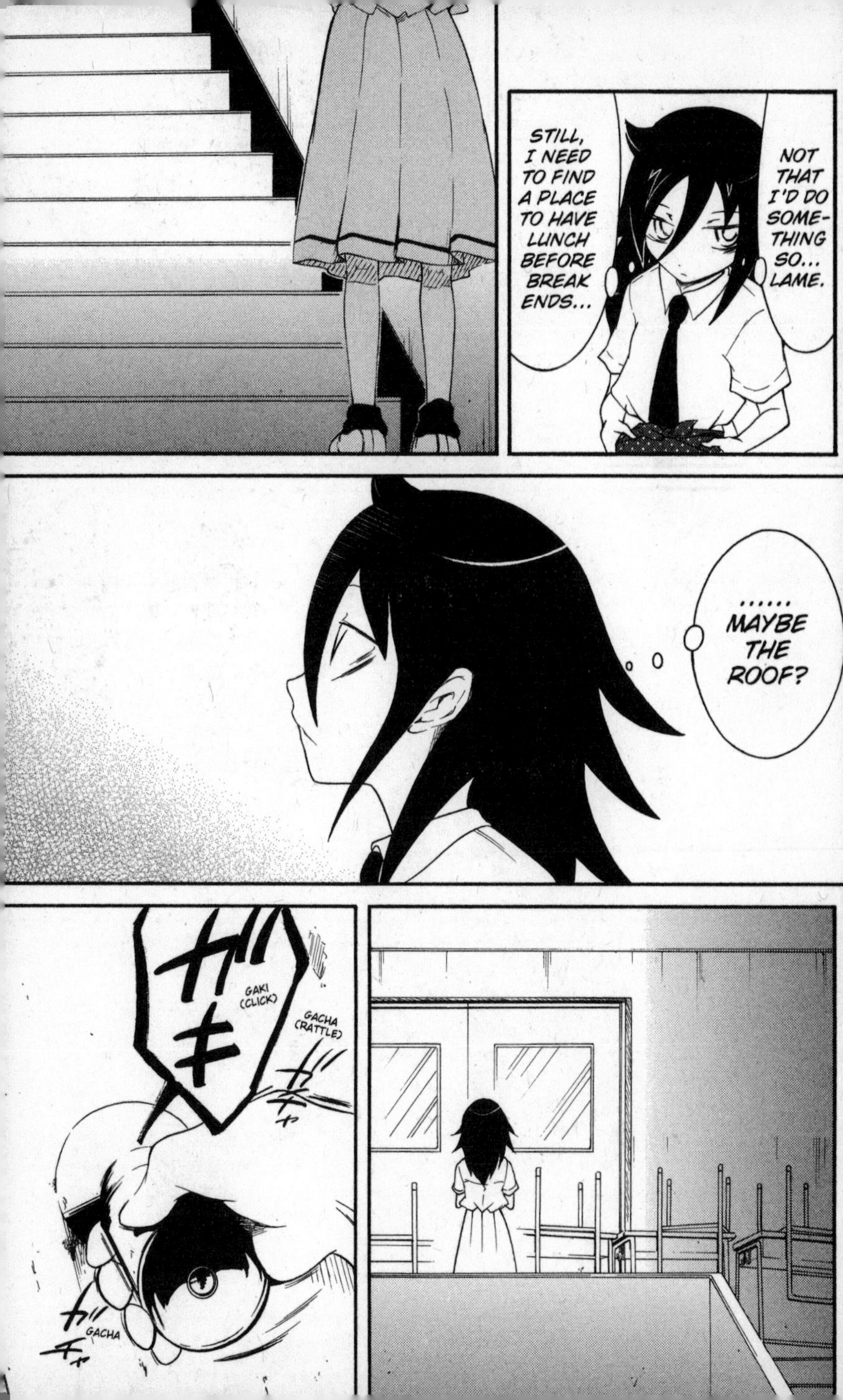
NOT THAT I'D DO SOME-THING SO... LAME.
STILL, I NEED TO FIND A PLACE TO HAVE LUNCH BEFORE BREAK ENDS...
...... MAYBE THE ROOF?
GAKI (CLICK)
GACHA (RATTLE)
GACHA

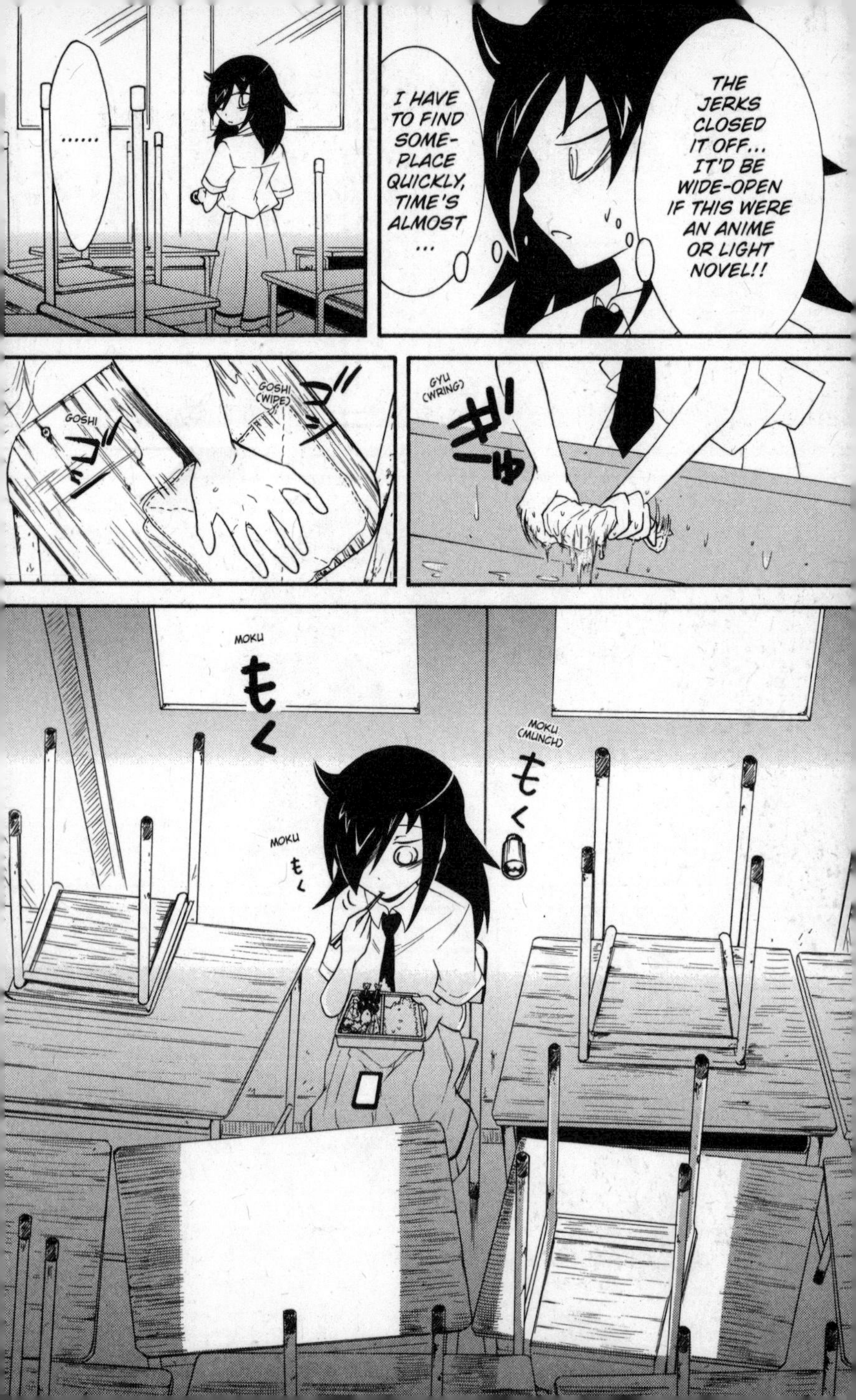
THE JERKS CLOSED IT OFF... IT'D BE WIDE-OPEN IF THIS WERE AN ANIME OR LIGHT NOVEL!!
I HAVE TO FIND SOME-PLACE QUICKLY, TIME'S ALMOST ...
......
GYU (WRING)
ぎゅ
GOSHI (WIPE)
ゴシ
GOSHI
ゴシ
MOKU
もく
MOKU (MUNCH)
もく
MOKU
もく

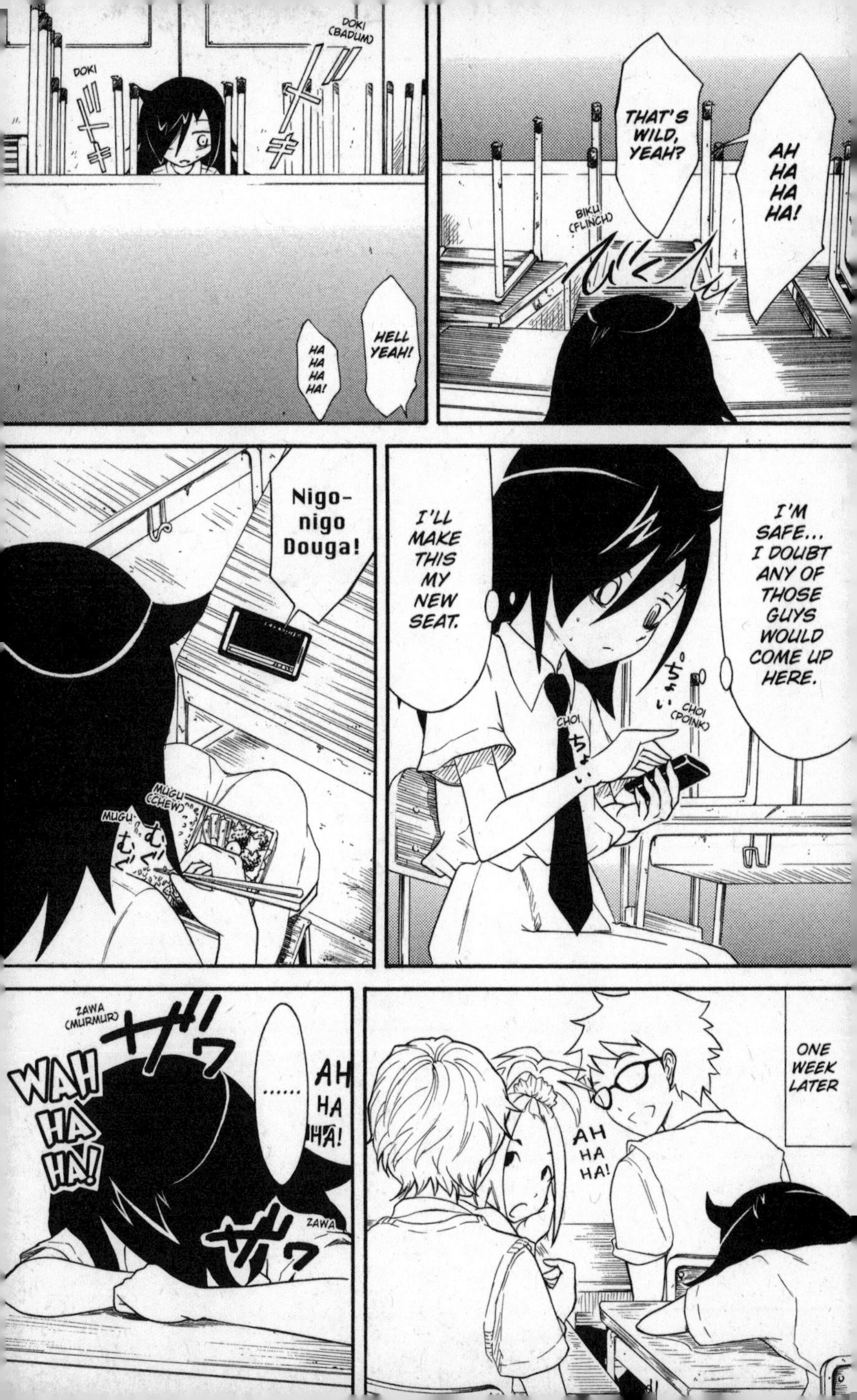
AH HA HA HA!
THAT'S WILD, YEAH?
BIKU (FLINCH)
DOKI (BADUM)
DOKI
HELL YEAH!
HA HA HA HA!
I'M SAFE... I DOUBT ANY OF THOSE GUYS WOULD COME UP HERE.
I'LL MAKE THIS MY NEW SEAT.
CHOI (POINK)
CHOI
Nigo-nigo Douga!
MUGU (CHEW)
MUGU
ONE WEEK LATER
AH HA HA!
AH HA HA!
......
ZAWA (MURMUR)
WAH HA HA HA!
ZAWA

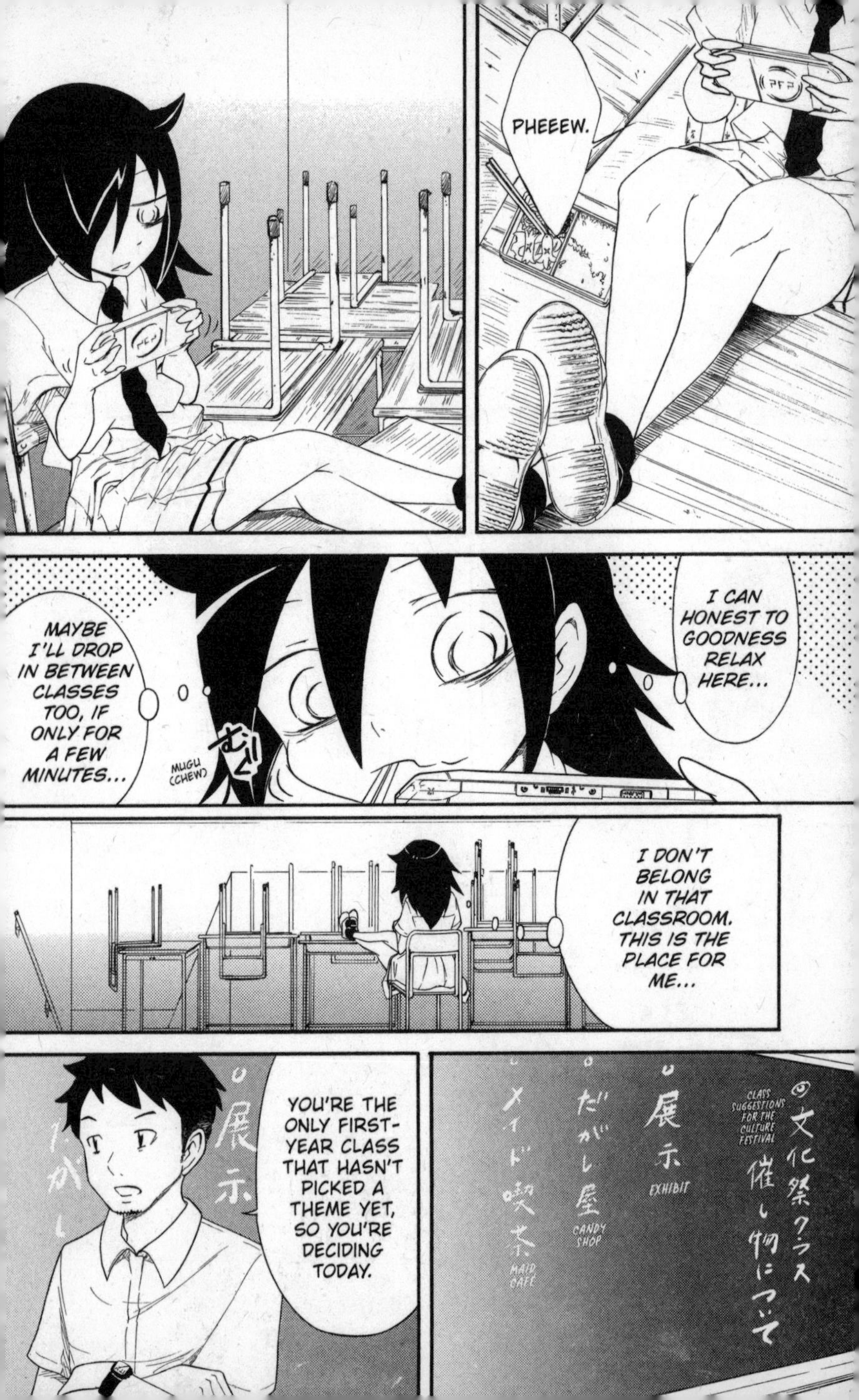
PHEEEW.
I CAN HONEST TO GOODNESS RELAX HERE...
MAYBE I'LL DROP IN BETWEEN CLASSES TOO, IF ONLY FOR A FEW MINUTES...
むぐ
MUGU (CHEW)
I DON'T BELONG IN THAT CLASSROOM. THIS IS THE PLACE FOR ME...
文化祭クラス催し物について
CLASS SUGGESTIONS FOR THE CULTURE FESTIVAL
展示
EXHIBIT
だがし屋
CANDY SHOP
メイド喫茶
MAID CAFE
YOU'RE THE ONLY FIRST-YEAR CLASS THAT HASN'T PICKED A THEME YET, SO YOU'RE DECIDING TODAY.

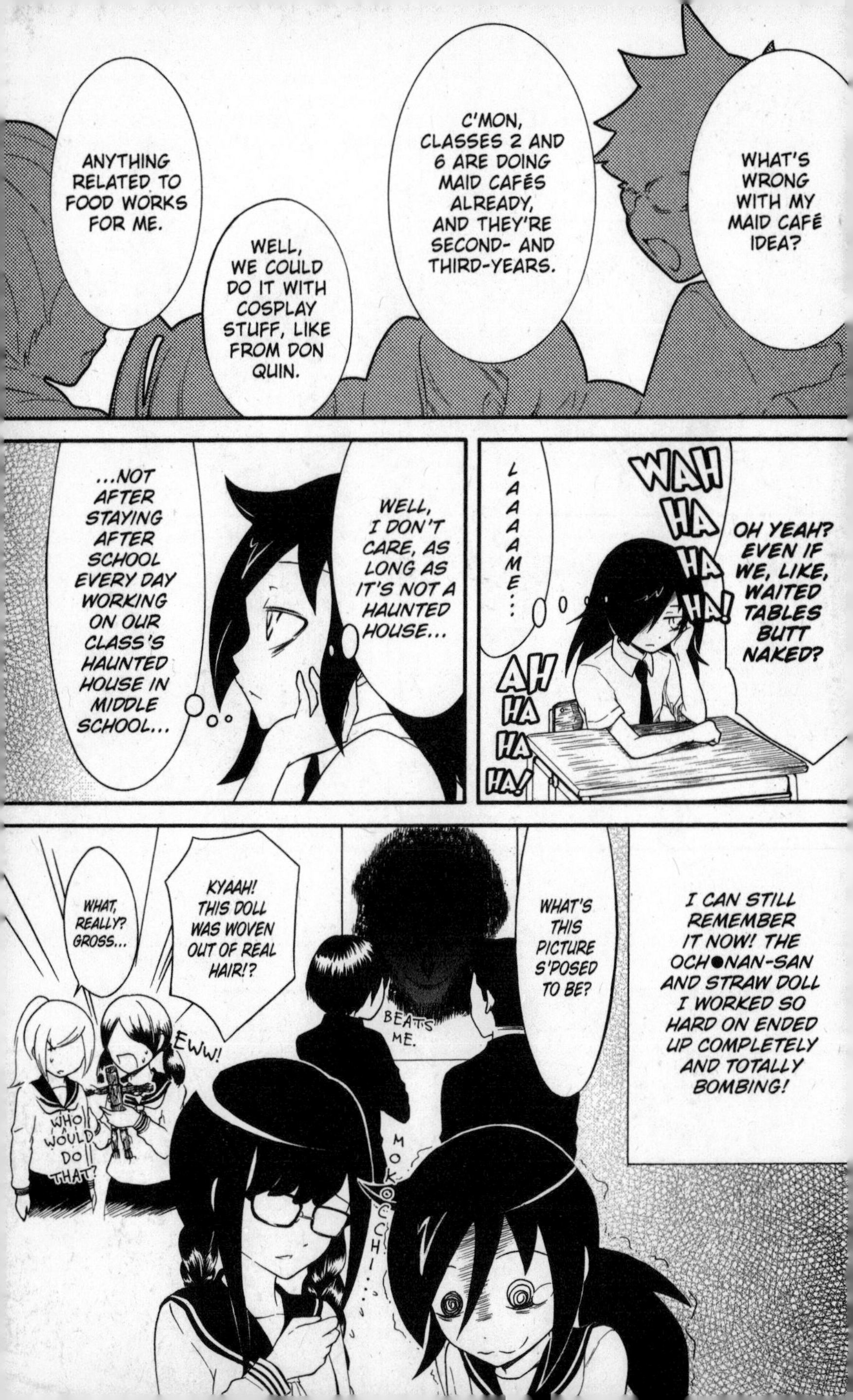
WHAT'S WRONG WITH MY MAID CAFÉ IDEA?
C'MON, CLASSES 2 AND 6 ARE DOING MAID CAFÉS ALREADY, AND THEY'RE SECOND- AND THIRD-YEARS.
WELL, WE COULD DO IT WITH COSPLAY STUFF, LIKE FROM DON QUIN.
ANYTHING RELATED TO FOOD WORKS FOR ME.
WAH HA HA HA!
OH YEAH? EVEN IF WE, LIKE, WAITED TABLES BUTT NAKED?
AH HA HA HA!
LAAAAAME...
WELL, I DON'T CARE, AS LONG AS IT'S NOT A HAUNTED HOUSE...
...NOT AFTER STAYING AFTER SCHOOL EVERY DAY WORKING ON OUR CLASS'S HAUNTED HOUSE IN MIDDLE SCHOOL...
I CAN STILL REMEMBER IT NOW! THE OCH●NAN-SAN AND STRAW DOLL I WORKED SO HARD ON ENDED UP COMPLETELY AND TOTALLY BOMBING!
WHAT'S THIS PICTURE S'POSED TO BE?
BEATS ME.
KYAAH! THIS DOLL WAS WOVEN OUT OF REAL HAIR!?
WHAT, REALLY? GROSS...
EWW!
WHO WOULD DO THAT?
MOKOCCHI...

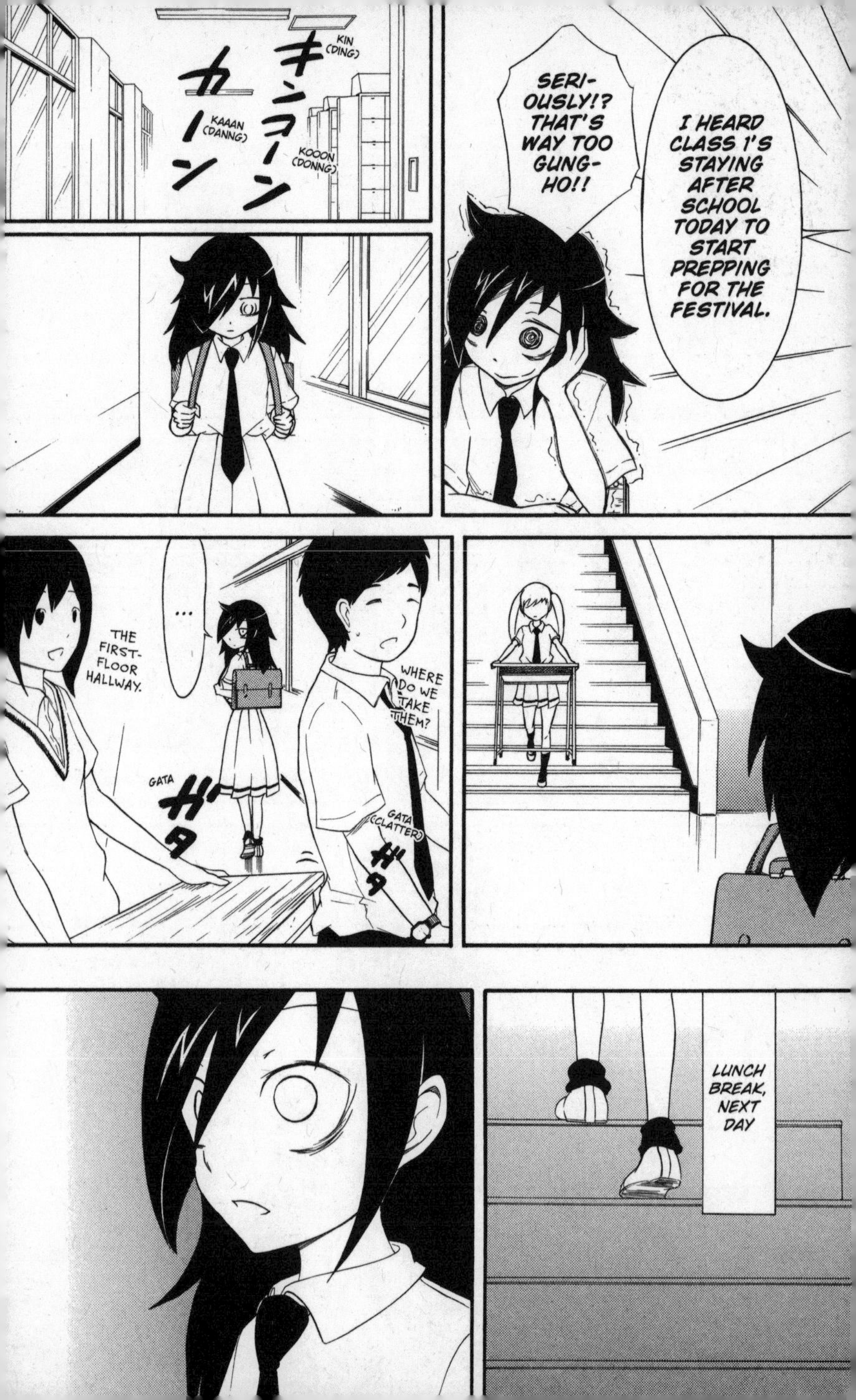
I HEARD CLASS 1'S STAYING AFTER SCHOOL TODAY TO START PREPPING FOR THE FESTIVAL.
SERI-OUSLY!? THAT'S WAY TOO GUNG-HO!!
KIN (DING)
KOOON (DONNG)
KAAAN (DANNG)
WHERE DO WE TAKE THEM?
...
THE FIRST-FLOOR HALLWAY.
GATA (CLATTER)
GATA
LUNCH BREAK, NEXT DAY

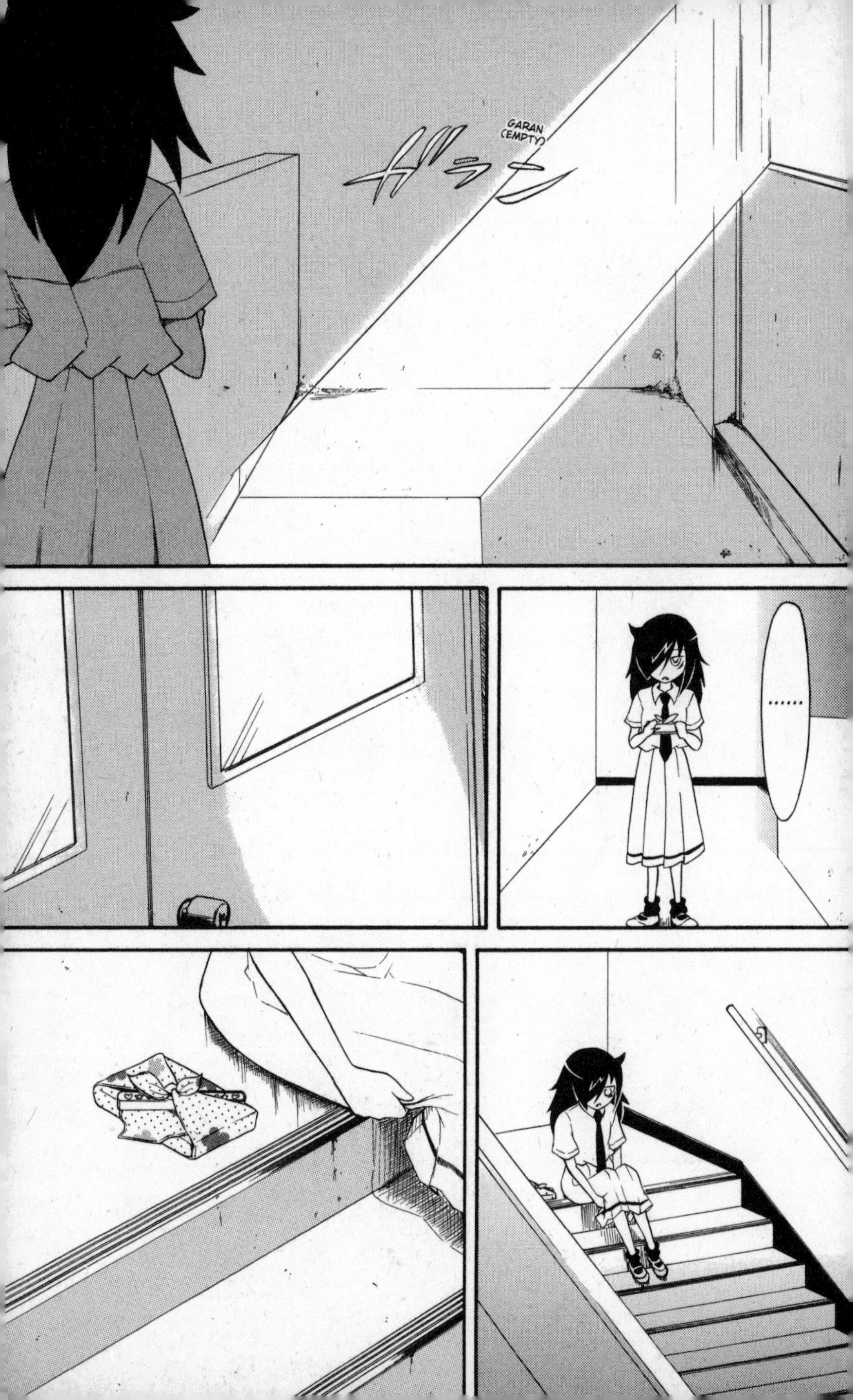
GARAN (EMPTY)
……

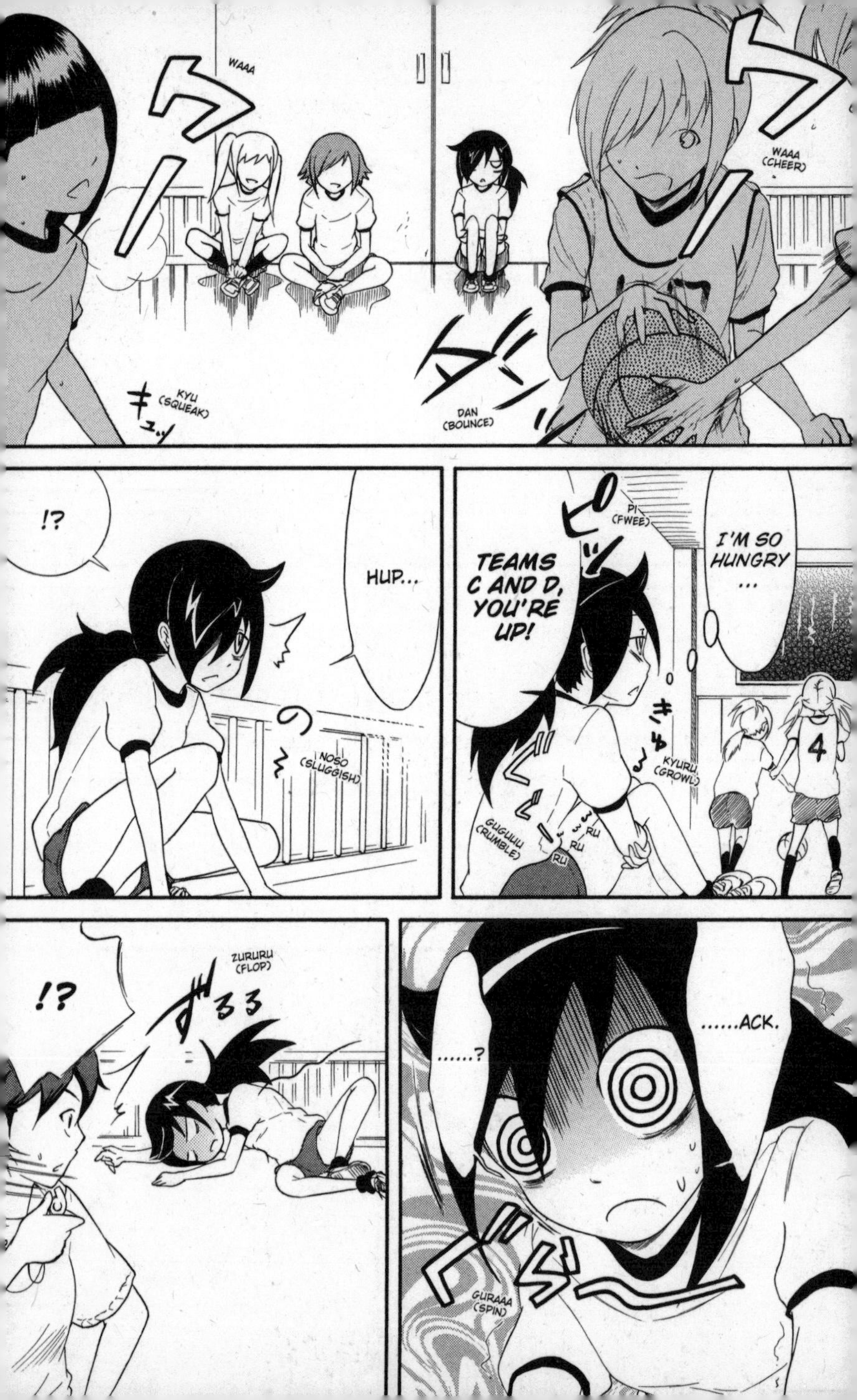
WAAA
(CHEER)
DAN
(BOUNCE)
WAAA
KYU
(SQUEAK)
PI
(FWEE)
I'M SO HUNGRY ...
TEAMS C AND D, YOU'RE UP!
KYURU
(GROWL)
GUGUUU
(RUMBLE)
RU
RU
RU
HUP...
!?
NOSO
(SLUGGISH)
......ACK.
......?
GURAAA
(SPIN)
ZURURU
(FLOP)
!?

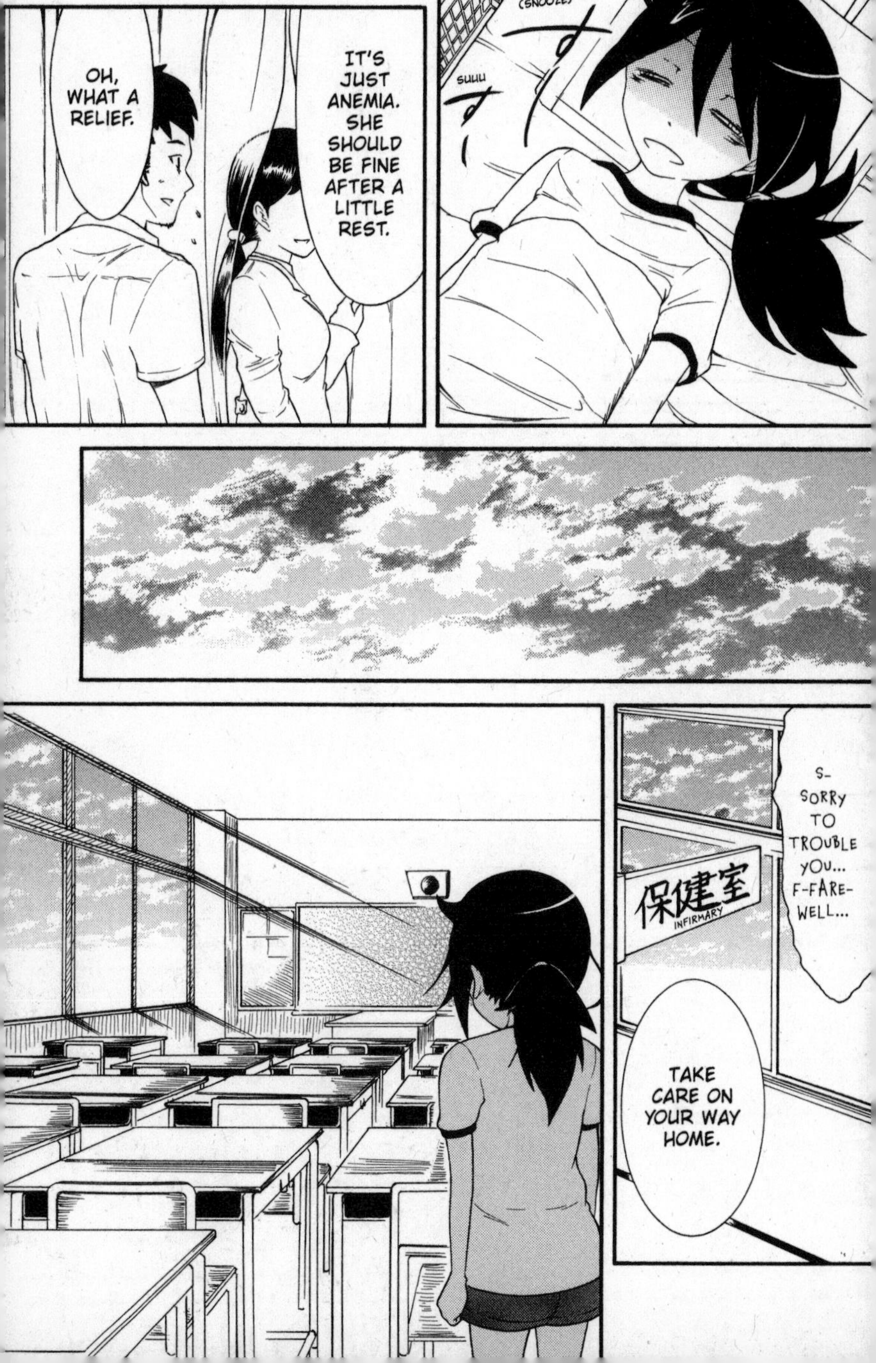
SUUU (SNOOZE)
SUUU
IT'S JUST ANEMIA. SHE SHOULD BE FINE AFTER A LITTLE REST.
OH, WHAT A RELIEF.
S-SORRY TO TROUBLE YOU... F-FAREWELL...
保健室
INFIRMARY
TAKE CARE ON YOUR WAY HOME.

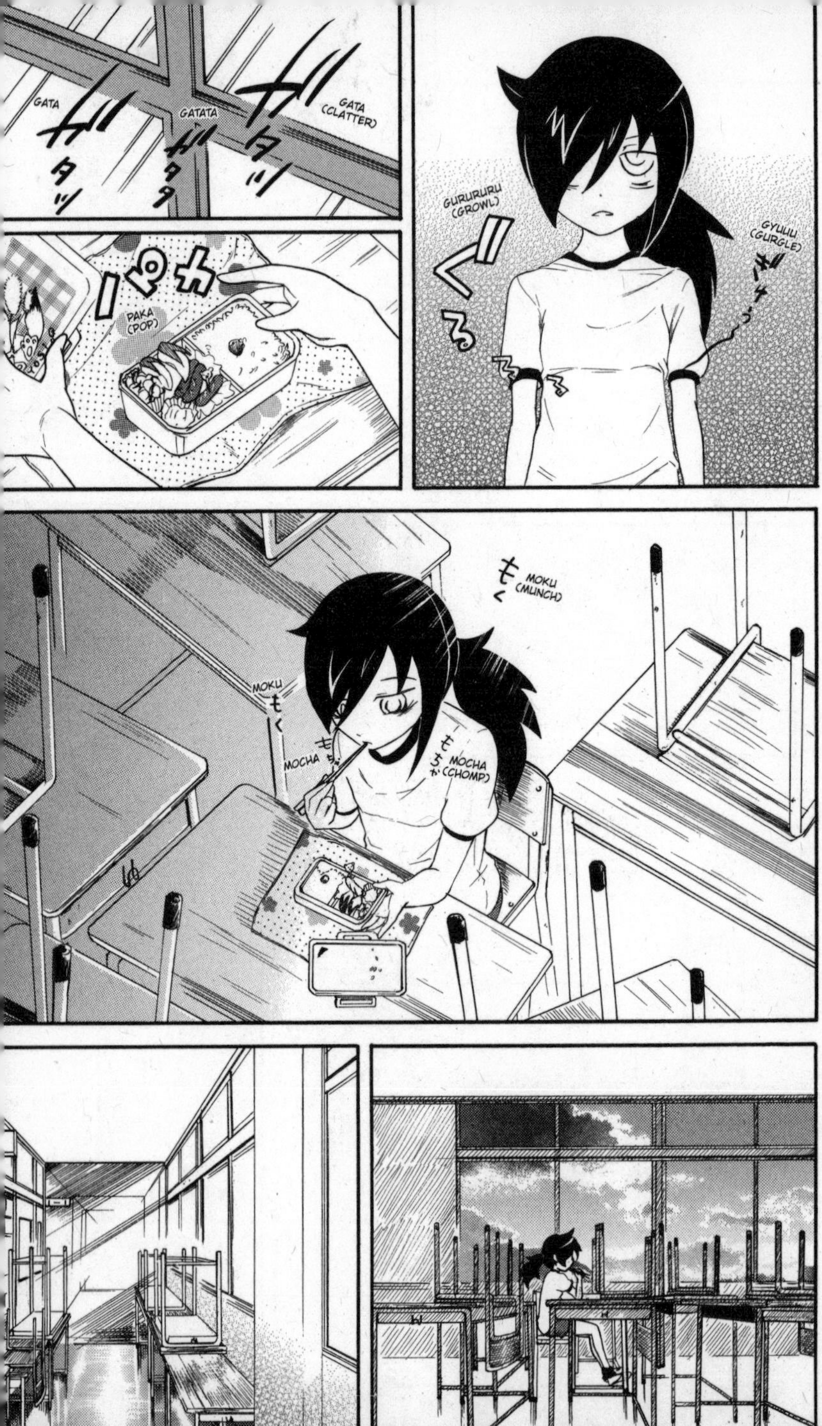
GURURURU (GROWL)
GYUUU (GURGLE)
GATA (CLATTER)
GATATA
GATA
PAKA (POP)
MOKU (MUNCH)
MOCHA (CHOMP)
MOKU
MOCHA

No Matter How I Look at It, It's You Guys' Fault I'm Not Popular!

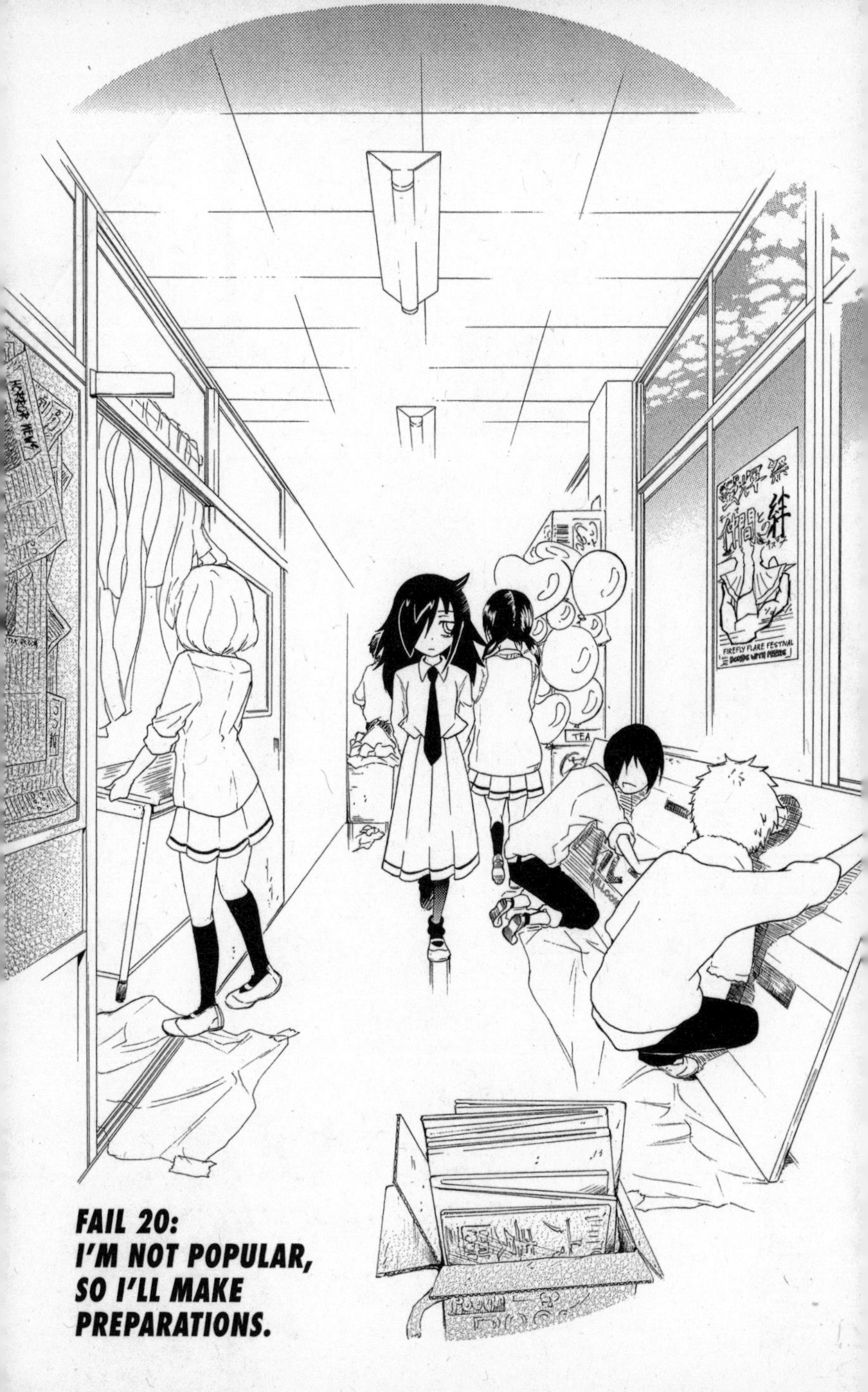
FIREFLY FLARE FESTIVAL
TEA

FAIL 20:
I'M NOT POPULAR, SO I'LL MAKE PREPARATIONS.

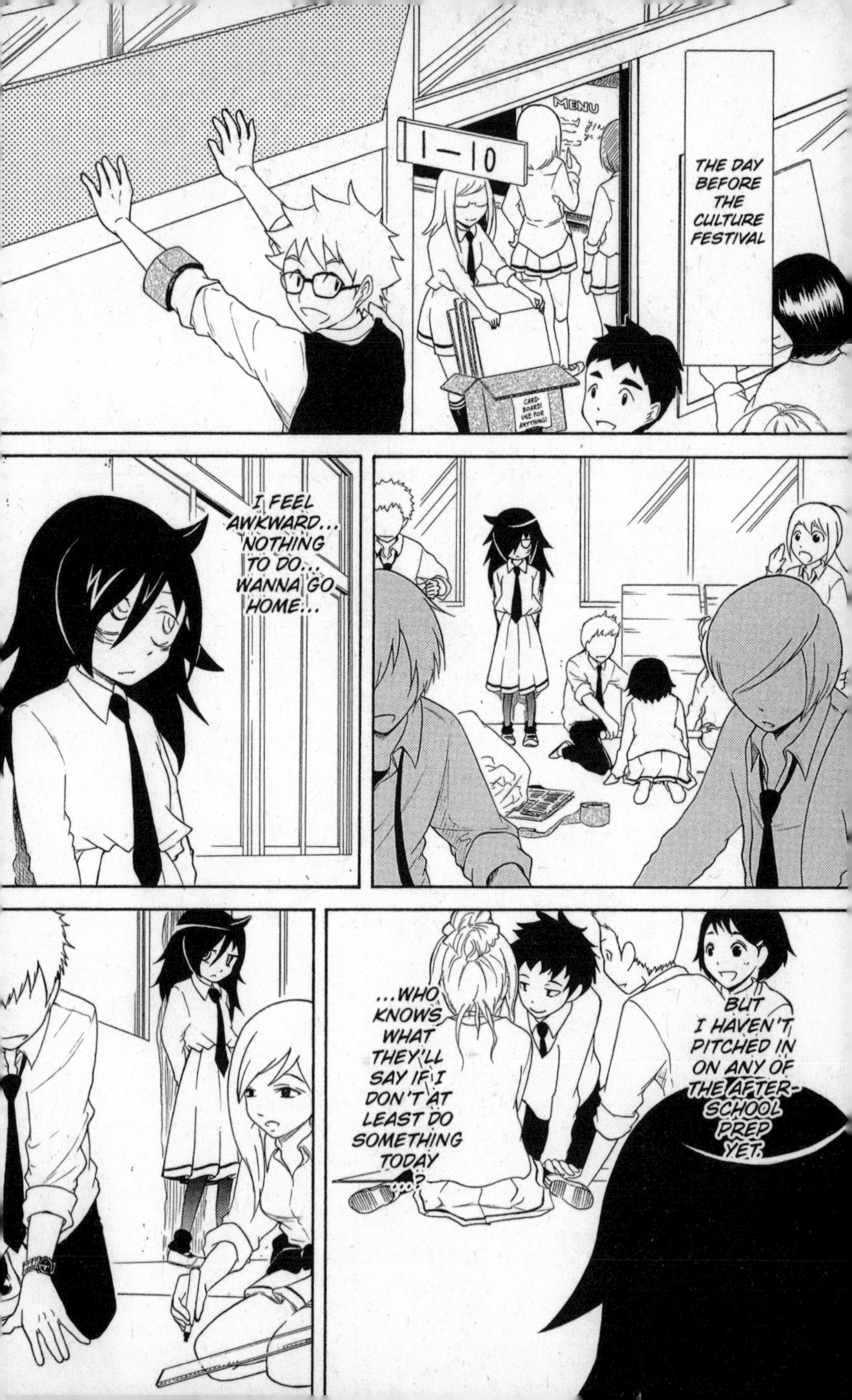
THE DAY BEFORE THE CULTURE FESTIVAL
MENU
1—10
CARD-BOARD! USE FOR ANYTHING!
I FEEL AWKWARD... NOTHING TO DO... WANNA GO HOME...
BUT I HAVEN'T PITCHED IN ON ANY OF THE AFTER-SCHOOL PREP YET.
...WHO KNOWS WHAT THEY'LL SAY IF I DON'T AT LEAST DO SOMETHING TODAY...?

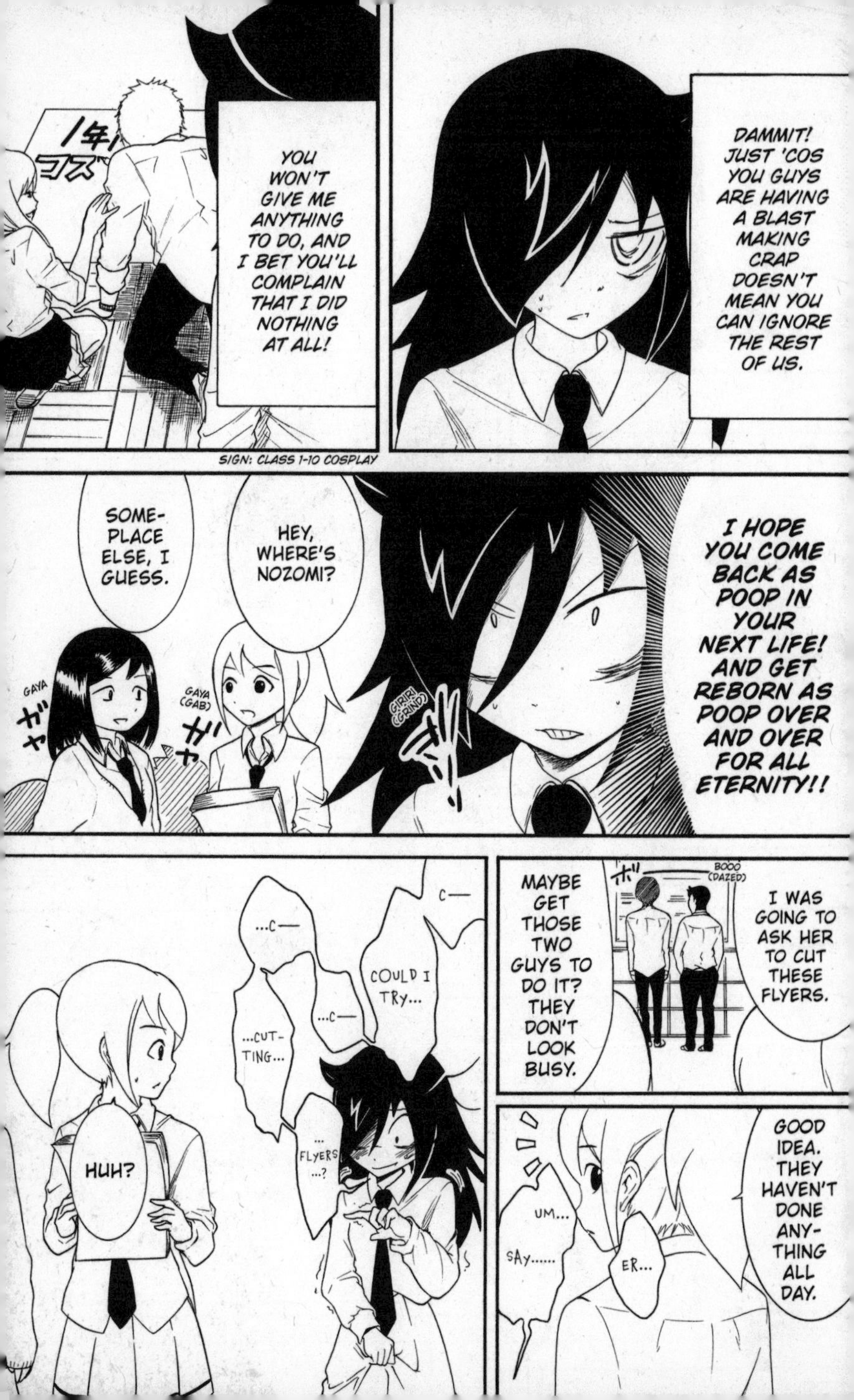

DAMMIT! JUST 'COS YOU GUYS ARE HAVING A BLAST MAKING CRAP DOESN'T MEAN YOU CAN IGNORE THE REST OF US.
YOU WON'T GIVE ME ANYTHING TO DO, AND I BET YOU'LL COMPLAIN THAT I DID NOTHING AT ALL!
SIGN: CLASS 1-10 COSPLAY
I HOPE YOU COME BACK AS POOP IN YOUR NEXT LIFE! AND GET REBORN AS POOP OVER AND OVER FOR ALL ETERNITY!!
GIRIRI (GRIND)
HEY, WHERE'S NOZOMI?
GAYA (GAB)
SOME-PLACE ELSE, I GUESS.
GAYA
I WAS GOING TO ASK HER TO CUT THESE FLYERS.
BOOO (DAZED)
MAYBE GET THOSE TWO GUYS TO DO IT? THEY DON'T LOOK BUSY.
GOOD IDEA. THEY HAVEN'T DONE ANY-THING ALL DAY.
ER...
UM...
SAY......
C—
COULD I TRY...
...C—
...C—
...CUT-TING...
...FLYERS...?
HUH?

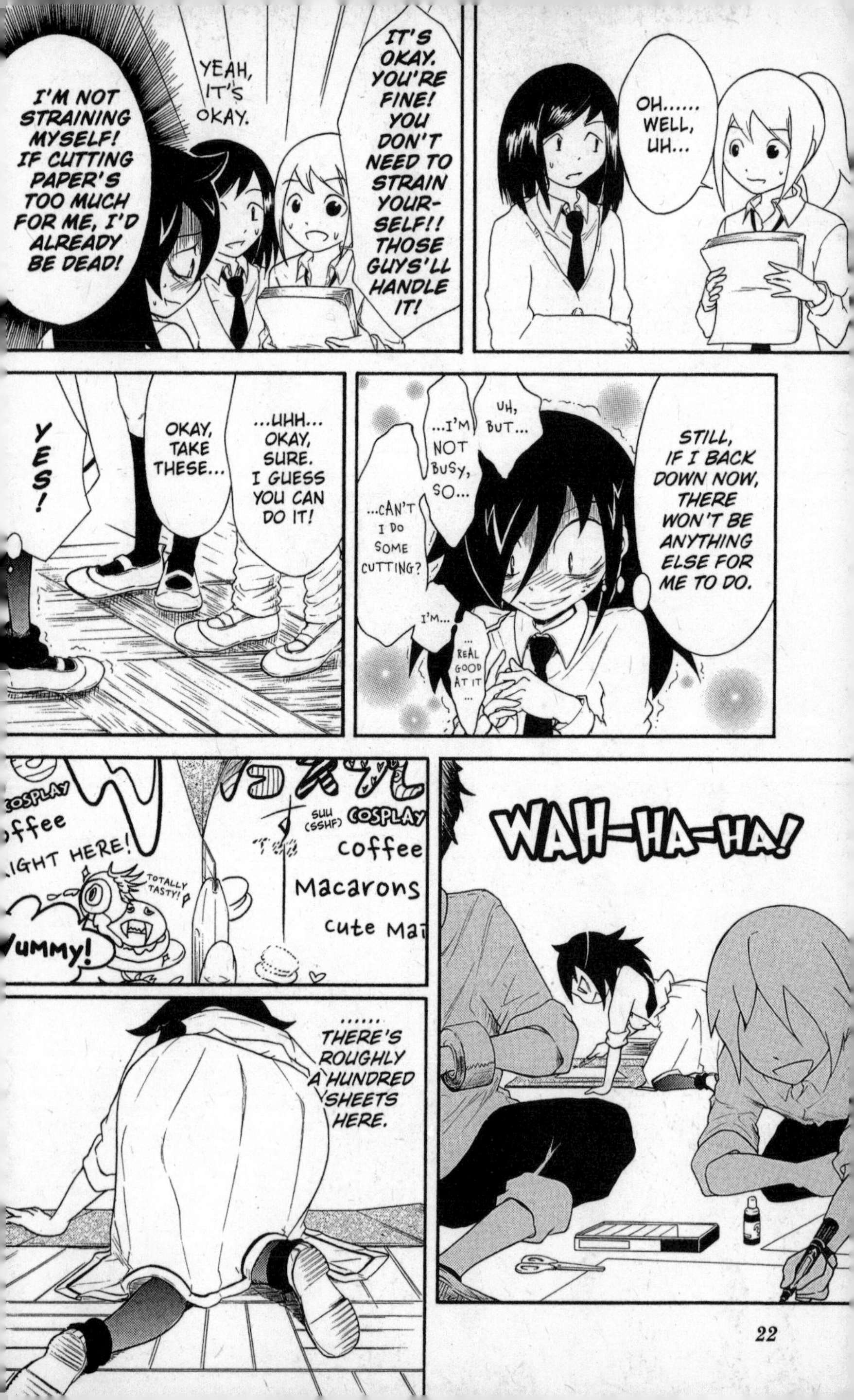
OH...... WELL, UH...
IT'S OKAY. YOU'RE FINE! YOU DON'T NEED TO STRAIN YOURSELF!! THOSE GUYS'LL HANDLE IT!
YEAH, IT'S OKAY.
I'M NOT STRAINING MYSELF! IF CUTTING PAPER'S TOO MUCH FOR ME, I'D ALREADY BE DEAD!
STILL, IF I BACK DOWN NOW, THERE WON'T BE ANYTHING ELSE FOR ME TO DO.
UH, BUT...
...I'M NOT BUSY, SO...
...CAN'T I DO SOME CUTTING?
I'M...
...REAL GOOD AT IT...
...UHH... OKAY, SURE. I GUESS YOU CAN DO IT!
OKAY, TAKE THESE...
YES!
WAH-HA-HA!
COSPLAY
TOTALLY TASTY!
Yummy!
SUU (SSHF)
COSPLAY
coffee
Macarons
...... THERE'S ROUGHLY A HUNDRED SHEETS HERE.

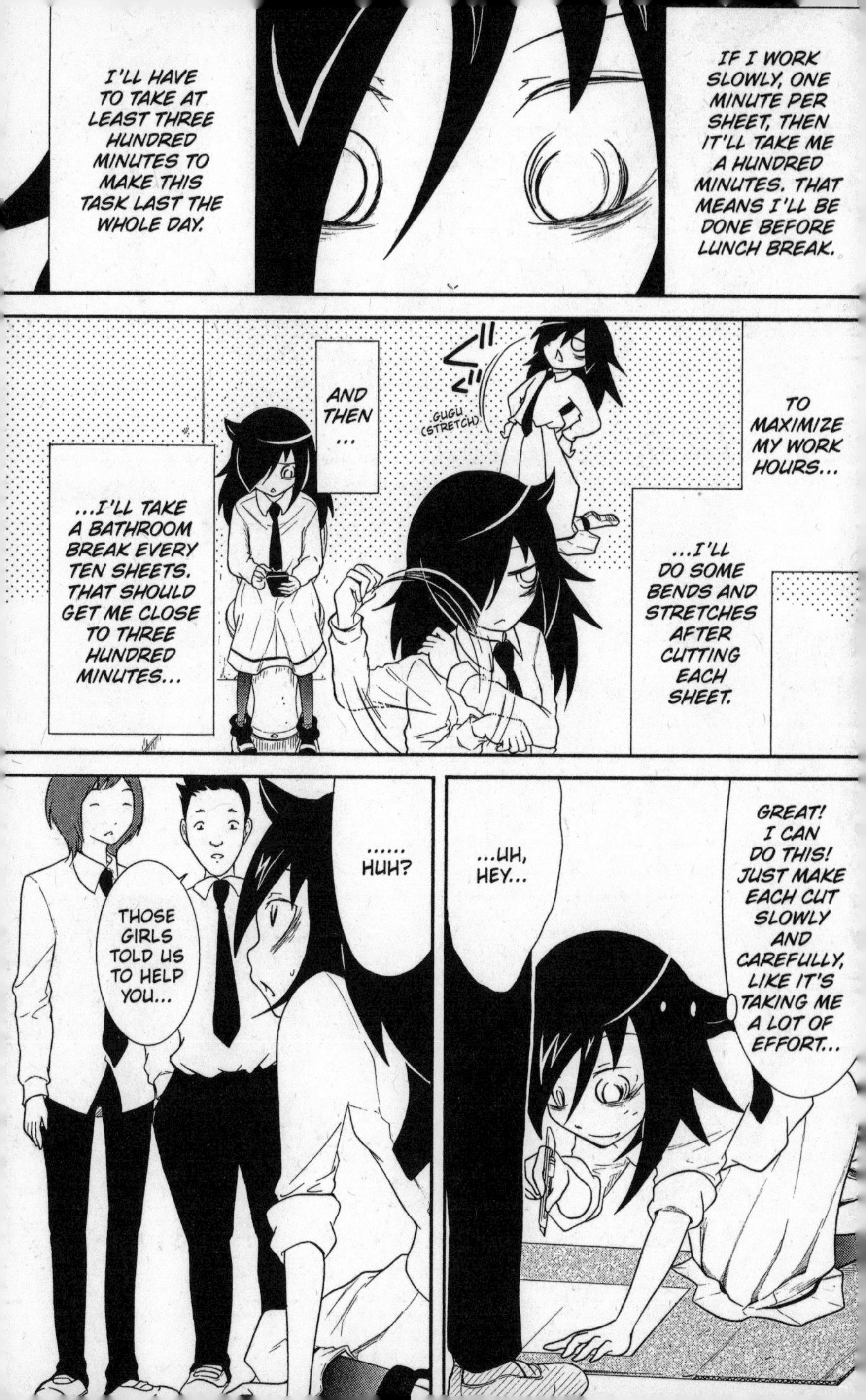
IF I WORK SLOWLY, ONE MINUTE PER SHEET, THEN IT'LL TAKE ME A HUNDRED MINUTES. THAT MEANS I'LL BE DONE BEFORE LUNCH BREAK.
I'LL HAVE TO TAKE AT LEAST THREE HUNDRED MINUTES TO MAKE THIS TASK LAST THE WHOLE DAY.
TO MAXIMIZE MY WORK HOURS...
...I'LL DO SOME BENDS AND STRETCHES AFTER CUTTING EACH SHEET.
GUGU (STRETCH)
AND THEN...
...I'LL TAKE A BATHROOM BREAK EVERY TEN SHEETS. THAT SHOULD GET ME CLOSE TO THREE HUNDRED MINUTES...
GREAT! I CAN DO THIS! JUST MAKE EACH CUT SLOWLY AND CAREFULLY, LIKE IT'S TAKING ME A LOT OF EFFORT...
...UH, HEY...
...... HUH?
THOSE GIRLS TOLD US TO HELP YOU...

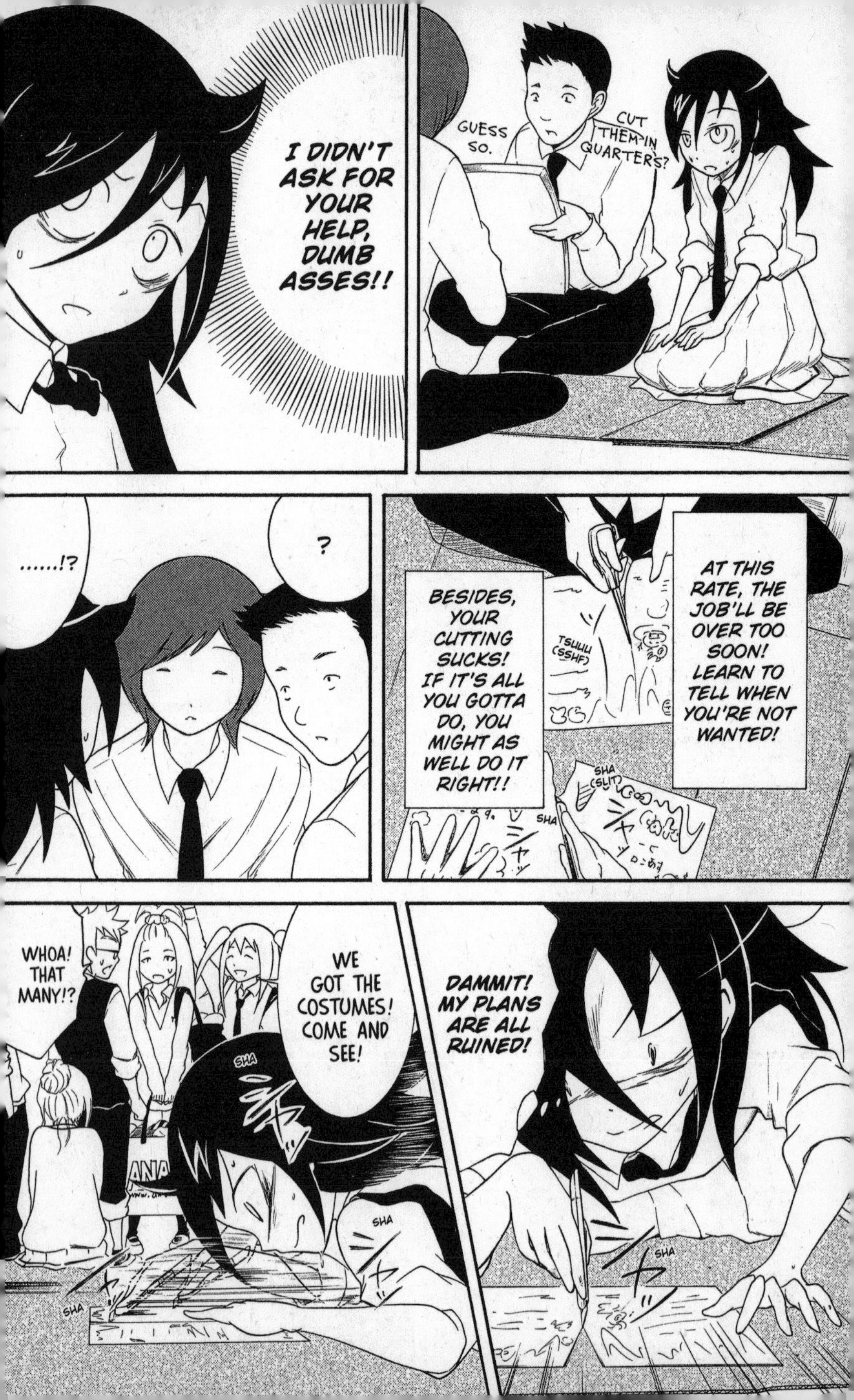
CUT THEM IN QUARTERS?
GUESS SO.
I DIDN'T ASK FOR YOUR HELP, DUMB ASSES!!
AT THIS RATE, THE JOB'LL BE OVER TOO SOON! LEARN TO TELL WHEN YOU'RE NOT WANTED!
BESIDES, YOUR CUTTING SUCKS! IF IT'S ALL YOU GOTTA DO, YOU MIGHT AS WELL DO IT RIGHT!!
TSUUU (SSHF)
SHA (SLIT)
SHA
?
......!?
DAMMIT! MY PLANS ARE ALL RUINED!
SHA
WE GOT THE COSTUMES! COME AND SEE!
WHOA! THAT MANY!?
SHA
SHA
SHA

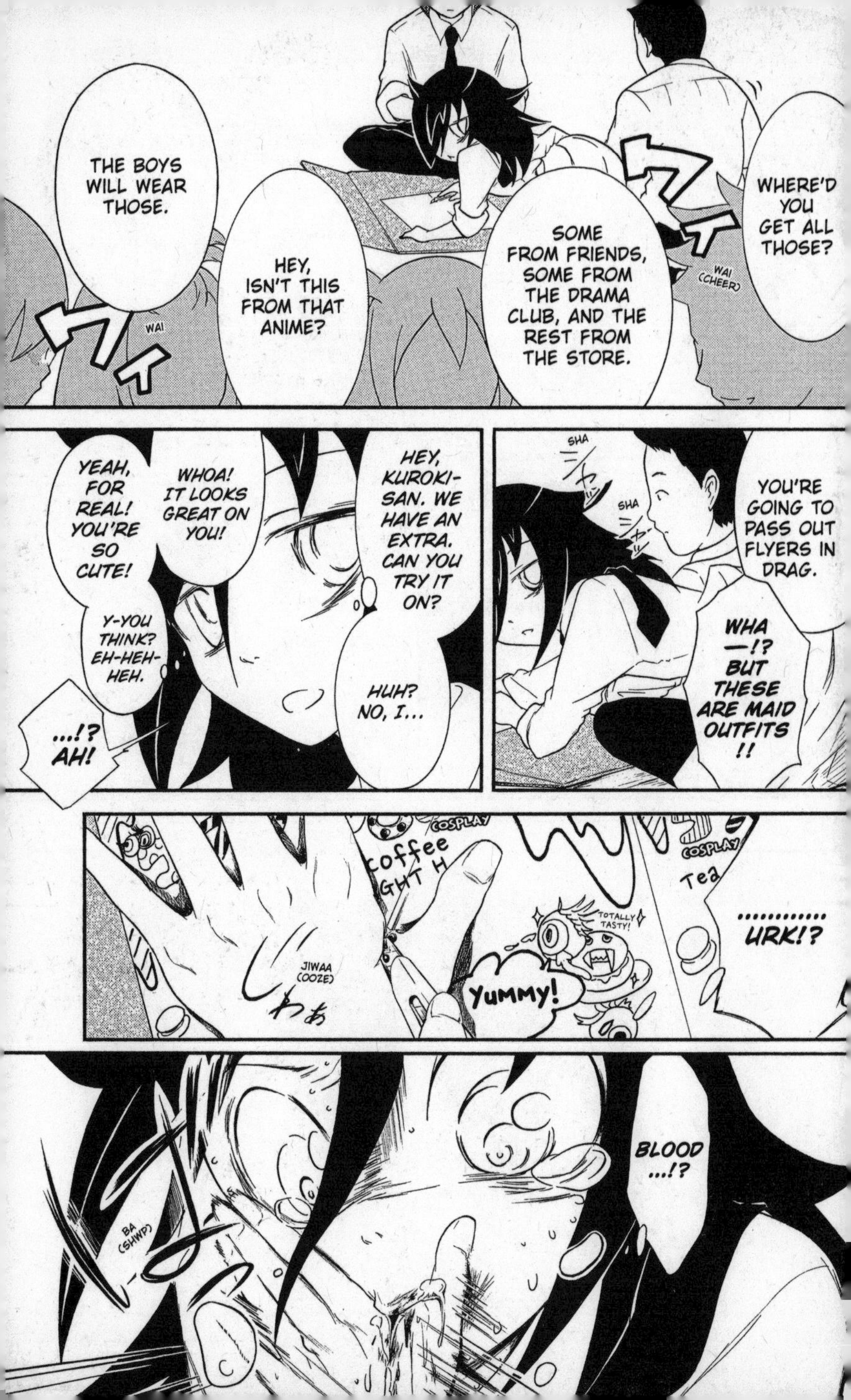
WHERE'D YOU GET ALL THOSE?
WAI (CHEER)
SOME FROM FRIENDS, SOME FROM THE DRAMA CLUB, AND THE REST FROM THE STORE.
HEY, ISN'T THIS FROM THAT ANIME?
THE BOYS WILL WEAR THOSE.
WAI
SHA
SHA
YOU'RE GOING TO PASS OUT FLYERS IN DRAG.
WHA—!? BUT THESE ARE MAID OUTFITS!!
HEY, KUROKI-SAN. WE HAVE AN EXTRA. CAN YOU TRY IT ON?
WHOA! IT LOOKS GREAT ON YOU!
YEAH, FOR REAL! YOU'RE SO CUTE!
HUH? NO, I...
Y-YOU THINK? EH-HEH-HEH.
...!? AH!
............URK!?
COSPLAY
COSPLAY
Tea
coffee
TOTALLY TASTY!
Yummy!
JIWAA (OOZE)
BLOOD ...!?
BA (SHWP)

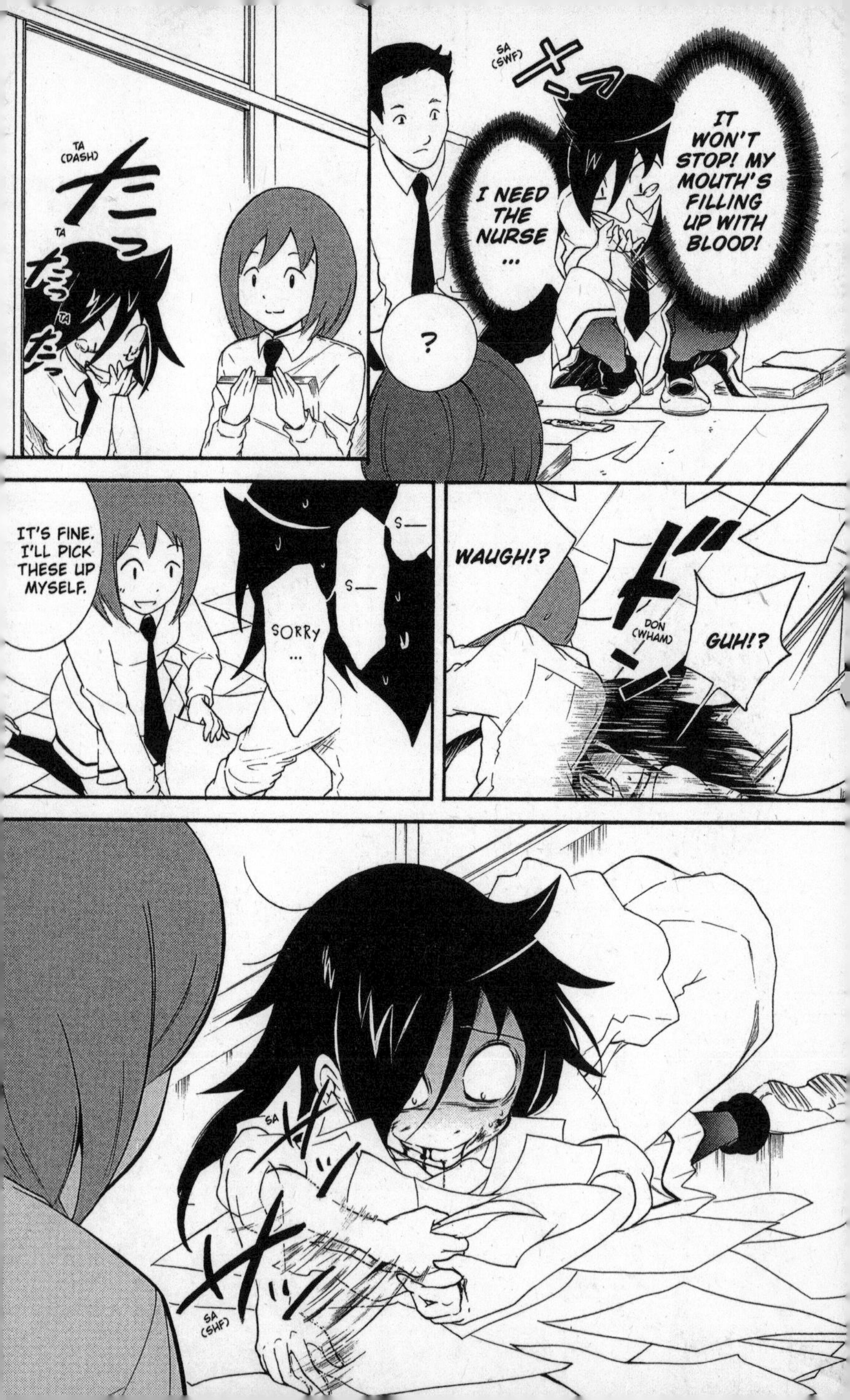
SA (SWF)
IT WON'T STOP! MY MOUTH'S FILLING UP WITH BLOOD!
I NEED THE NURSE ...
?
TA (DASH)
TA
TA
WAUGH!?
DON (WHAM)
GUH!?
S—
S—
SORRY ...
IT'S FINE. I'LL PICK THESE UP MYSELF.
SA
SA (SHF)

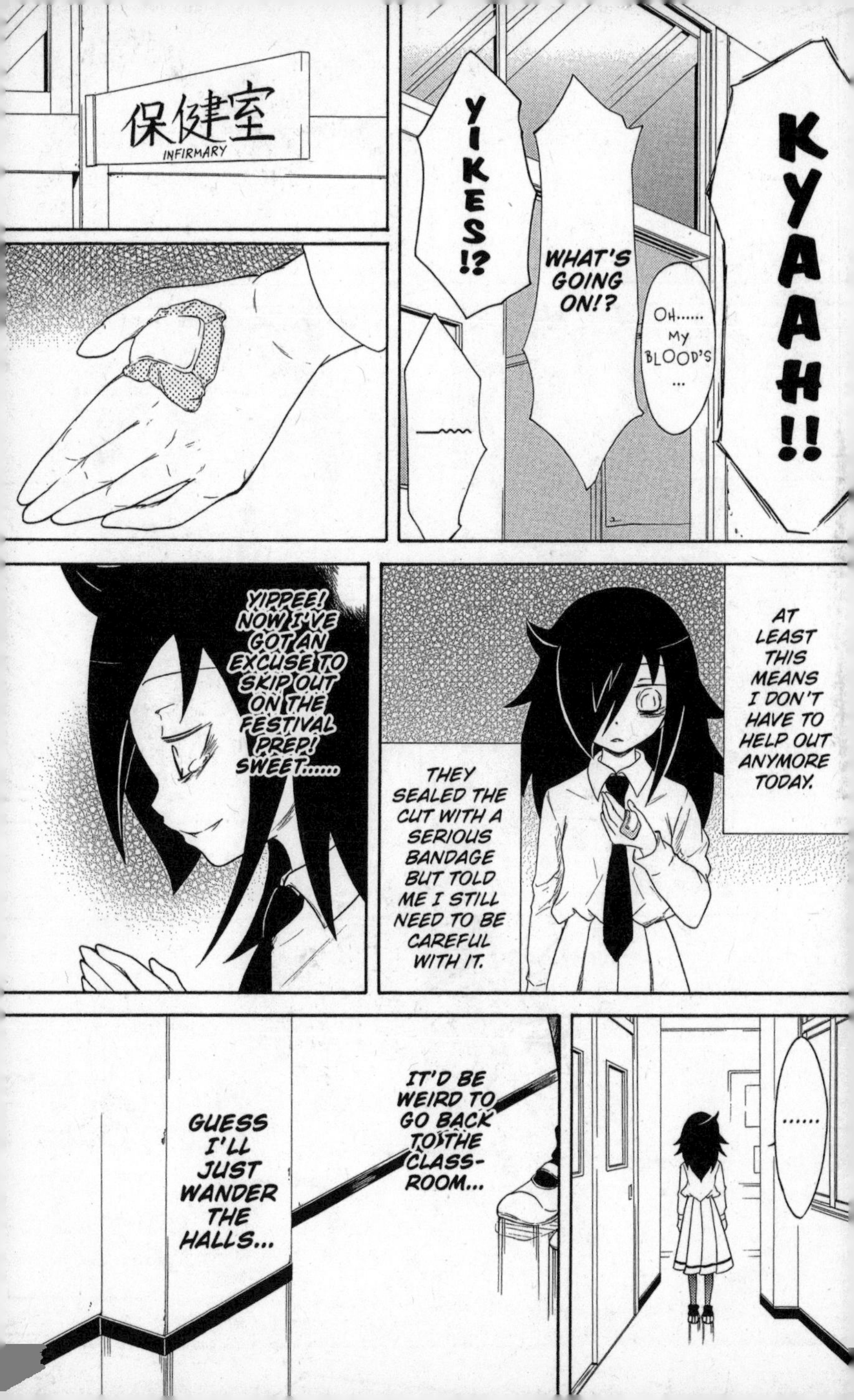
KYAAAH!!
OH...... MY BLOOD'S...
WHAT'S GOING ON!?
YIKES!?
—~~~
保健室
INFIRMARY
AT LEAST THIS MEANS I DON'T HAVE TO HELP OUT ANYMORE TODAY.
THEY SEALED THE CUT WITH A SERIOUS BANDAGE BUT TOLD ME I STILL NEED TO BE CAREFUL WITH IT.
YIPPEE! NOW I'VE GOT AN EXCUSE TO SKIP OUT ON THE FESTIVAL PREP! SWEET......
......
IT'D BE WEIRD TO GO BACK TO THE CLASS-ROOM...
GUESS I'LL JUST WANDER THE HALLS...

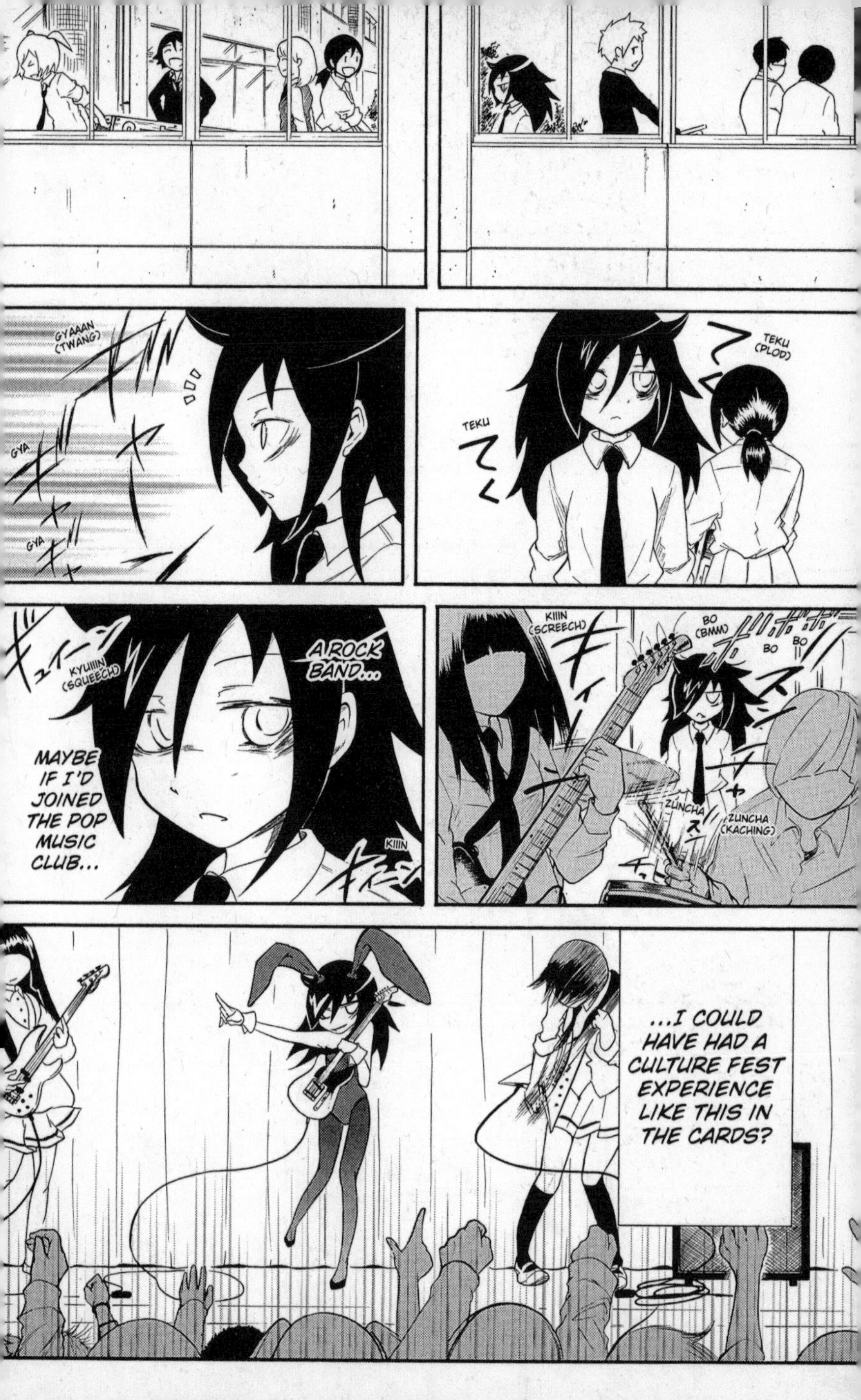
TEKU (PLOD)
TEKU
GYAAAN (TWANG)
GYA
GYA
KIIIN (SCREECH)
BO (BMM)
BO
BO
ZUNCHA (KACHING)
ZUNCHA
A ROCK BAND...
KYUIIIN (SQUEECH)
MAYBE IF I'D JOINED THE POP MUSIC CLUB...
KIIIN
...I COULD HAVE HAD A CULTURE FEST EXPERIENCE LIKE THIS IN THE CARDS?

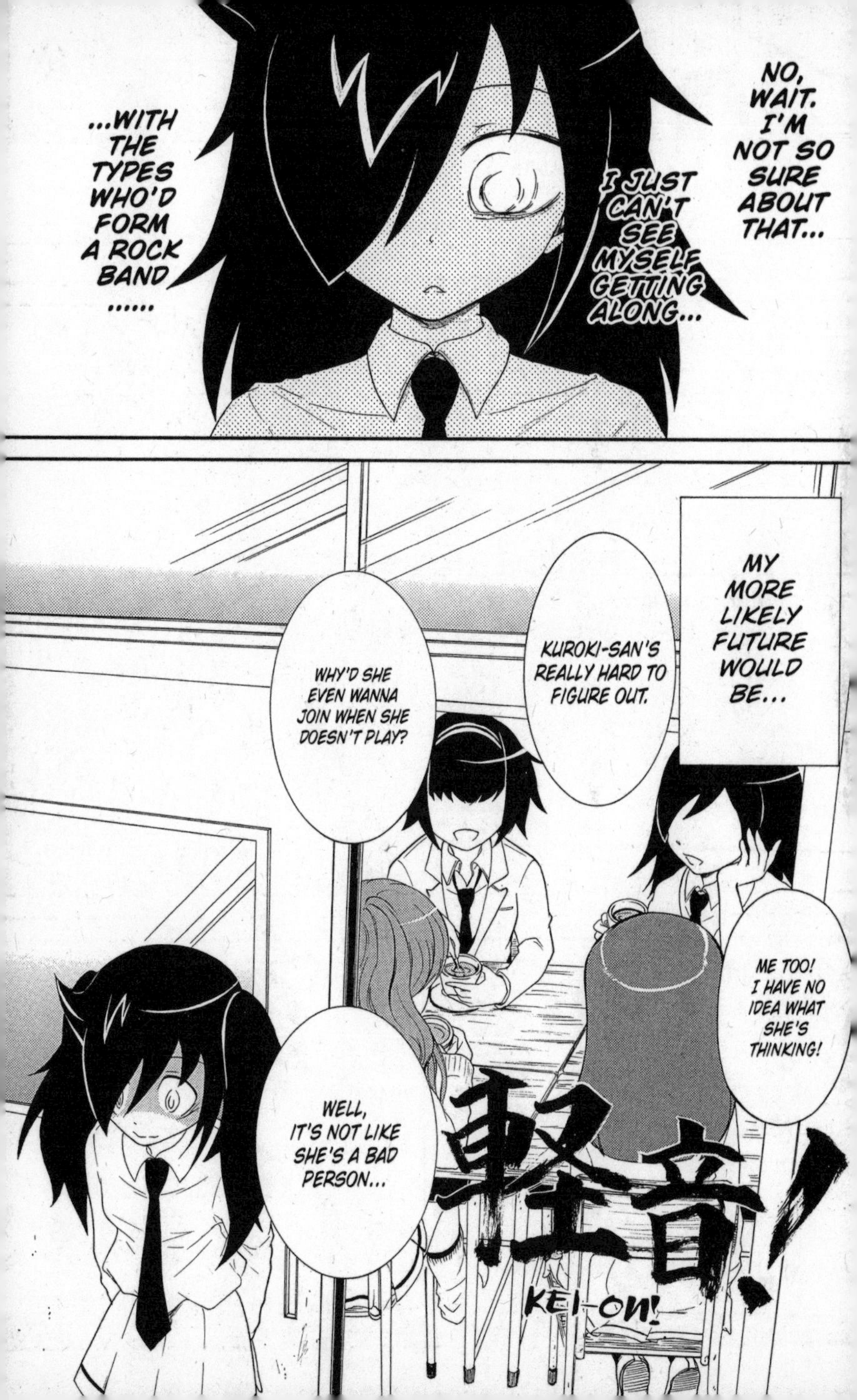
NO, WAIT. I'M NOT SO SURE ABOUT THAT...
I JUST CAN'T SEE MYSELF GETTING ALONG...
...WITH THE TYPES WHO'D FORM A ROCK BAND ......
MY MORE LIKELY FUTURE WOULD BE...
KUROKI-SAN'S REALLY HARD TO FIGURE OUT.
WHY'D SHE EVEN WANNA JOIN WHEN SHE DOESN'T PLAY?
ME TOO! I HAVE NO IDEA WHAT SHE'S THINKING!
WELL, IT'S NOT LIKE SHE'S A BAD PERSON...
軽音!
KEI-ON!

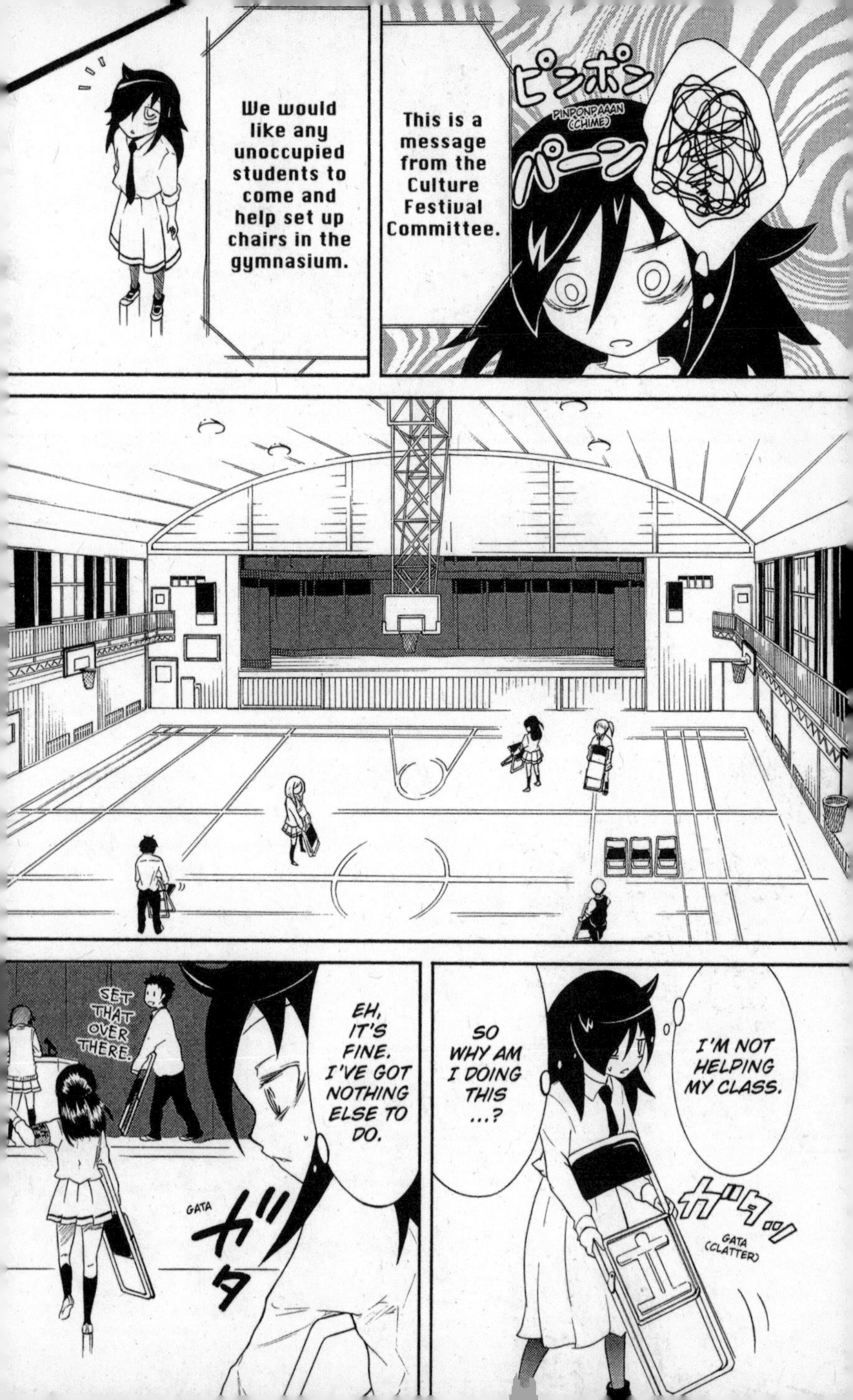
ピンポンパーン
PINPONPAAAN (CHIME)
This is a message from the Culture Festival Committee.
We would like any unoccupied students to come and help set up chairs in the gymnasium.
I'M NOT HELPING MY CLASS.
SO WHY AM I DOING THIS ...?
ガタッ
GATA (CLATTER)
EH, IT'S FINE. I'VE GOT NOTHING ELSE TO DO.
SET THAT OVER THERE.
ガタ
GATA

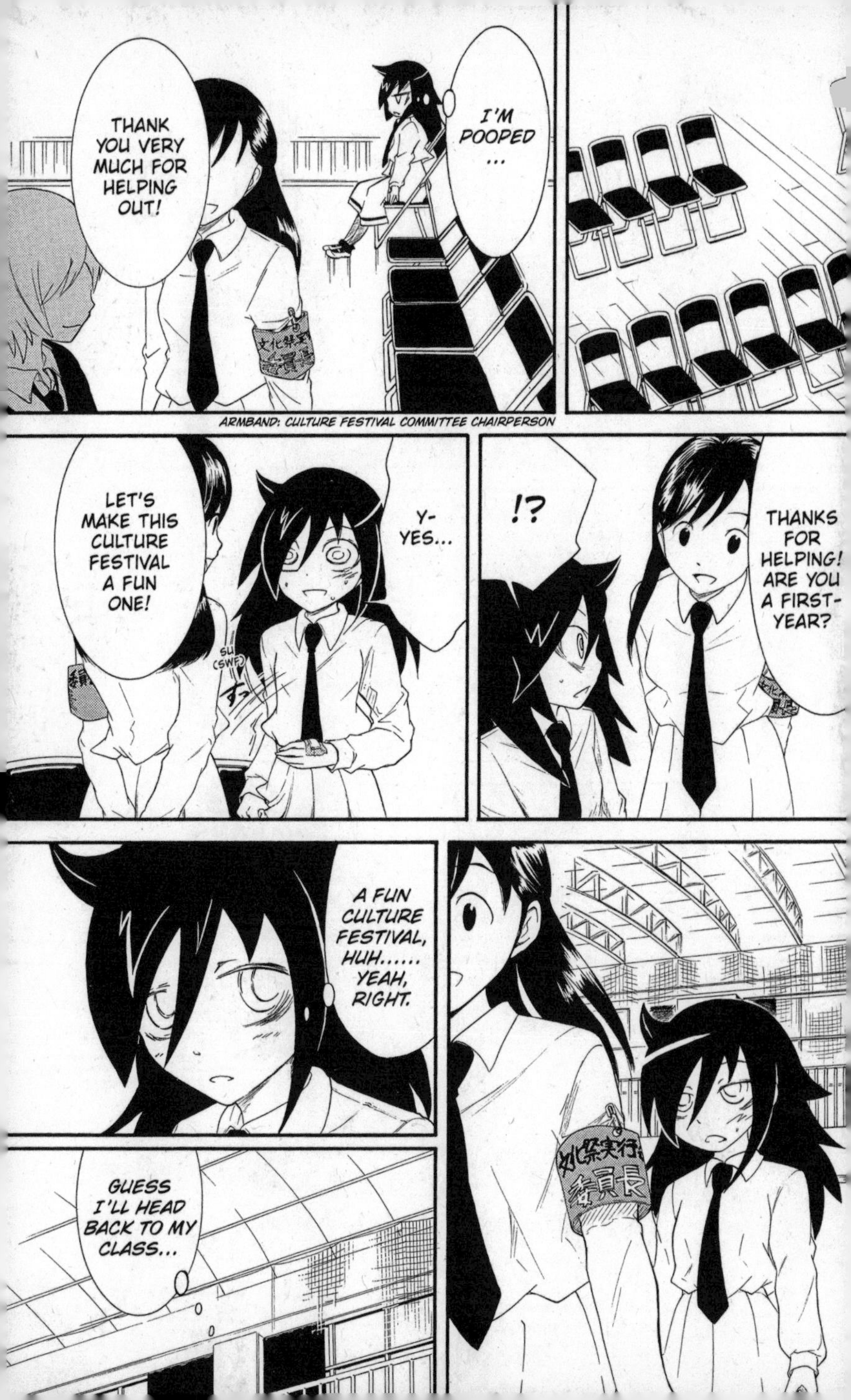
I'M POOPED ...
THANK YOU VERY MUCH FOR HELPING OUT!
ARMBAND: CULTURE FESTIVAL COMMITTEE CHAIRPERSON
THANKS FOR HELPING! ARE YOU A FIRST-YEAR?
!?
LET'S MAKE THIS CULTURE FESTIVAL A FUN ONE!
Y-YES...
SU (SWF)
A FUN CULTURE FESTIVAL, HUH...... YEAH, RIGHT.
GUESS I'LL HEAD BACK TO MY CLASS...

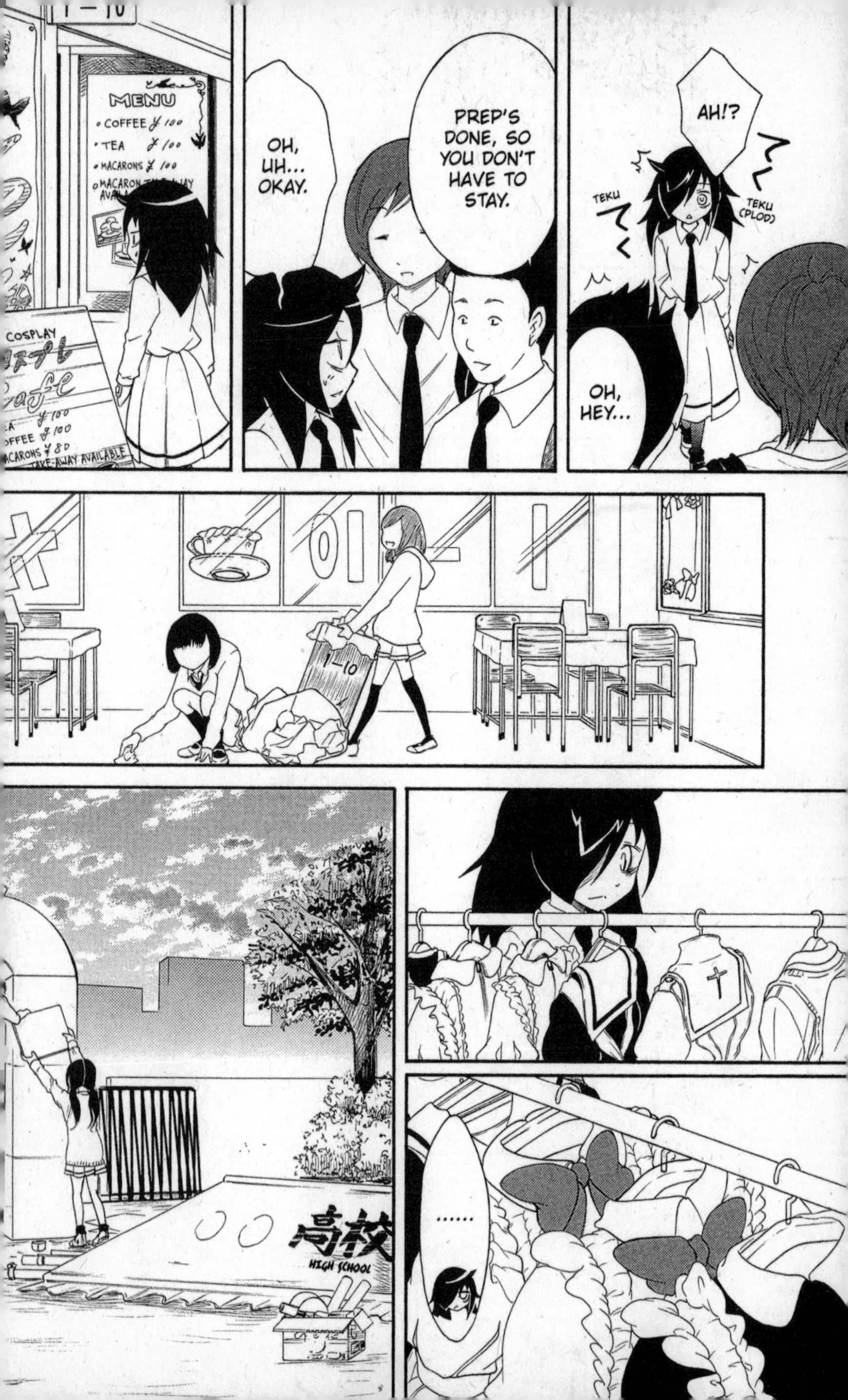

AH!?
TEKU (PLOD)
TEKU
OH, HEY...
PREP'S DONE, SO YOU DON'T HAVE TO STAY.
OH, UH... OKAY.
MENU
• COFFEE ¥100
• TEA ¥100
• MACARONS ¥100
COSPLAY
TAKE-AWAY AVAILABLE
1-10
......
高校
HIGH SCHOOL

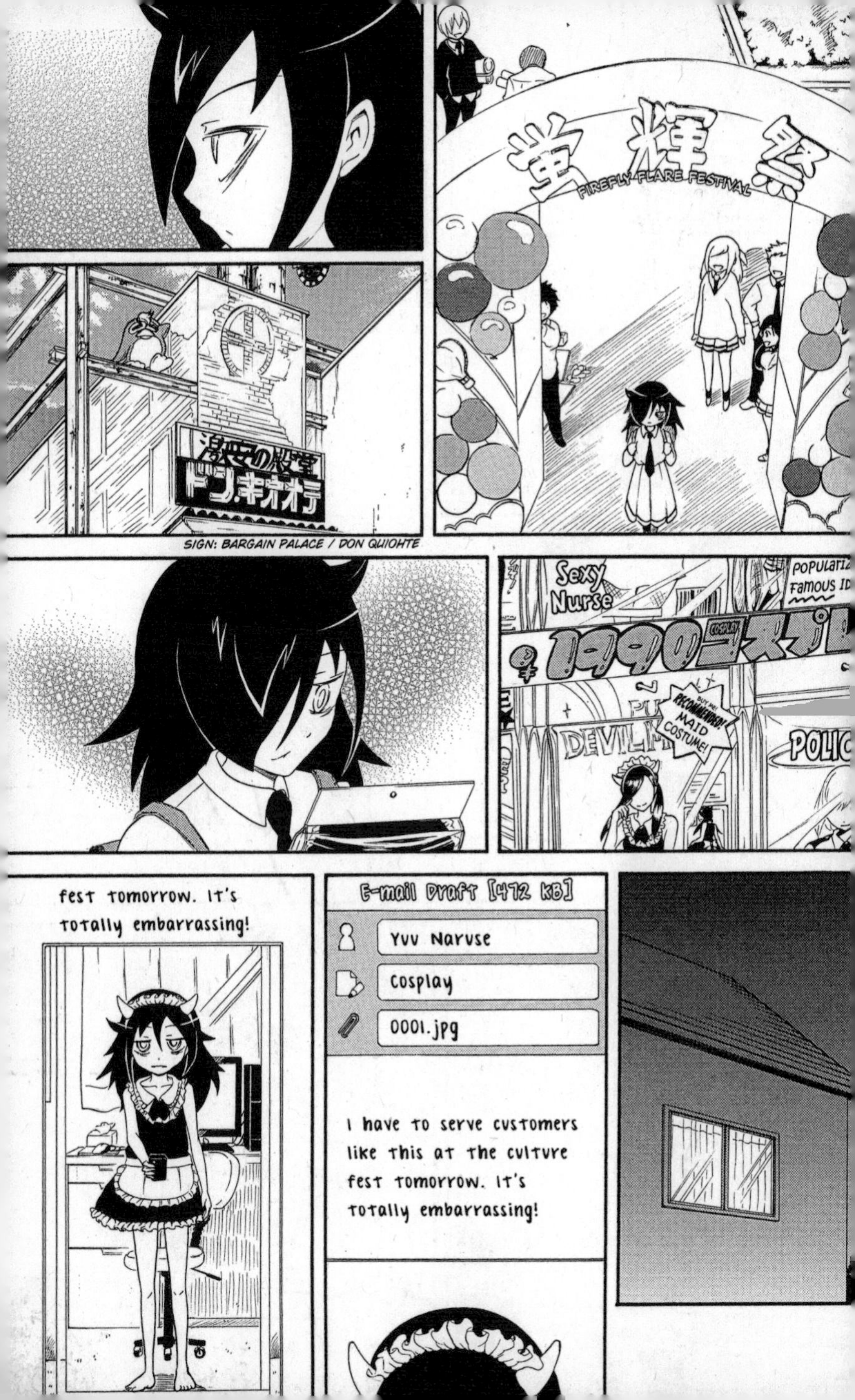

蛍輝祭
FIREFLY FLARE FESTIVAL
SIGN: BARGAIN PALACE / DON QUIOHTE
Sexy Nurse
POPULARIZ
Famous ID
COSPLAY
BUY ME! RECOMMENDED! MAID COSTUME!
DEVILM
POLIC
E-mail Draft [472 KB]
Yuu Naruse
cosplay
0001.jpg
I have to serve customers like this at the culture fest tomorrow. It's totally embarrassing!
fest tomorrow. It's totally embarrassing!

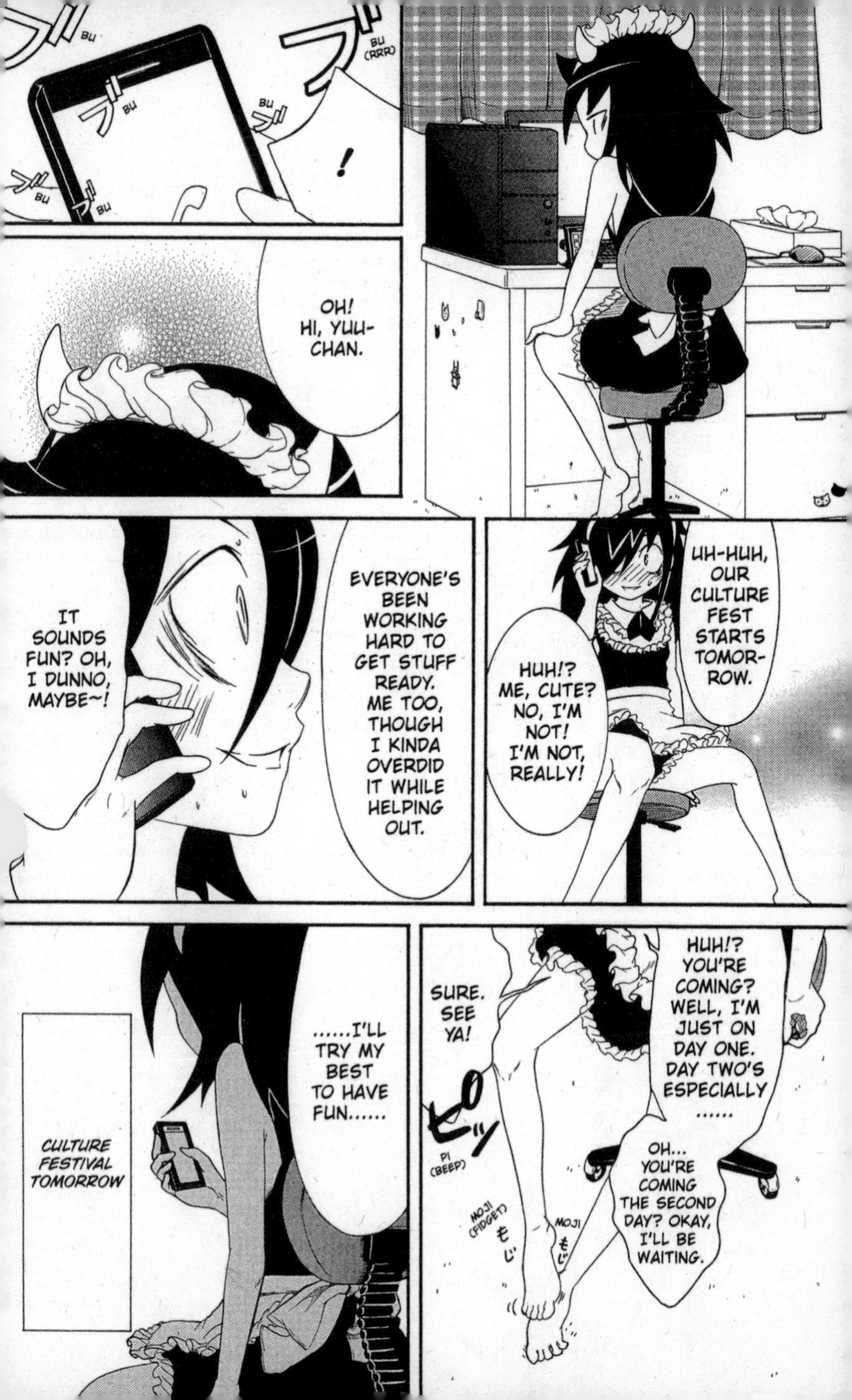

ブ
BU
ブ
BU (RRR)
ブ
BU
ブ
BU
ブ
BU
ブ
BU
!
OH! HI, YUU-CHAN.
UH-HUH, OUR CULTURE FEST STARTS TOMORROW.
HUH!? ME, CUTE? NO, I'M NOT! I'M NOT, REALLY!
EVERYONE'S BEEN WORKING HARD TO GET STUFF READY. ME TOO, THOUGH I KINDA OVERDID IT WHILE HELPING OUT.
IT SOUNDS FUN? OH, I DUNNO, MAYBE~!
HUH!? YOU'RE COMING? WELL, I'M JUST ON DAY ONE. DAY TWO'S ESPECIALLY ......
OH... YOU'RE COMING THE SECOND DAY? OKAY, I'LL BE WAITING.
SURE. SEE YA!
ピッ
PI (BEEP)
もじ
MOJI (FIDGET)
もじ
MOJI
......I'LL TRY MY BEST TO HAVE FUN......
CULTURE FESTIVAL TOMORROW

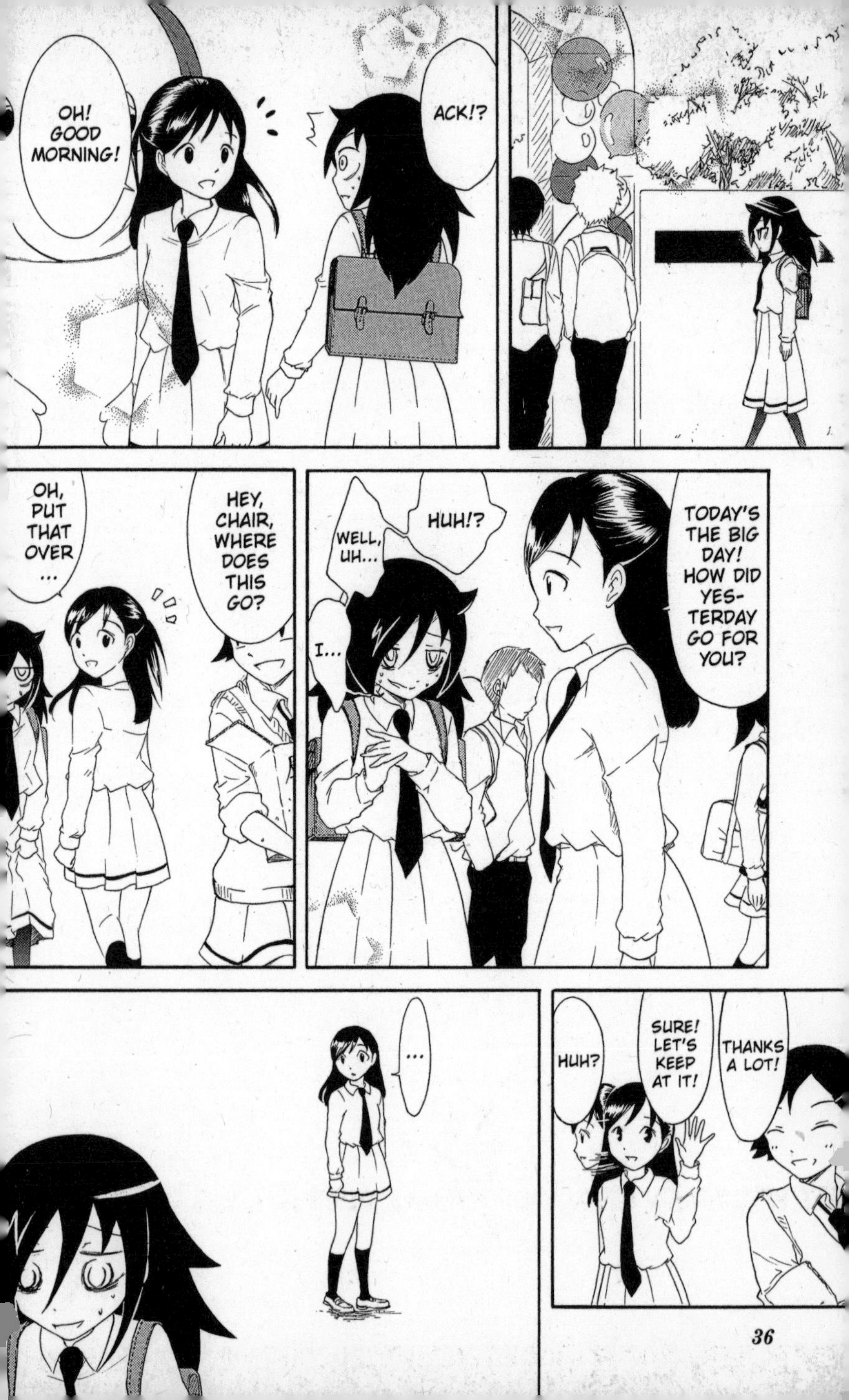

ACK!?
OH! GOOD MORNING!
TODAY'S THE BIG DAY! HOW DID YES-TERDAY GO FOR YOU?
HUH!?
WELL, UH...
I...
HEY, CHAIR, WHERE DOES THIS GO?
OH, PUT THAT OVER ...
THANKS A LOT!
SURE! LET'S KEEP AT IT!
HUH?
...

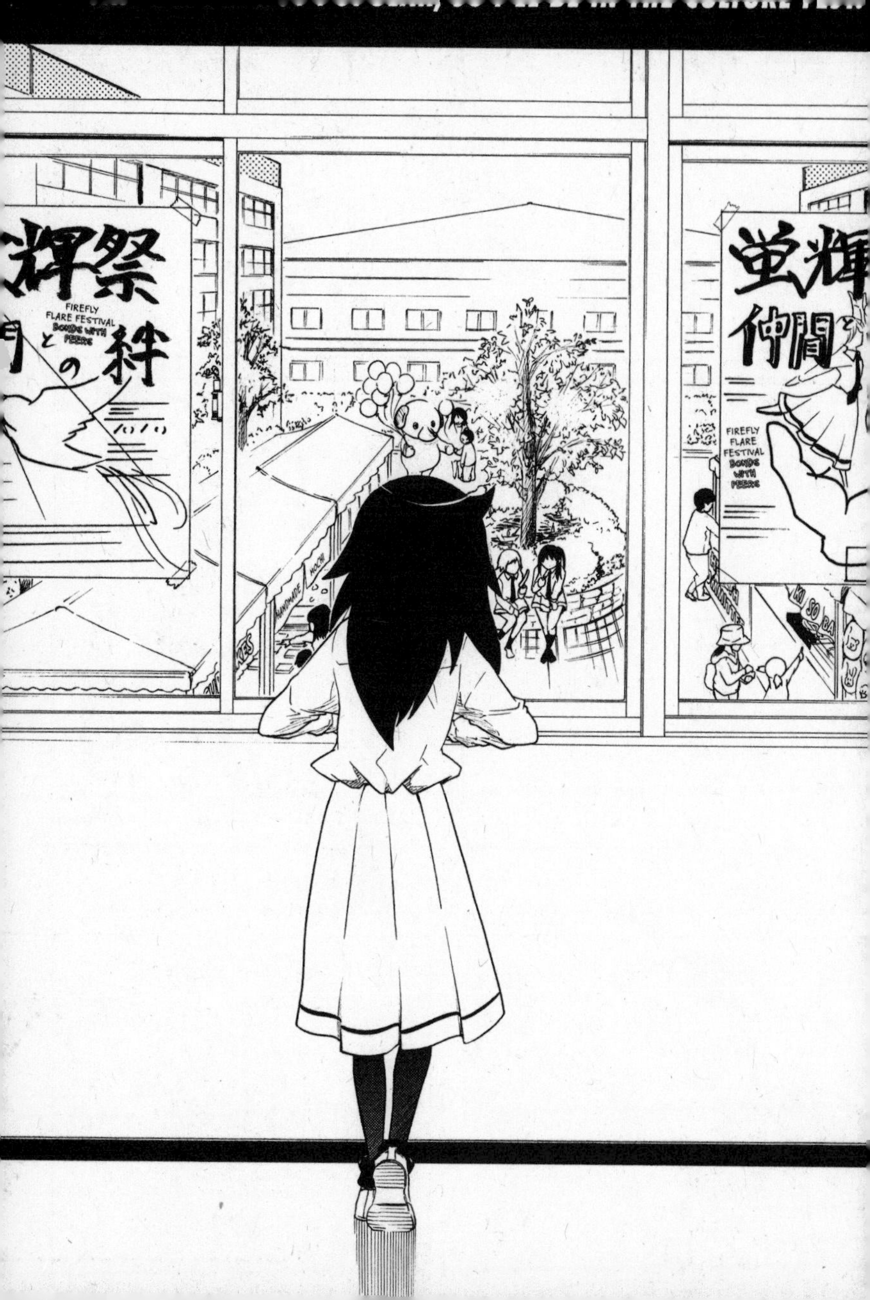
仲間と
FIREFLY FLARE FESTIVAL BONDS WITH PEERS
KI SO BA
FIREFLY FLARE FESTIVAL BONDS WITH PEERS
HANDMADE
MOCHI

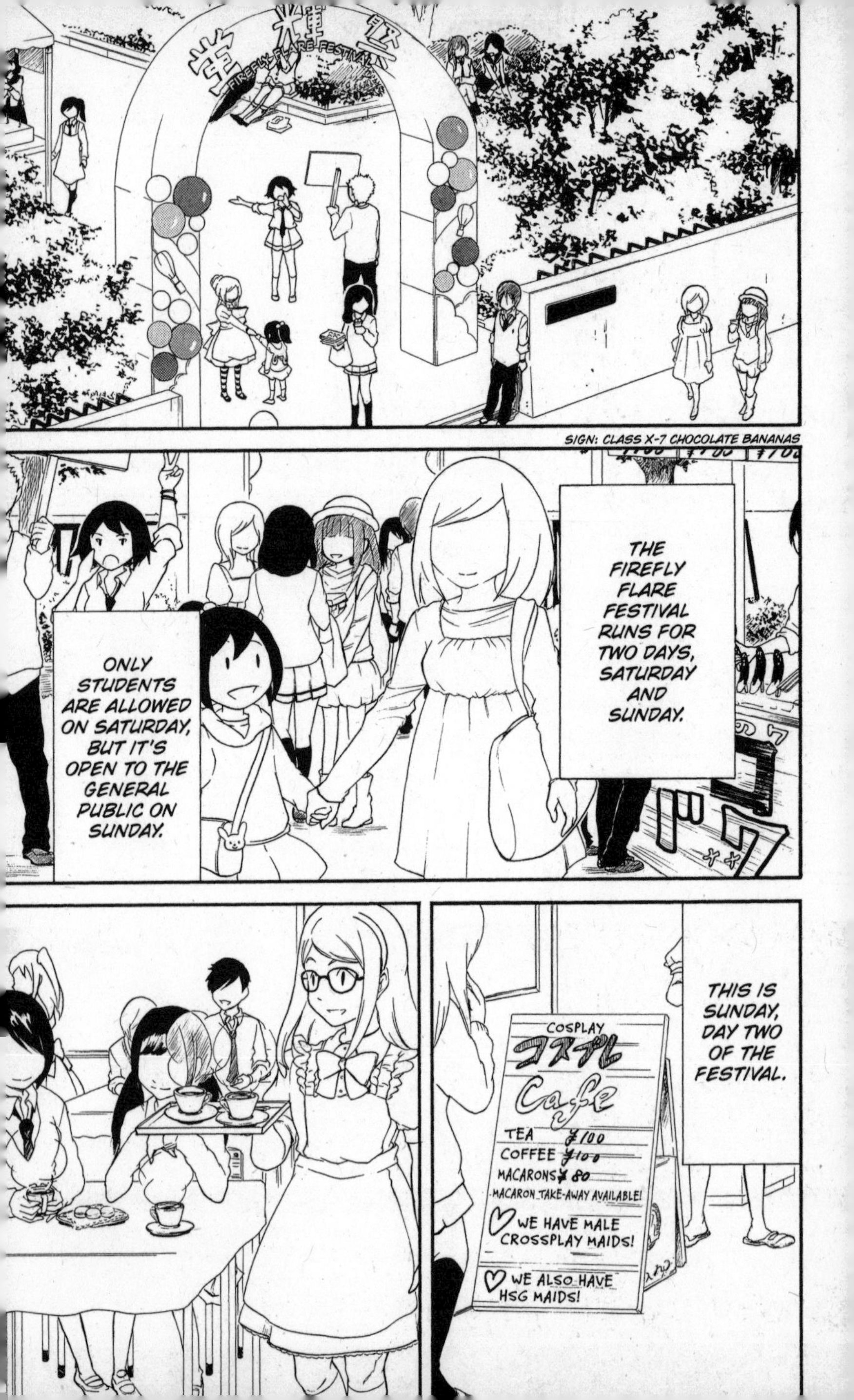
FIREFLY FLARE FESTIVAL
SIGN: CLASS X-7 CHOCOLATE BANANAS
THE FIREFLY FLARE FESTIVAL RUNS FOR TWO DAYS, SATURDAY AND SUNDAY.
ONLY STUDENTS ARE ALLOWED ON SATURDAY, BUT IT'S OPEN TO THE GENERAL PUBLIC ON SUNDAY.
THIS IS SUNDAY, DAY TWO OF THE FESTIVAL.
COSPLAY
コスプレ
Cafe
TEA ¥100
COFFEE ¥100
MACARONS ¥80
MACARON TAKE-AWAY AVAILABLE!
♡ WE HAVE MALE CROSSPLAY MAIDS!
♡ WE ALSO HAVE HSG MAIDS!

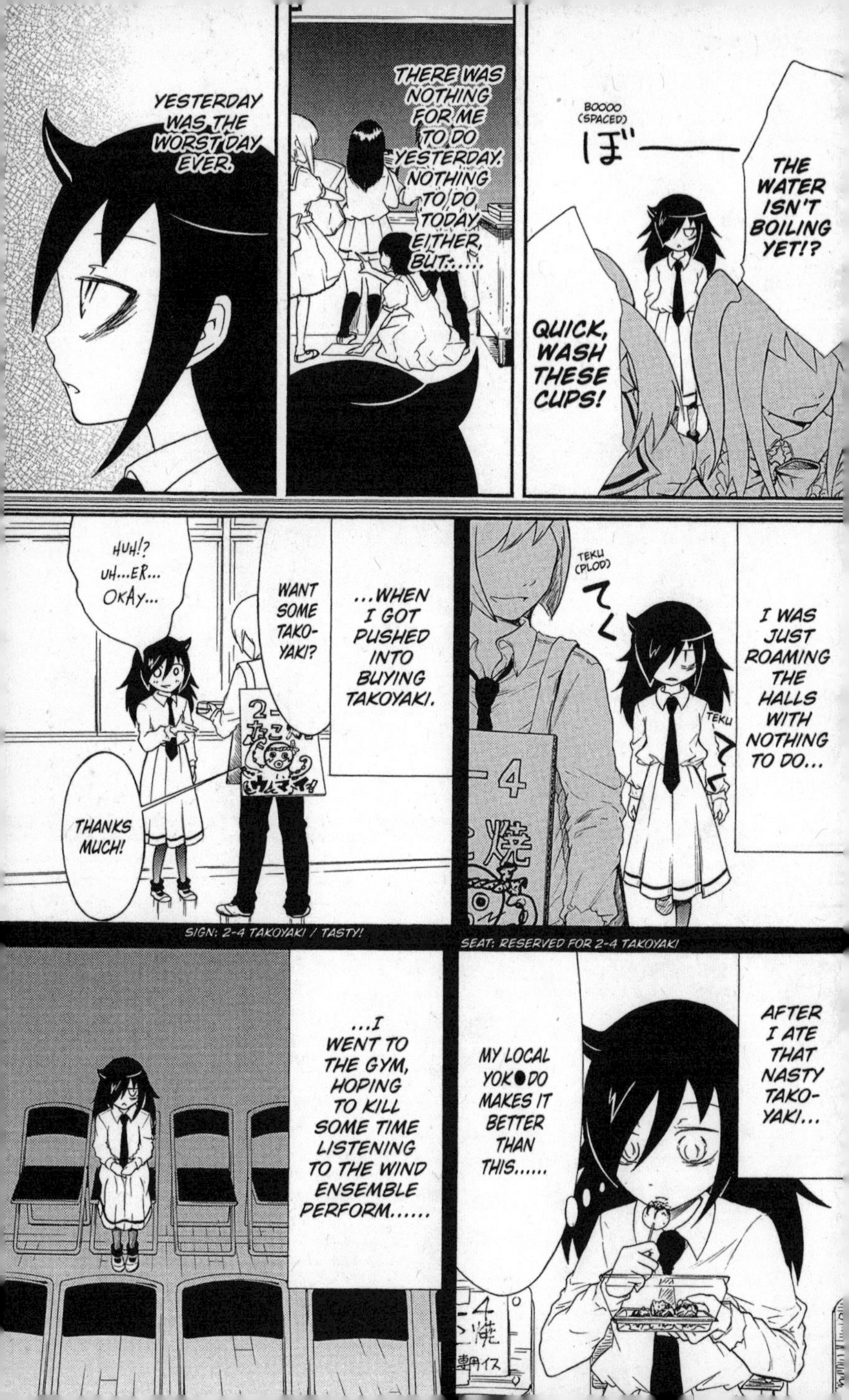
BOOOO (SPACED)
ぼーーー
THE WATER ISN'T BOILING YET!?
QUICK, WASH THESE CUPS!
THERE WAS NOTHING FOR ME TO DO YESTERDAY. NOTHING TO DO TODAY, EITHER, BUT......
YESTERDAY WAS THE WORST DAY EVER.
I WAS JUST ROAMING THE HALLS WITH NOTHING TO DO...
TEKU (PLOD)
TEKU
SEAT: RESERVED FOR 2-4 TAKOYAKI
...WHEN I GOT PUSHED INTO BUYING TAKOYAKI.
WANT SOME TAKO-YAKI?
HUH!? UH...ER... OKAY...
THANKS MUCH!
SIGN: 2-4 TAKOYAKI / TASTY!
AFTER I ATE THAT NASTY TAKO-YAKI...
MY LOCAL YOKO●DO MAKES IT BETTER THAN THIS......
...I WENT TO THE GYM, HOPING TO KILL SOME TIME LISTENING TO THE WIND ENSEMBLE PERFORM......

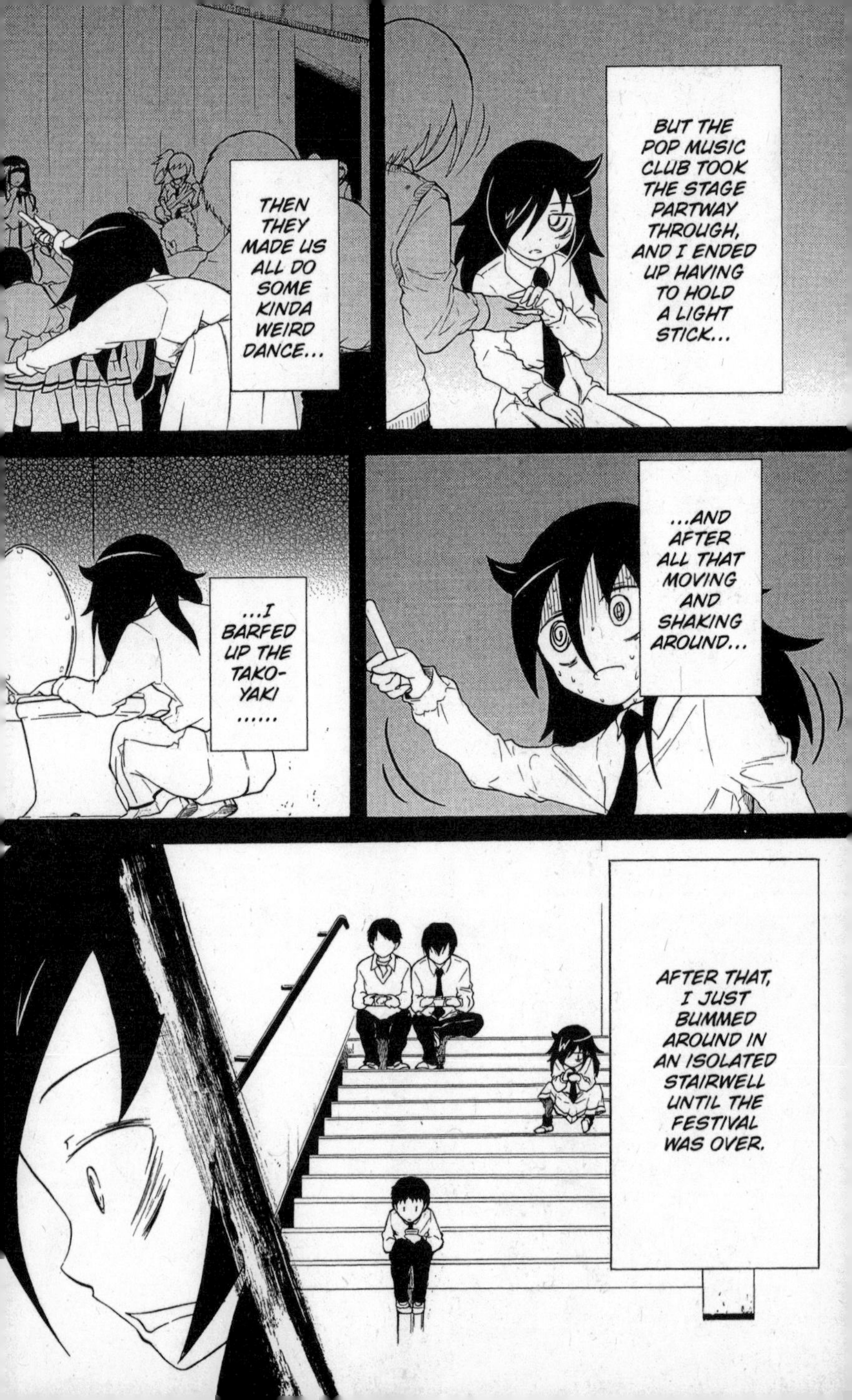
BUT THE POP MUSIC CLUB TOOK THE STAGE PARTWAY THROUGH, AND I ENDED UP HAVING TO HOLD A LIGHT STICK...
THEN THEY MADE US ALL DO SOME KINDA WEIRD DANCE...
...AND AFTER ALL THAT MOVING AND SHAKING AROUND...
...I BARFED UP THE TAKO-YAKI ......
AFTER THAT, I JUST BUMMED AROUND IN AN ISOLATED STAIRWELL UNTIL THE FESTIVAL WAS OVER.

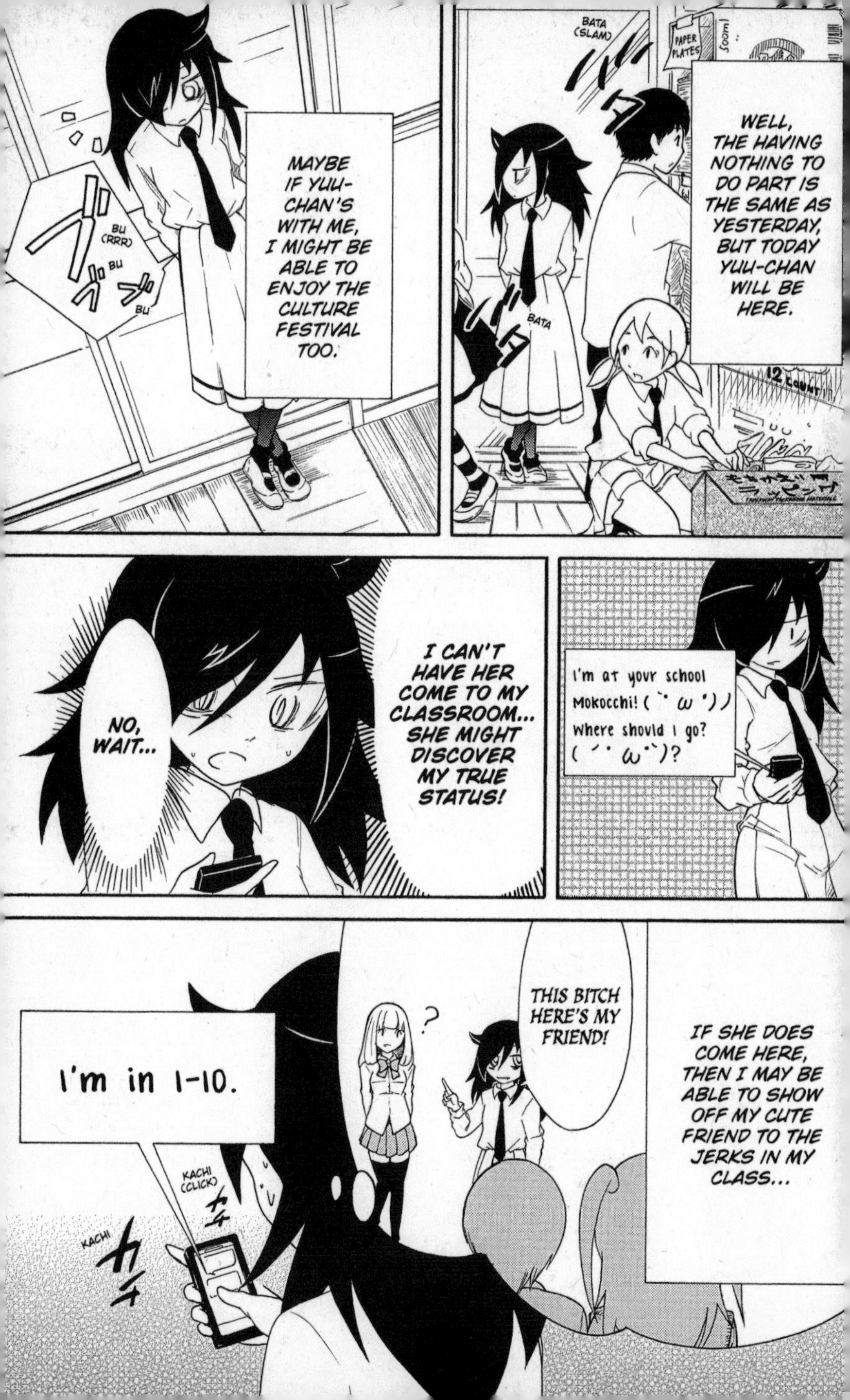
BATA (SLAM)
PAPER PLATES
WELL, THE HAVING NOTHING TO DO PART IS THE SAME AS YESTERDAY, BUT TODAY YUU-CHAN WILL BE HERE.
BATA
12 COUNT
MAYBE IF YUU-CHAN'S WITH ME, I MIGHT BE ABLE TO ENJOY THE CULTURE FESTIVAL TOO.
BU (RRR)
BU
BU
I'm at your school Mokocchi! (´˙ω˙))
Where should I go? (´・ω・`)?
I CAN'T HAVE HER COME TO MY CLASSROOM... SHE MIGHT DISCOVER MY TRUE STATUS!
NO, WAIT...
IF SHE DOES COME HERE, THEN I MAY BE ABLE TO SHOW OFF MY CUTE FRIEND TO THE JERKS IN MY CLASS...
THIS BITCH HERE'S MY FRIEND!
?
I'm in 1-10.
KACHI (CLICK)
KACHI

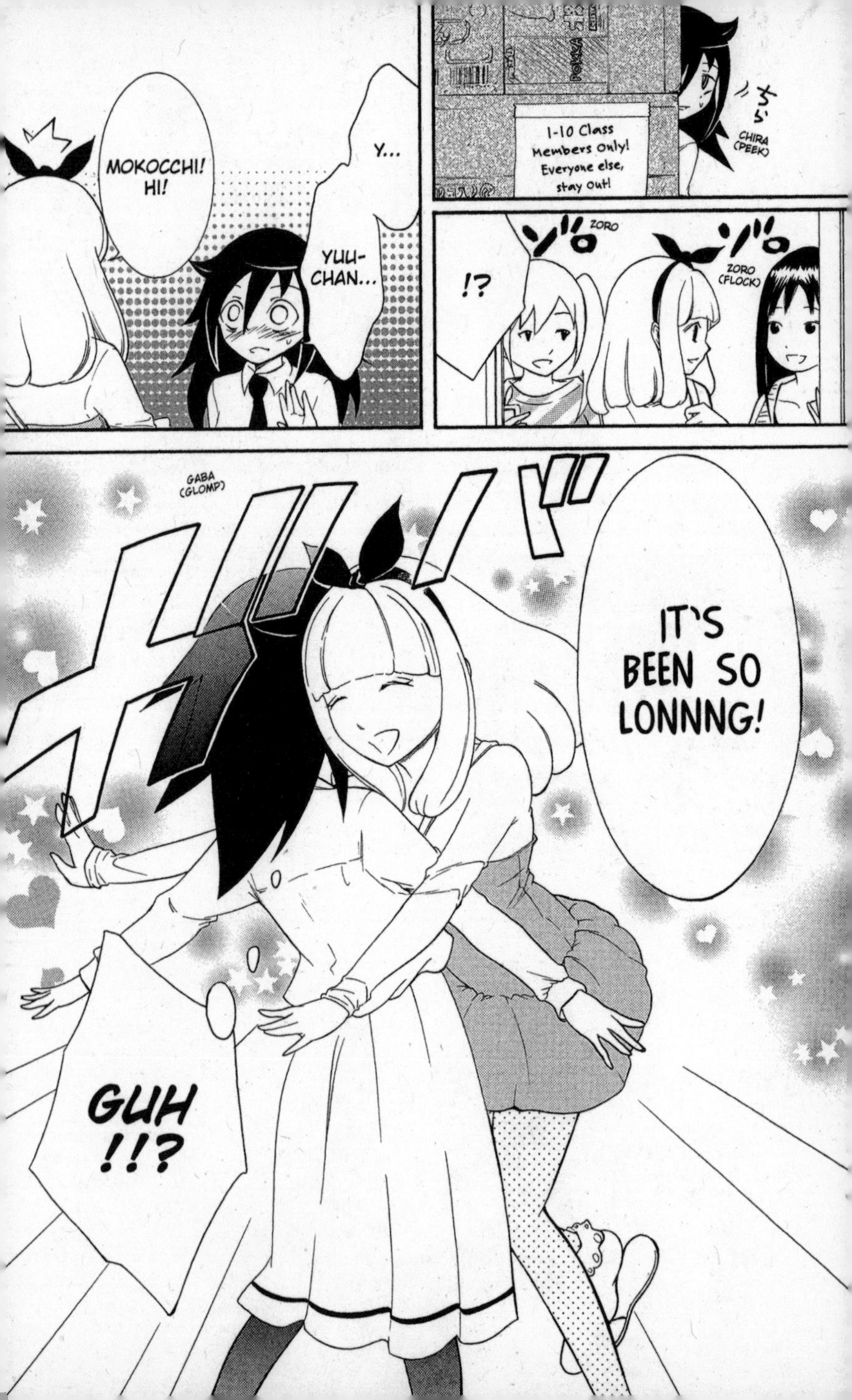
1-10 Class Members Only! Everyone else, stay out!
ちら
CHIRA (PEEK)
ゾロ
ZORO
ゾロ
ZORO (FLOCK)
!?
MOKOCCHI! HI!
Y...
YUU-CHAN...
IT'S BEEN SO LONNNG!
GABA (GLOMP)
GUH !!?

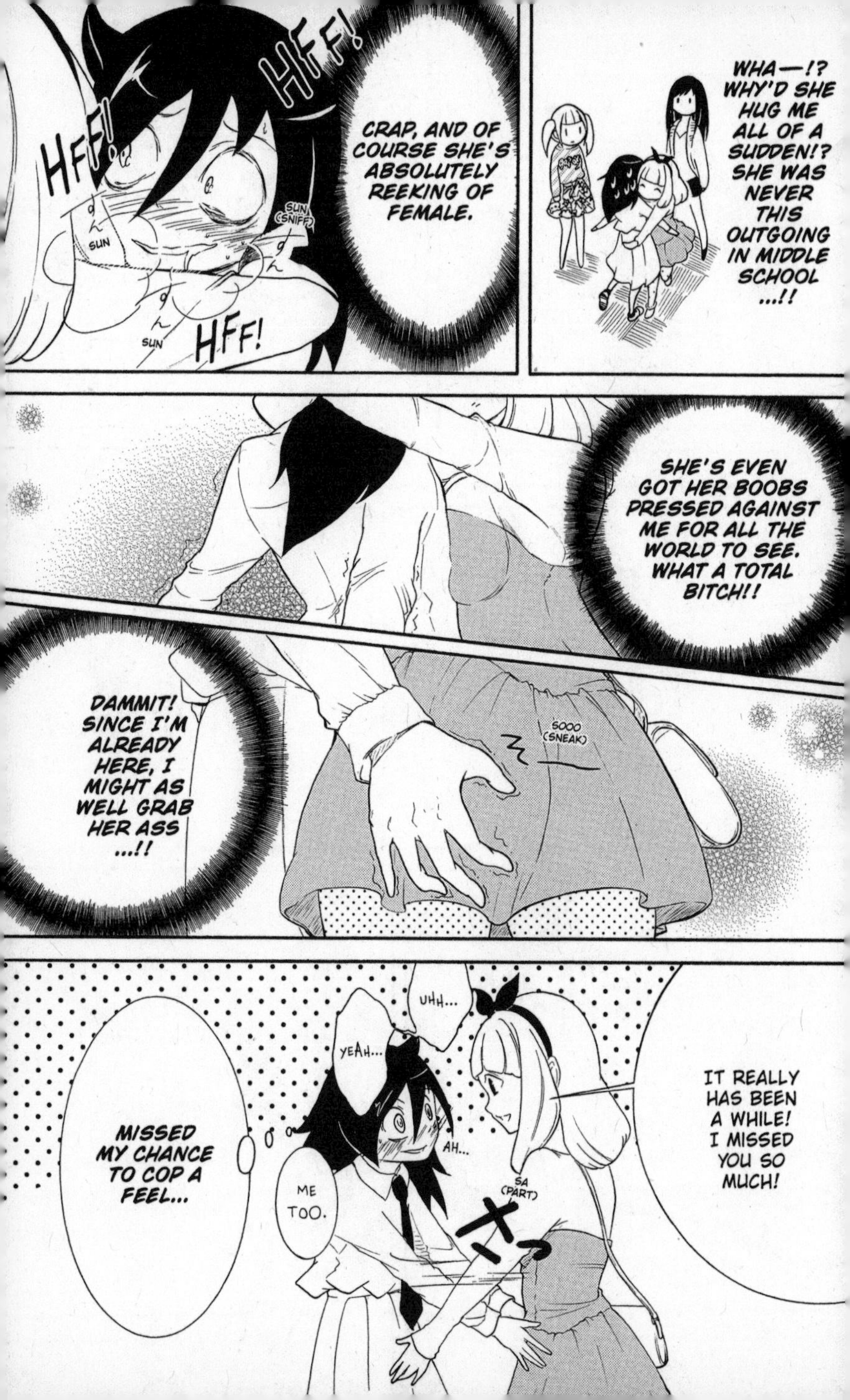
WHA—!? WHY'D SHE HUG ME ALL OF A SUDDEN!? SHE WAS NEVER THIS OUTGOING IN MIDDLE SCHOOL ...!!
HFF!
HFF!
CRAP, AND OF COURSE SHE'S ABSOLUTELY REEKING OF FEMALE.
SUN (SNIFF)
SUN
SUN
HFF!
SHE'S EVEN GOT HER BOOBS PRESSED AGAINST ME FOR ALL THE WORLD TO SEE. WHAT A TOTAL BITCH!!
SOOO (SNEAK)
DAMMIT! SINCE I'M ALREADY HERE, I MIGHT AS WELL GRAB HER ASS ...!!
IT REALLY HAS BEEN A WHILE! I MISSED YOU SO MUCH!
UHH...
YEAH...
AH...
SA (PART)
ME TOO.
MISSED MY CHANCE TO COP A FEEL...

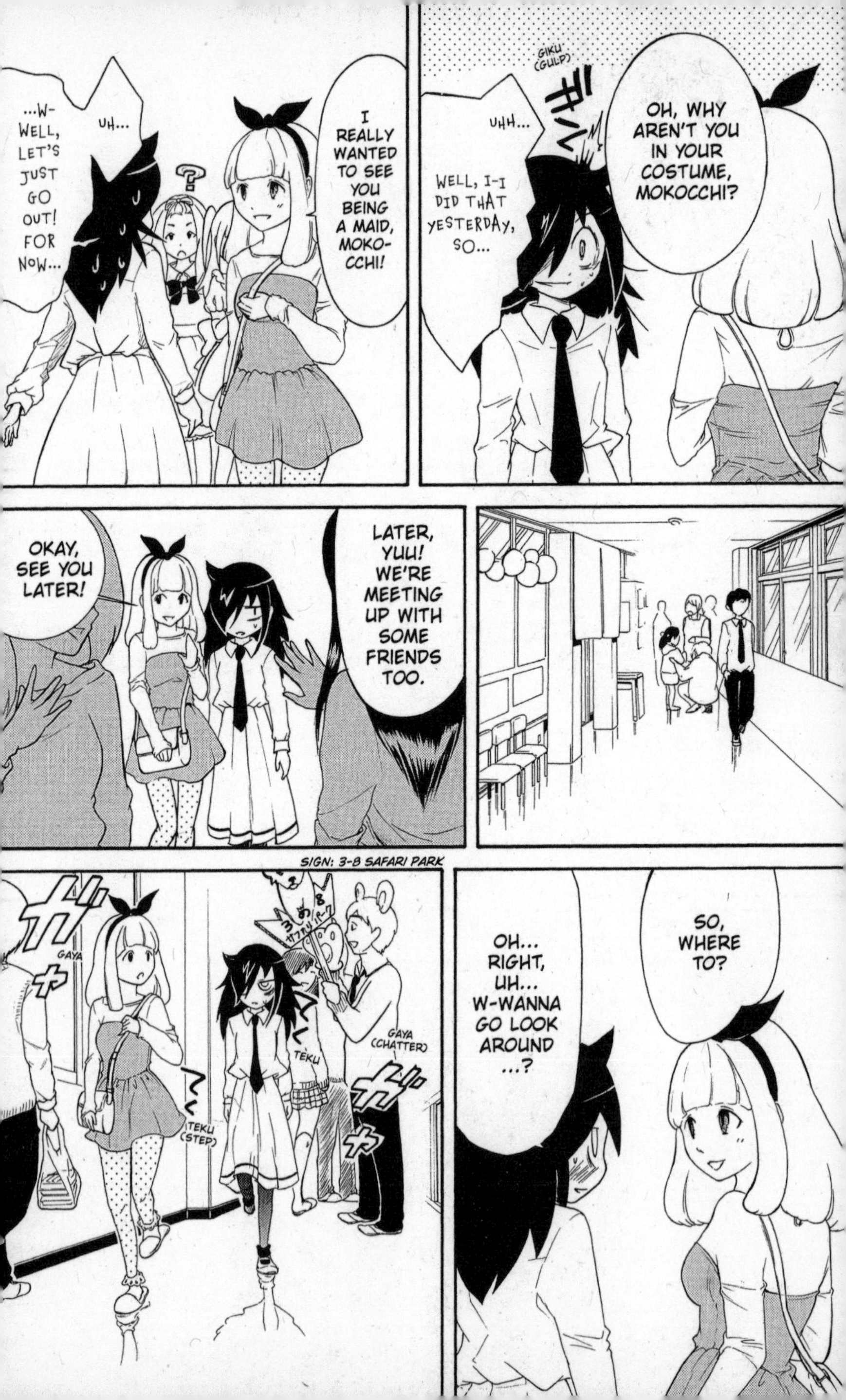
OH, WHY AREN'T YOU IN YOUR COSTUME, MOKOCCHI?
GIKU (GULP)
UHH...
WELL, I-I DID THAT YESTERDAY, SO...
I REALLY WANTED TO SEE YOU BEING A MAID, MOKO-CCHI!
UH...
...W-WELL, LET'S JUST GO OUT! FOR NOW...
LATER, YUU! WE'RE MEETING UP WITH SOME FRIENDS TOO.
OKAY, SEE YOU LATER!
SIGN: 3-8 SAFARI PARK
SO, WHERE TO?
OH... RIGHT, UH... W-WANNA GO LOOK AROUND ...?
GAYA (CHATTER)
TEKU
TEKU (STEP)
GAYA

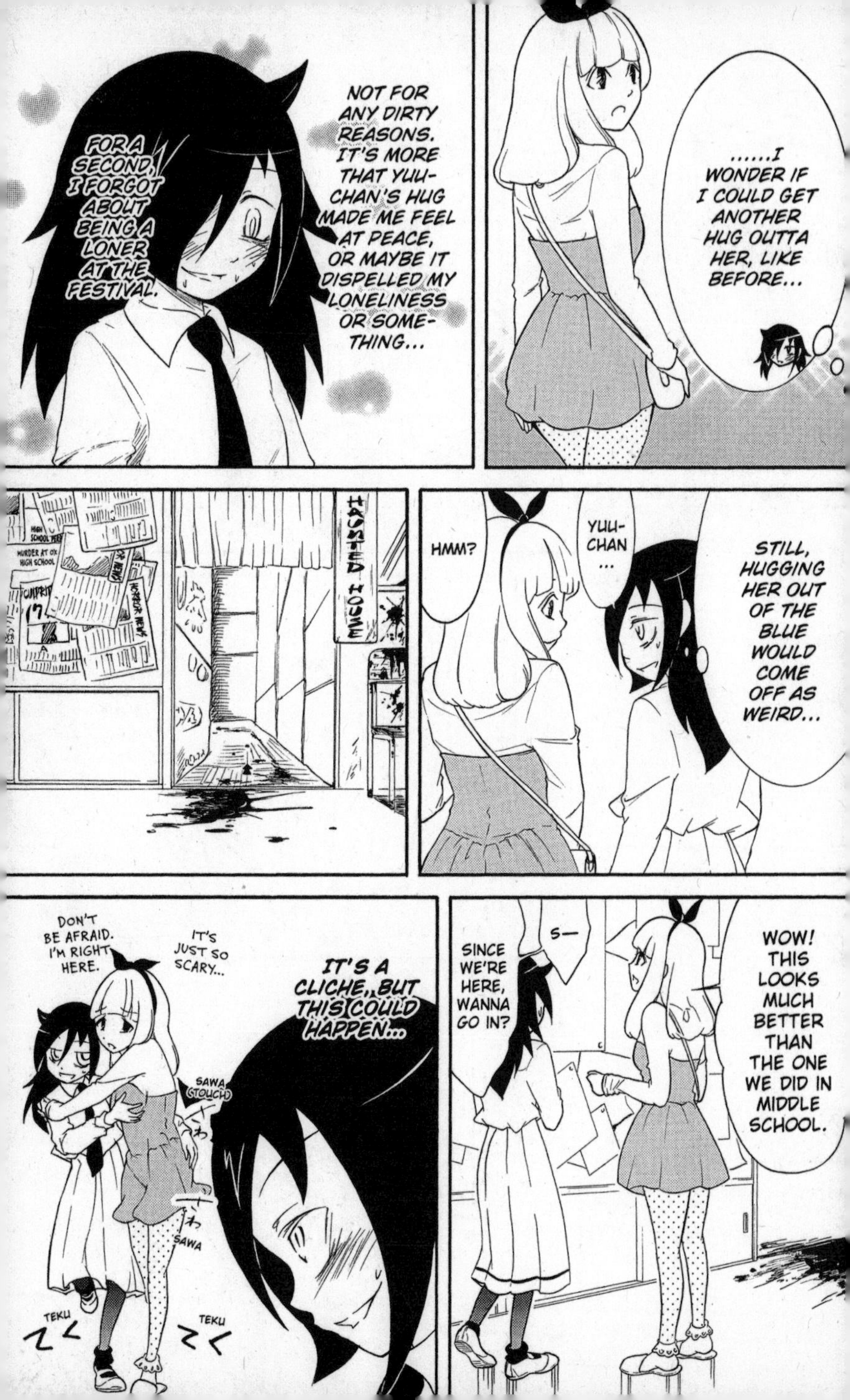

......I WONDER IF I COULD GET ANOTHER HUG OUTTA HER, LIKE BEFORE...
NOT FOR ANY DIRTY REASONS. IT'S MORE THAT YUU-CHAN'S HUG MADE ME FEEL AT PEACE, OR MAYBE IT DISPELLED MY LONELINESS OR SOME-THING...
FOR A SECOND, I FORGOT ABOUT BEING A LONER AT THE FESTIVAL.
STILL, HUGGING HER OUT OF THE BLUE WOULD COME OFF AS WEIRD...
YUU-CHAN...
HMM?
HAUNTED HOUSE
HORROR NEWS
MURDER AT OX HIGH SCHOOL
WOW! THIS LOOKS MUCH BETTER THAN THE ONE WE DID IN MIDDLE SCHOOL.
S—
SINCE WE'RE HERE, WANNA GO IN?
IT'S A CLICHE, BUT THIS COULD HAPPEN...
IT'S JUST SO SCARY...
DON'T BE AFRAID. I'M RIGHT HERE.
SAWA (TOUCH)
SAWA
TEKU
TEKU

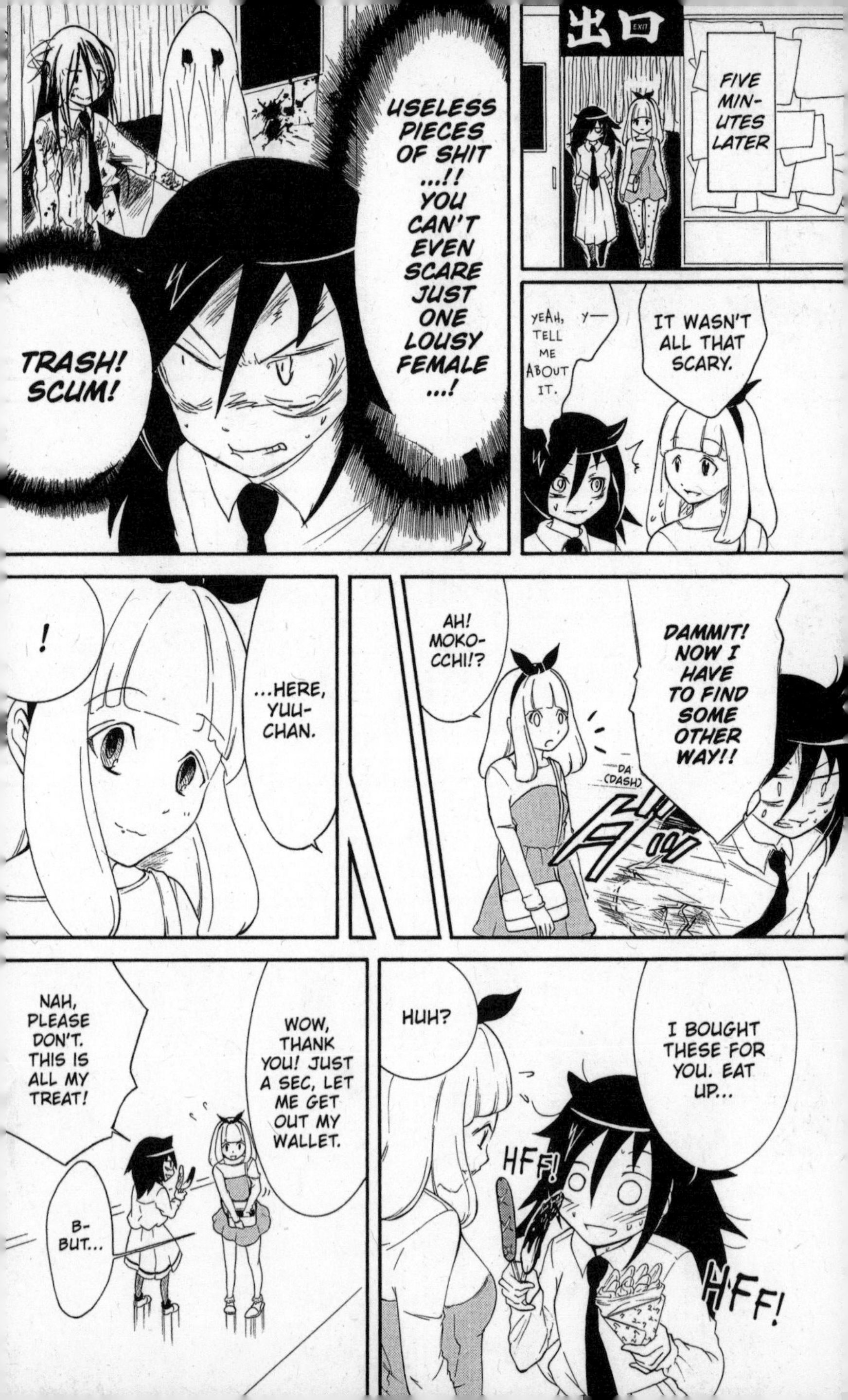
出口
EXIT
FIVE MIN-UTES LATER
IT WASN'T ALL THAT SCARY.
YEAH, TELL ME ABOUT IT. Y—
USELESS PIECES OF SHIT ...!! YOU CAN'T EVEN SCARE JUST ONE LOUSY FEMALE ...!
TRASH! SCUM!
DAMMIT! NOW I HAVE TO FIND SOME OTHER WAY!!
AH! MOKO-CCHI!?
DA (DASH)
...HERE, YUU-CHAN.
!
I BOUGHT THESE FOR YOU. EAT UP...
HUH?
HFF!
HFF!
WOW, THANK YOU! JUST A SEC, LET ME GET OUT MY WALLET.
NAH, PLEASE DON'T. THIS IS ALL MY TREAT!
B-BUT...

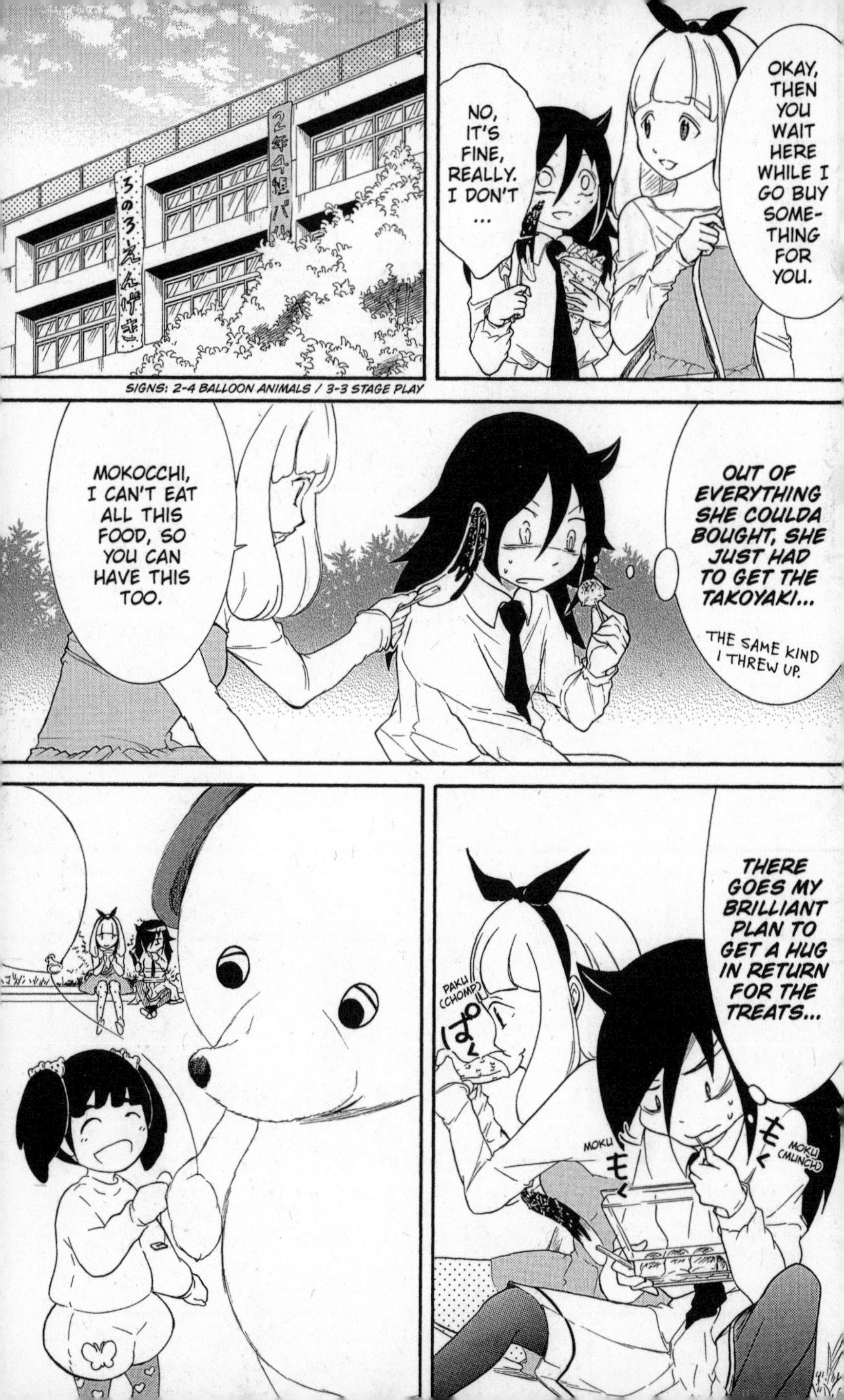
OKAY, THEN YOU WAIT HERE WHILE I GO BUY SOMETHING FOR YOU.
NO, IT'S FINE, REALLY. I DON'T ...
SIGNS: 2-4 BALLOON ANIMALS / 3-3 STAGE PLAY
OUT OF EVERYTHING SHE COULDA BOUGHT, SHE JUST HAD TO GET THE TAKOYAKI...
THE SAME KIND I THREW UP.
MOKOCCHI, I CAN'T EAT ALL THIS FOOD, SO YOU CAN HAVE THIS TOO.
THERE GOES MY BRILLIANT PLAN TO GET A HUG IN RETURN FOR THE TREATS...
MOKU (MUNCH)
MOKU
PAKU (CHOMP)

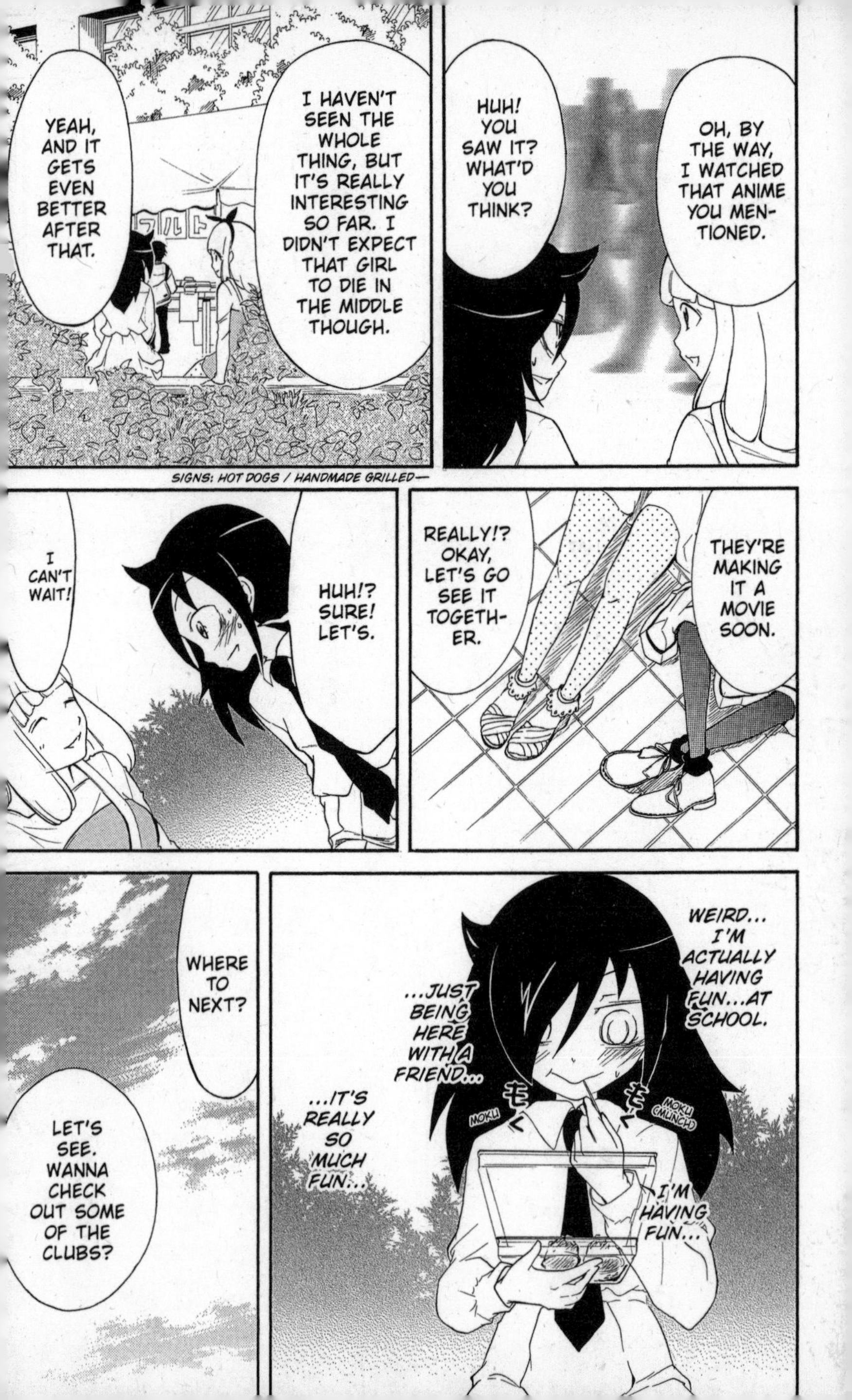
OH, BY THE WAY, I WATCHED THAT ANIME YOU MENTIONED.
HUH! YOU SAW IT? WHAT'D YOU THINK?
I HAVEN'T SEEN THE WHOLE THING, BUT IT'S REALLY INTERESTING SO FAR. I DIDN'T EXPECT THAT GIRL TO DIE IN THE MIDDLE THOUGH.
YEAH, AND IT GETS EVEN BETTER AFTER THAT.
SIGNS: HOT DOGS / HANDMADE GRILLED—
THEY'RE MAKING IT A MOVIE SOON.
REALLY!? OKAY, LET'S GO SEE IT TOGETH-ER.
HUH!? SURE! LET'S.
I CAN'T WAIT!
WEIRD... I'M ACTUALLY HAVING FUN...AT SCHOOL.
...JUST BEING HERE WITH A FRIEND...
MOKU (MUNCH)
MOKU
...IT'S REALLY SO MUCH FUN...
I'M HAVING FUN...
WHERE TO NEXT?
LET'S SEE. WANNA CHECK OUT SOME OF THE CLUBS?

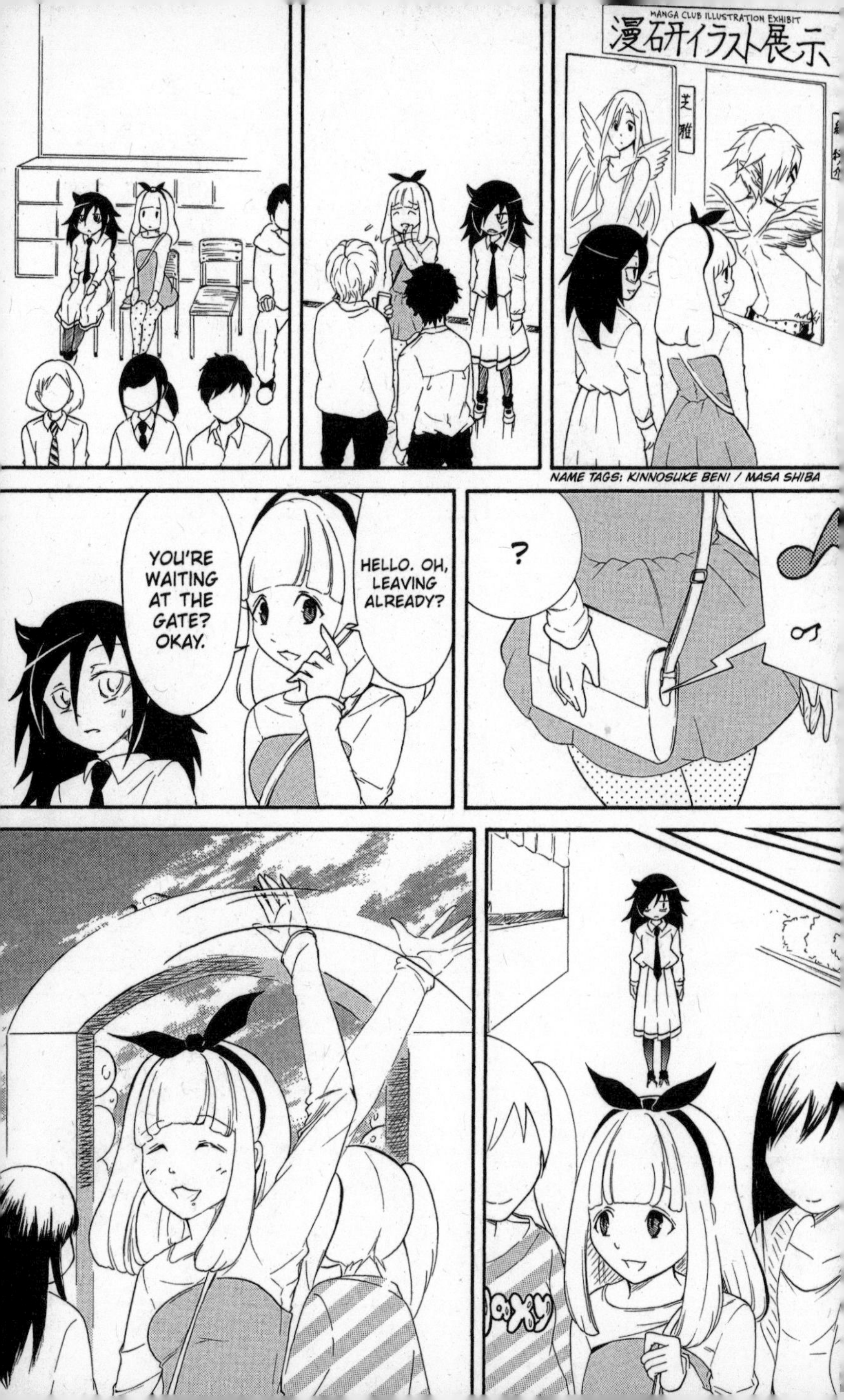
MANGA CLUB ILLUSTRATION EXHIBIT
漫研イラスト展示
NAME TAGS: KINNOSUKE BENI / MASA SHIBA
?
HELLO. OH, LEAVING ALREADY?
YOU'RE WAITING AT THE GATE? OKAY.

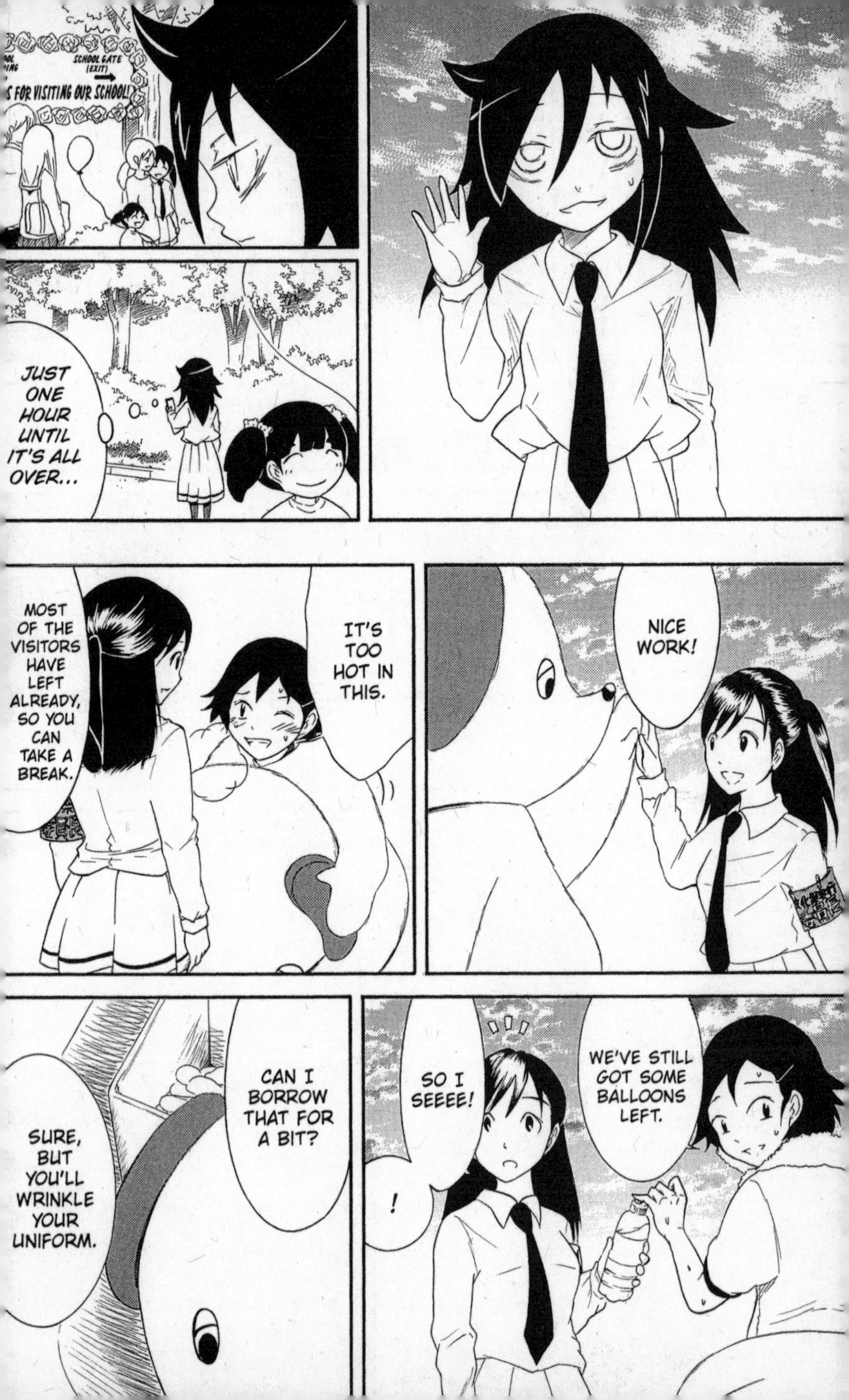
SCHOOL GATE (EXIT)
S FOR VISITING OUR SCHOOL!
JUST ONE HOUR UNTIL IT'S ALL OVER...
NICE WORK!
IT'S TOO HOT IN THIS.
MOST OF THE VISITORS HAVE LEFT ALREADY, SO YOU CAN TAKE A BREAK.
WE'VE STILL GOT SOME BALLOONS LEFT.
SO I SEEEE!
!
CAN I BORROW THAT FOR A BIT?
SURE, BUT YOU'LL WRINKLE YOUR UNIFORM.

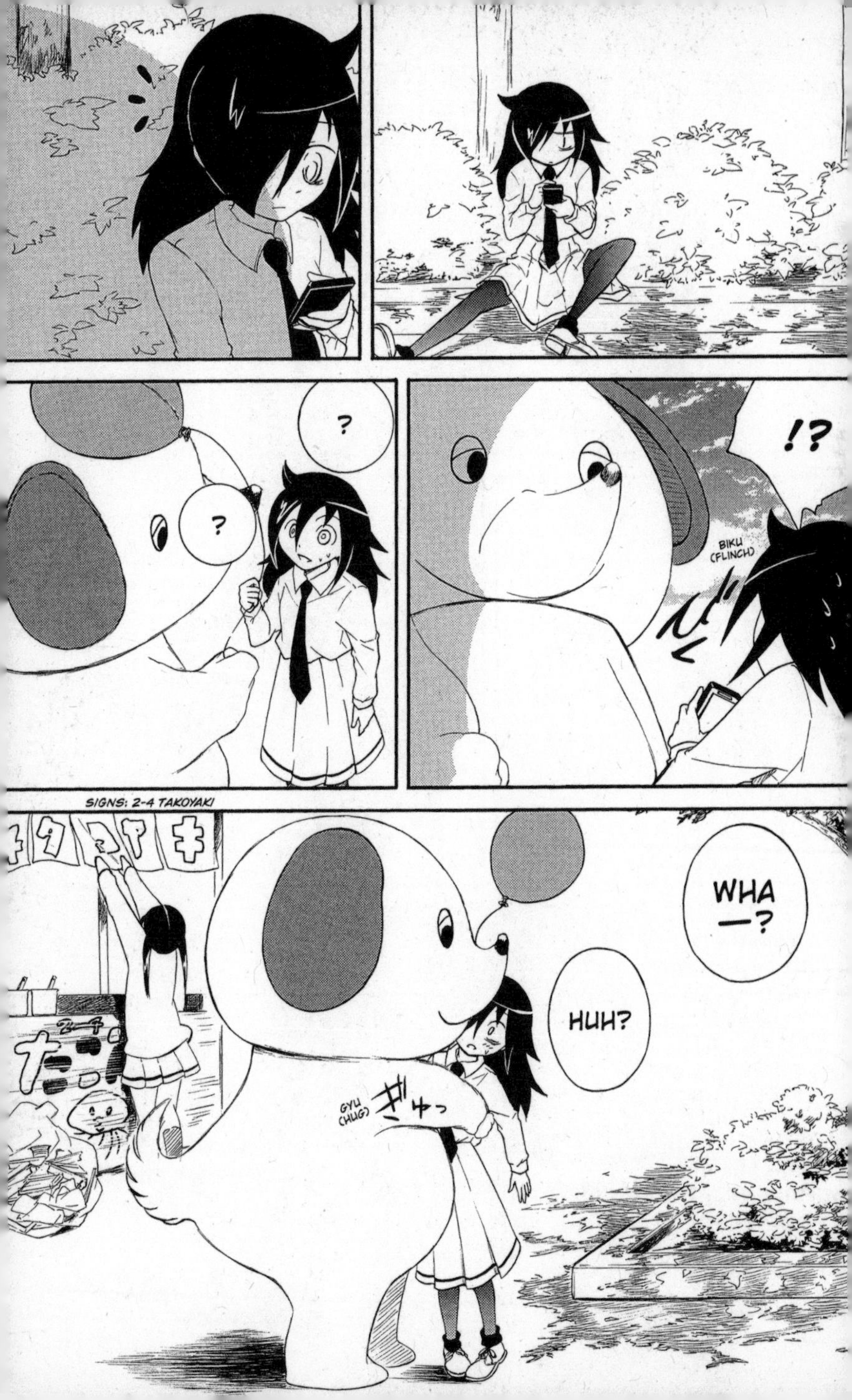
!?
BIKU (FLINCH)
?
?
SIGNS: 2-4 TAKOYAKI
WHA—?
HUH?
GYU (HUG)

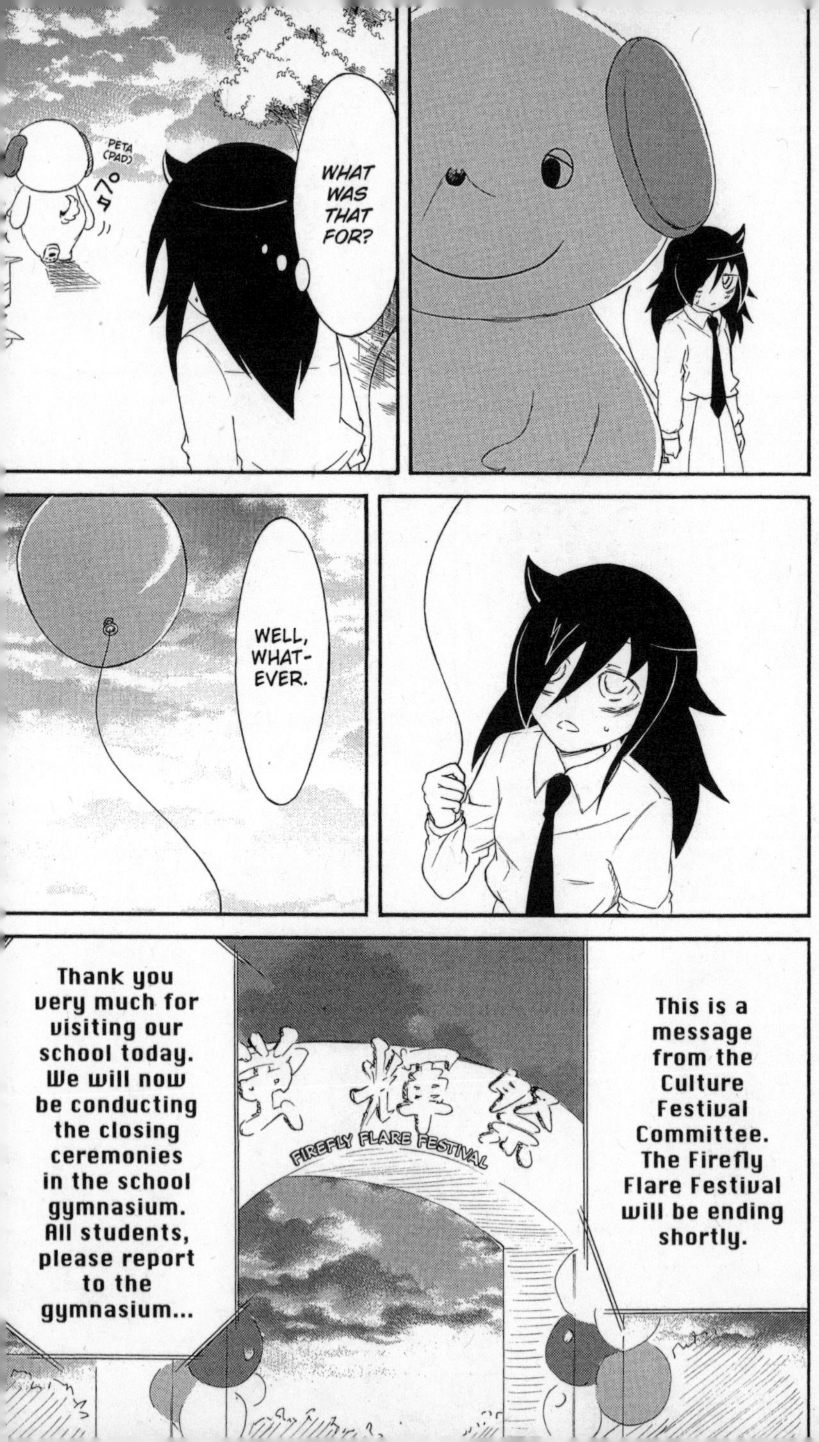
WHAT WAS THAT FOR?
PETA (PAD)
WELL, WHAT-EVER.
This is a message from the Culture Festival Committee. The Firefly Flare Festival will be ending shortly.
Thank you very much for visiting our school today. We will now be conducting the closing ceremonies in the school gymnasium. All students, please report to the gymnasium...
FIREFLY FLARE FESTIVAL

No Matter How I Look at It, It's You Guys' Fault I'm Not Popular!

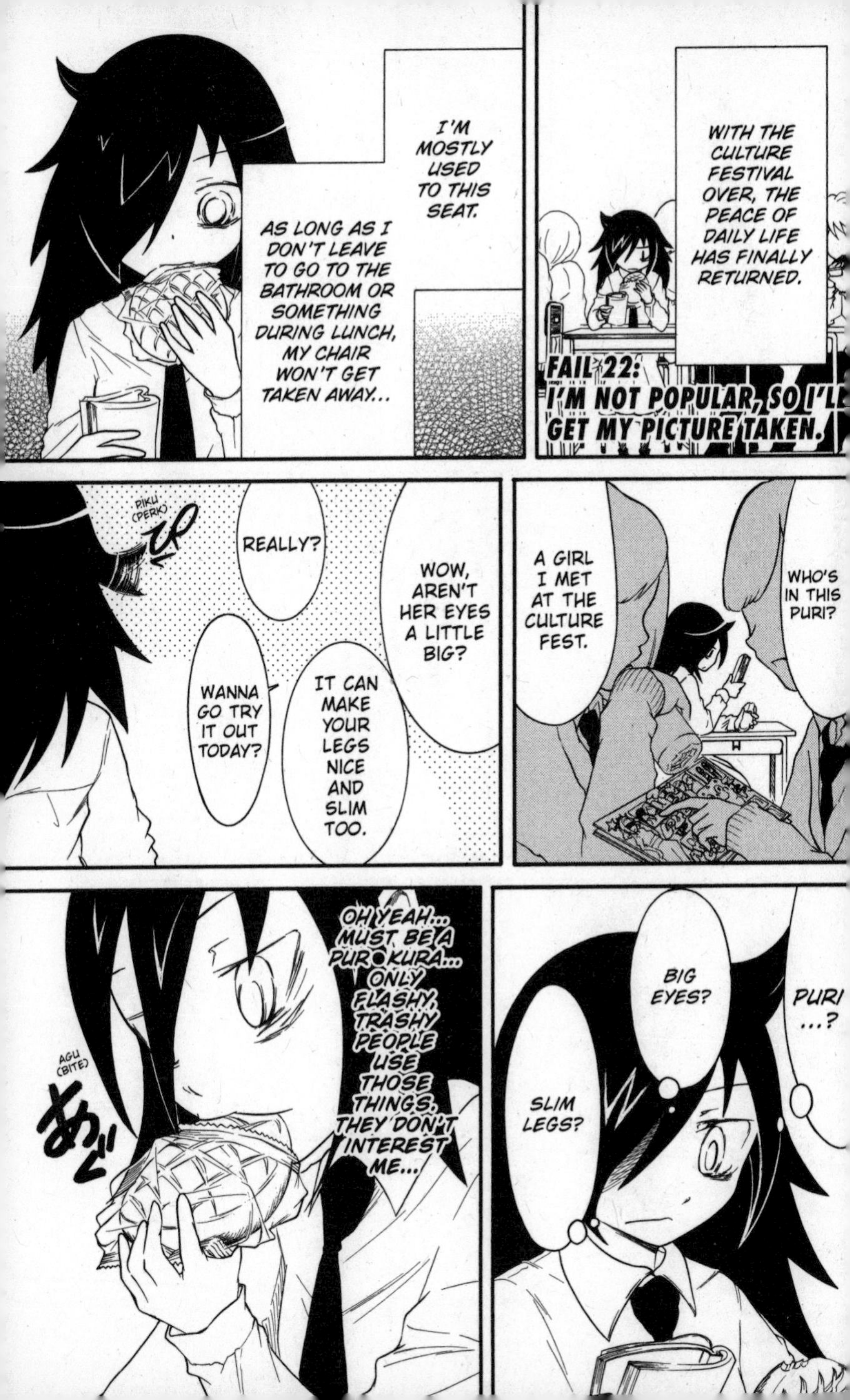
WITH THE CULTURE FESTIVAL OVER, THE PEACE OF DAILY LIFE HAS FINALLY RETURNED.
FAIL 22: I'M NOT POPULAR, SO I'LL GET MY PICTURE TAKEN.
I'M MOSTLY USED TO THIS SEAT.
AS LONG AS I DON'T LEAVE TO GO TO THE BATHROOM OR SOMETHING DURING LUNCH, MY CHAIR WON'T GET TAKEN AWAY...
WHO'S IN THIS PURI?
A GIRL I MET AT THE CULTURE FEST.
WOW, AREN'T HER EYES A LITTLE BIG?
REALLY?
IT CAN MAKE YOUR LEGS NICE AND SLIM TOO.
WANNA GO TRY IT OUT TODAY?
PIKU (PERK)
PURI ...?
BIG EYES?
SLIM LEGS?
OH YEAH... MUST BE A PURI KURA... ONLY FLASHY, TRASHY PEOPLE USE THOSE THINGS. THEY DON'T INTEREST ME...
AGU (BITE)
あぐ

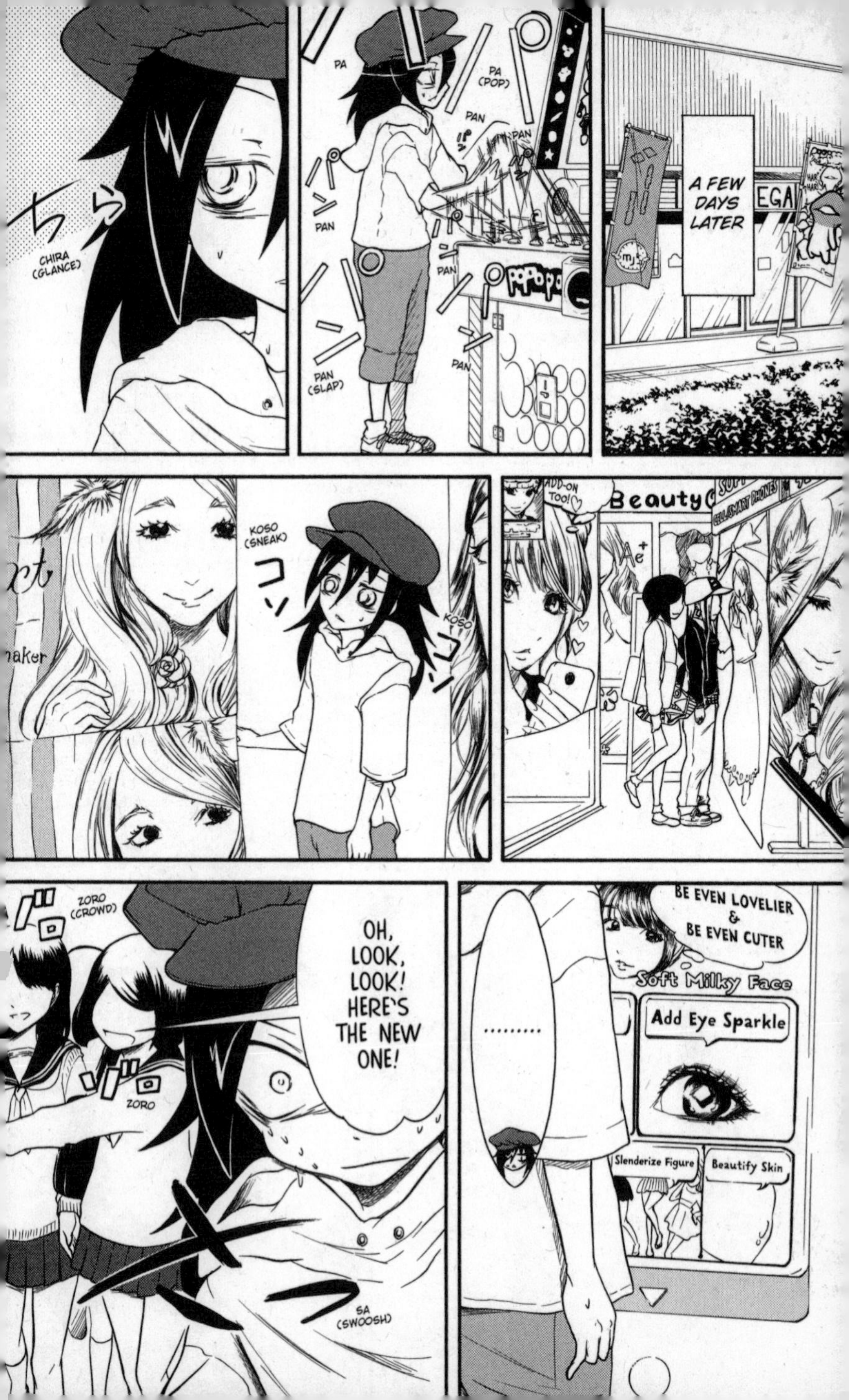
A FEW DAYS LATER
EGA
PA
PA (POP)
PAN
PAN
PAN
PAN
PAN
PAN (SLAP)
POPOPO
CHIRA (GLANCE)
ADD-ON TOO!
Beauty
CELL&SMART PHONES
KOSO (SNEAK)
KOSO
BE EVEN LOVELIER & BE EVEN CUTER
Soft Milky Face
Add Eye Sparkle
Slenderize Figure
Beautify Skin
....
OH, LOOK, LOOK! HERE'S THE NEW ONE!
ZORO (CROWD)
ZORO
SA (SWOOSH)

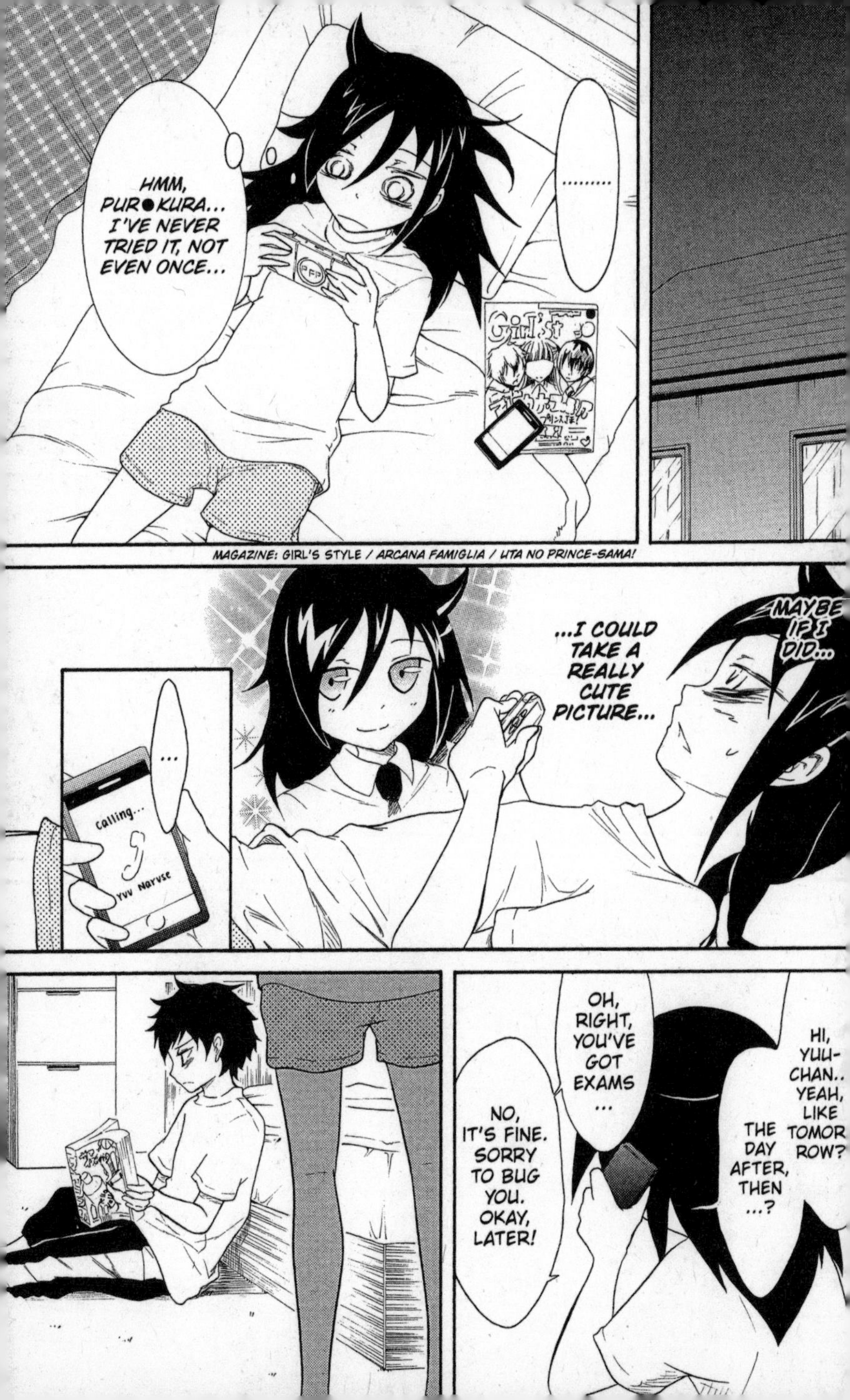
....
HMM, PUR●KURA... I'VE NEVER TRIED IT, NOT EVEN ONCE...
MAGAZINE: GIRL'S STYLE / ARCANA FAMIGLIA / UTA NO PRINCE-SAMA!
MAYBE IF I DID...
...I COULD TAKE A REALLY CUTE PICTURE...
...
Calling...
Yuu Naruse
HI, YUU-CHAN.. YEAH, LIKE TOMOR ROW?
OH, RIGHT, YOU'VE GOT EXAMS ...
THE DAY AFTER, THEN ...?
NO, IT'S FINE. SORRY TO BUG YOU. OKAY, LATER!

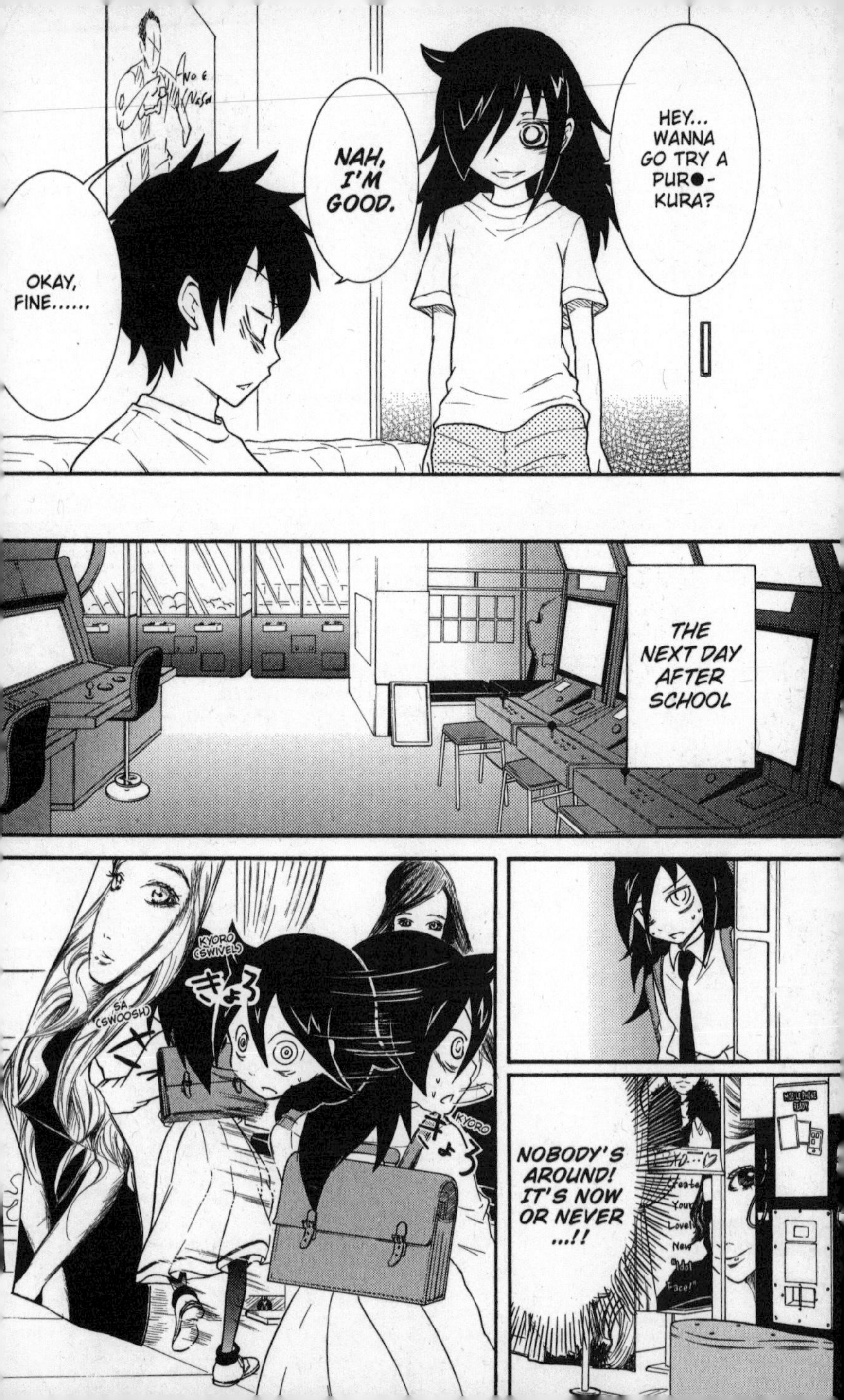
HEY... WANNA GO TRY A PURO●-KURA?
NAH, I'M GOOD.
OKAY, FINE......
THE NEXT DAY AFTER SCHOOL
NOBODY'S AROUND! IT'S NOW OR NEVER ...!!
KYORO (SWIVEL)
SA (SWOOSH)
KYORO

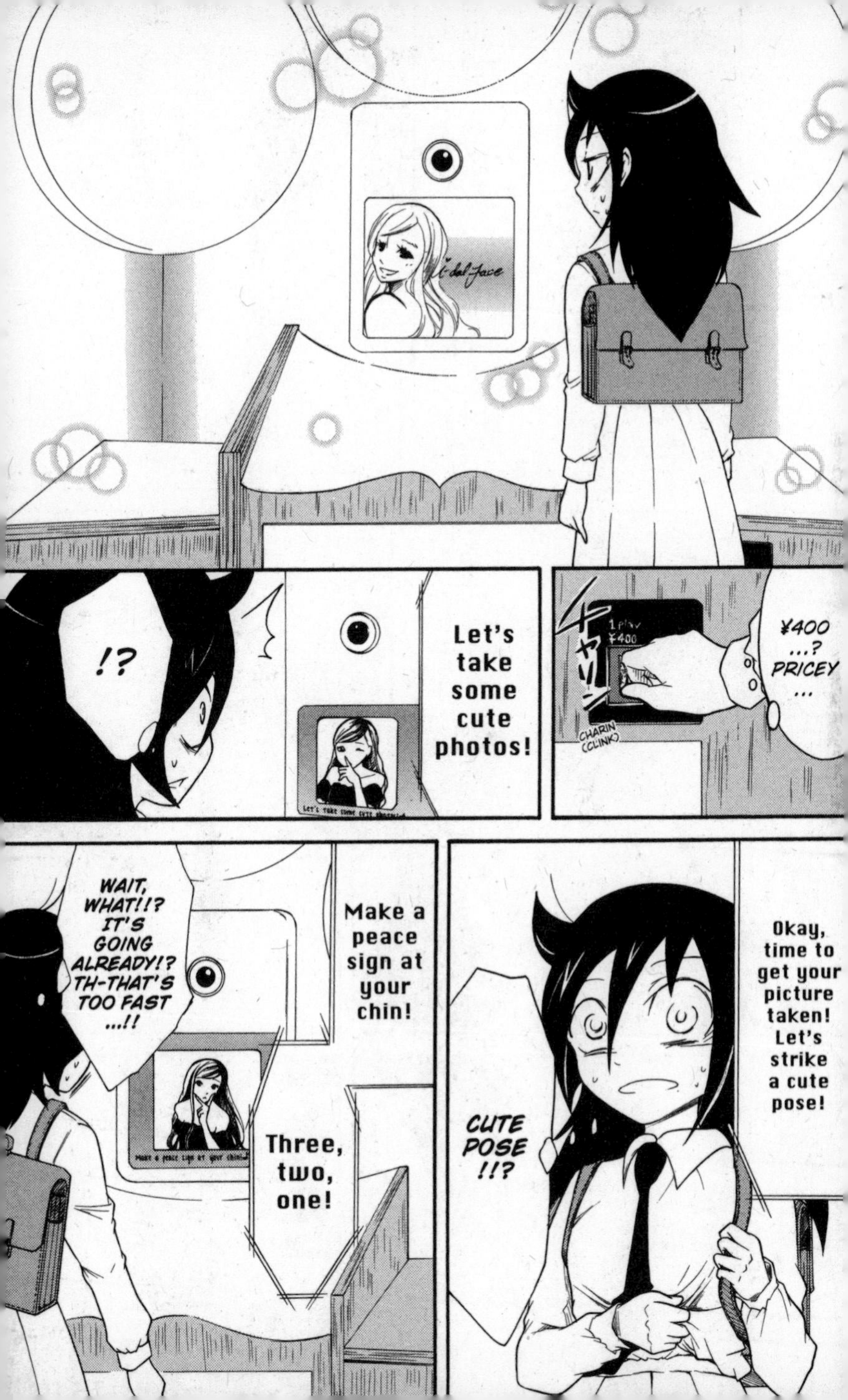
1 play
¥400
CHARIN (CLINK)
¥400 ...? PRICEY ...
Let's take some cute photos!
!?
Okay, time to get your picture taken! Let's strike a cute pose!
CUTE POSE !!?
Make a peace sign at your chin!
WAIT, WHAT!!? IT'S GOING ALREADY!? TH-THAT'S TOO FAST ...!!
Three, two, one!

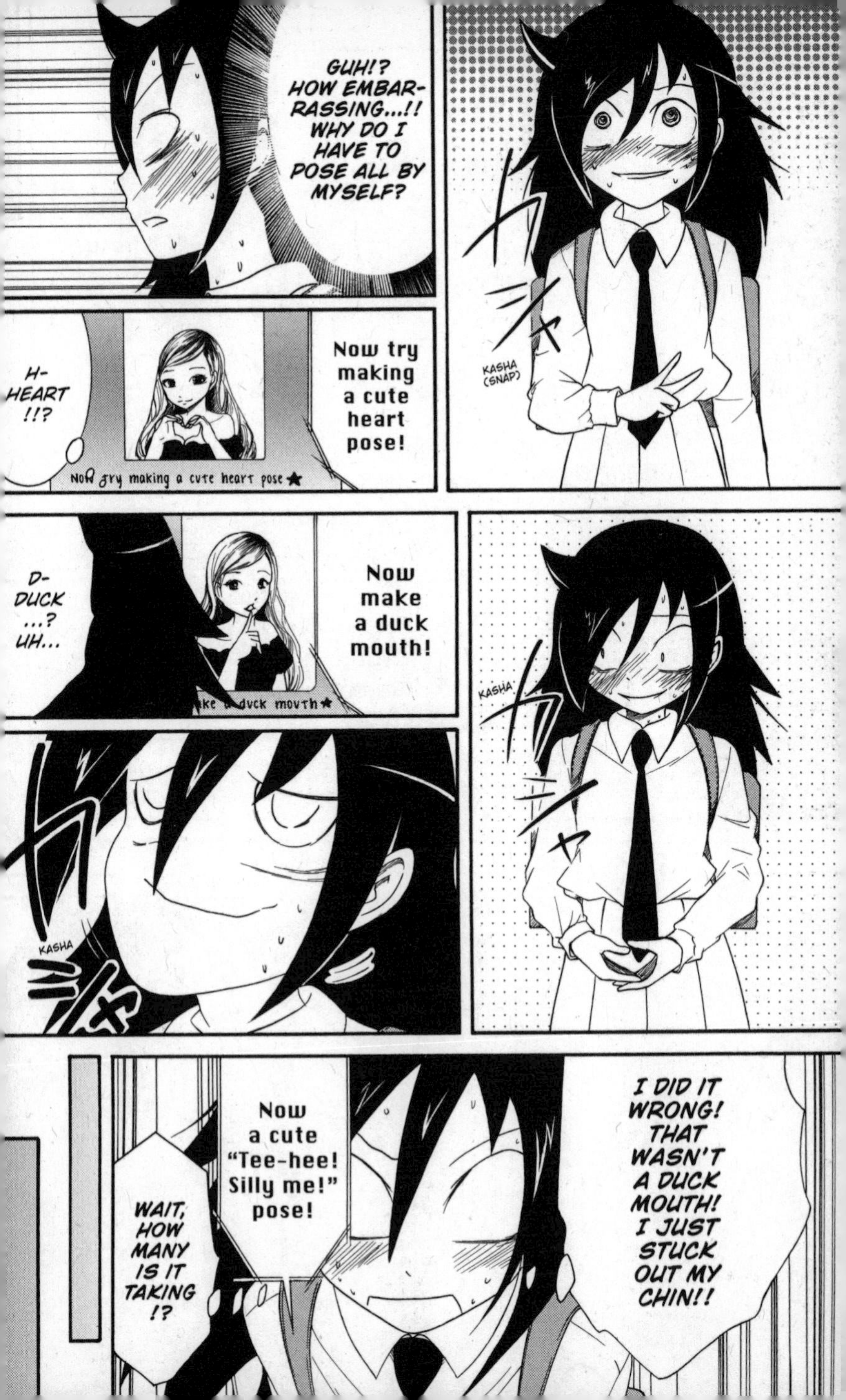
KASHA (SNAP)
GUH!? HOW EMBARRASSING...!! WHY DO I HAVE TO POSE ALL BY MYSELF?
Now try making a cute heart pose!
Now try making a cute heart pose★
H-HEART!!?
KASHA
Now make a duck mouth!
ake a duck mouth★
D-DUCK...? UH...
KASHA
I DID IT WRONG! THAT WASN'T A DUCK MOUTH! I JUST STUCK OUT MY CHIN!!
Now a cute "Tee-hee! Silly me!" pose!
WAIT, HOW MANY IS IT TAKING!?

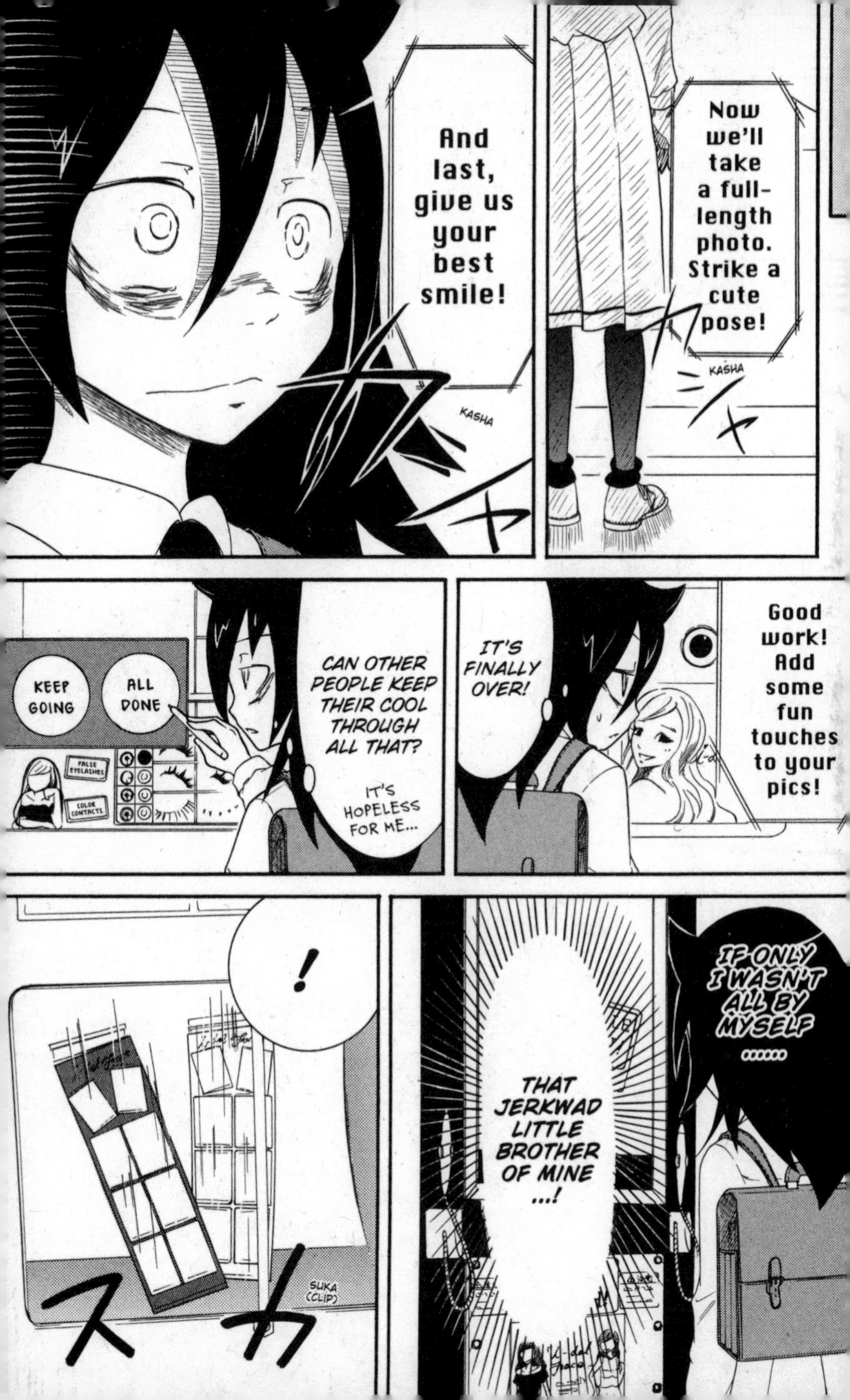
Now we'll take a full-length photo. Strike a cute pose!
KASHA
And last, give us your best smile!
KASHA
Good work! Add some fun touches to your pics!
IT'S FINALLY OVER!
CAN OTHER PEOPLE KEEP THEIR COOL THROUGH ALL THAT?
IT'S HOPELESS FOR ME...
KEEP GOING
ALL DONE
FALSE EYELASHES
COLOR CONTACTS
IF ONLY I WASN'T ALL BY MYSELF ......
THAT JERKWAD LITTLE BROTHER OF MINE ...!
!
SUKA (CLIP)

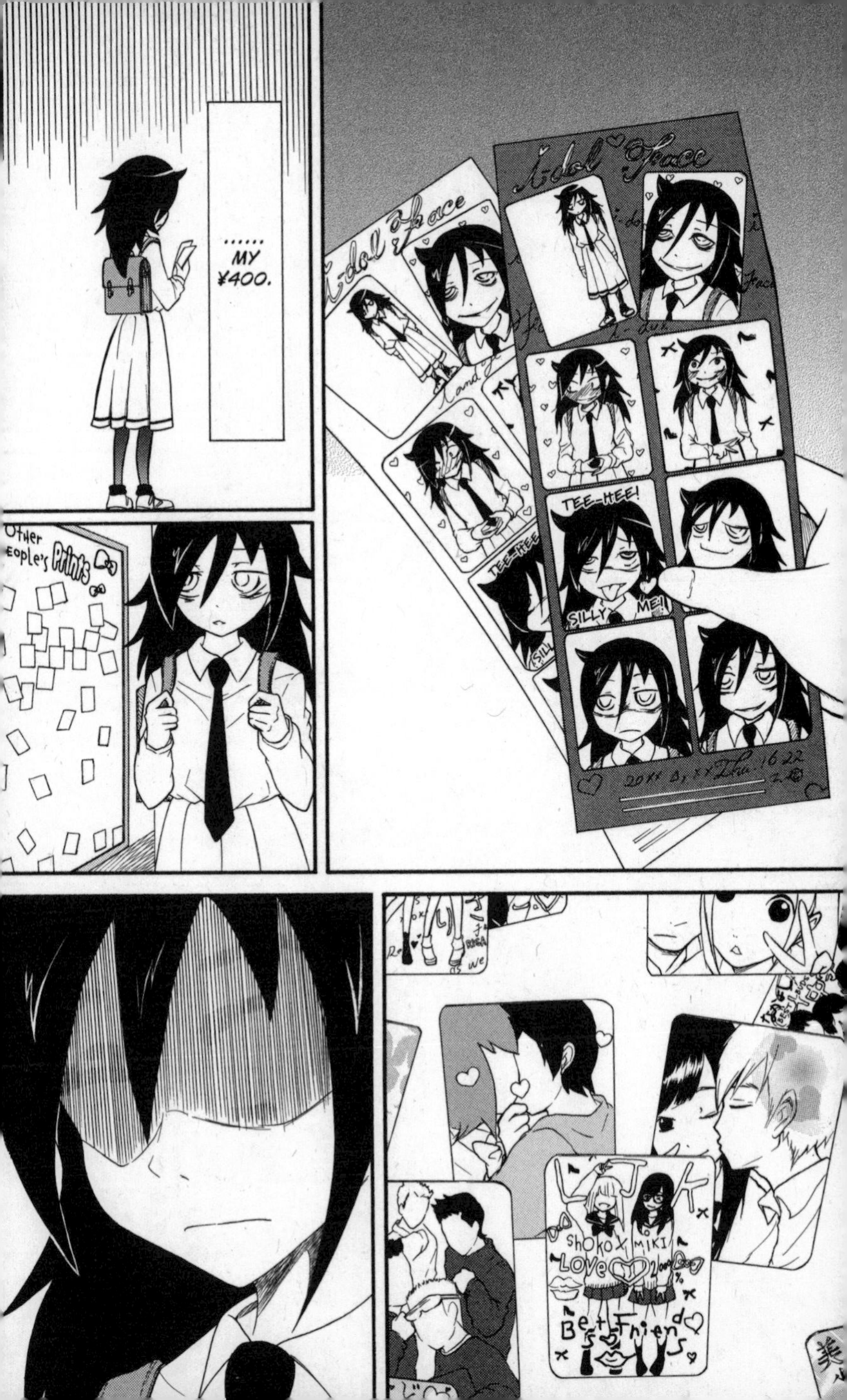
TEE-HEE!
SILLY ME!
...... MY ¥400.
Other
eople's Prints
SHOKO x MIKI
LOVE 2000%
Best Friends

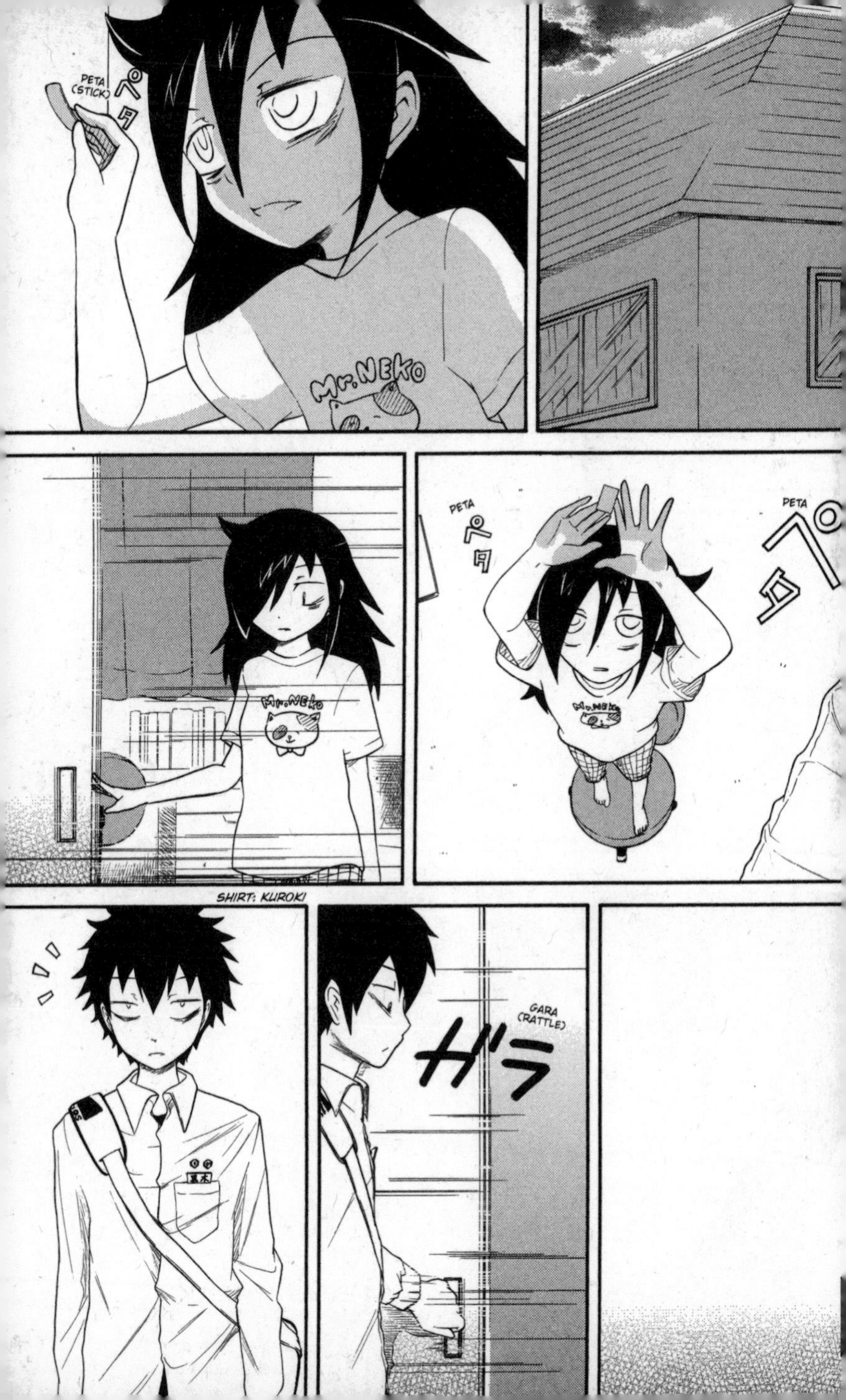
PETA (STICK)
ペタ
PETA
ペタ
PETA
ペタ
SHIRT: KUROKI
GARA (RATTLE)
ガラ

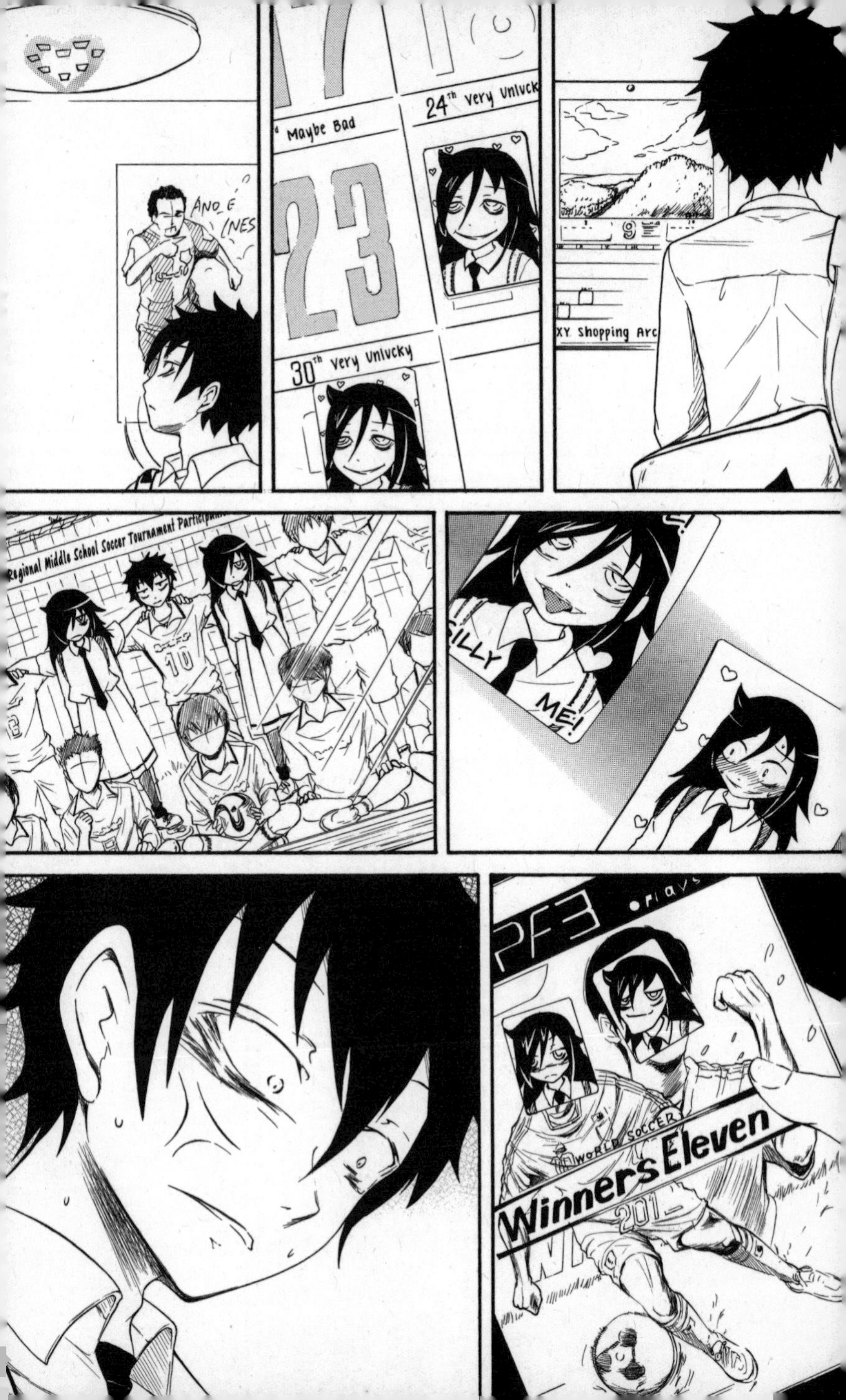
XY Shopping Arc
24th Very Unluck
Maybe Bad
23
30th Very Unlucky
SILLY ME!
Regional Middle School Soccer Tournament Participa
WORLD SOCCER
Winners Eleven
201_

No Matter How I Look at It, It's You Guys' Fault I'm Not Popular!

FAIL 23: I'M NOT POPULAR, SO THE WEATHER'S LOUSY.

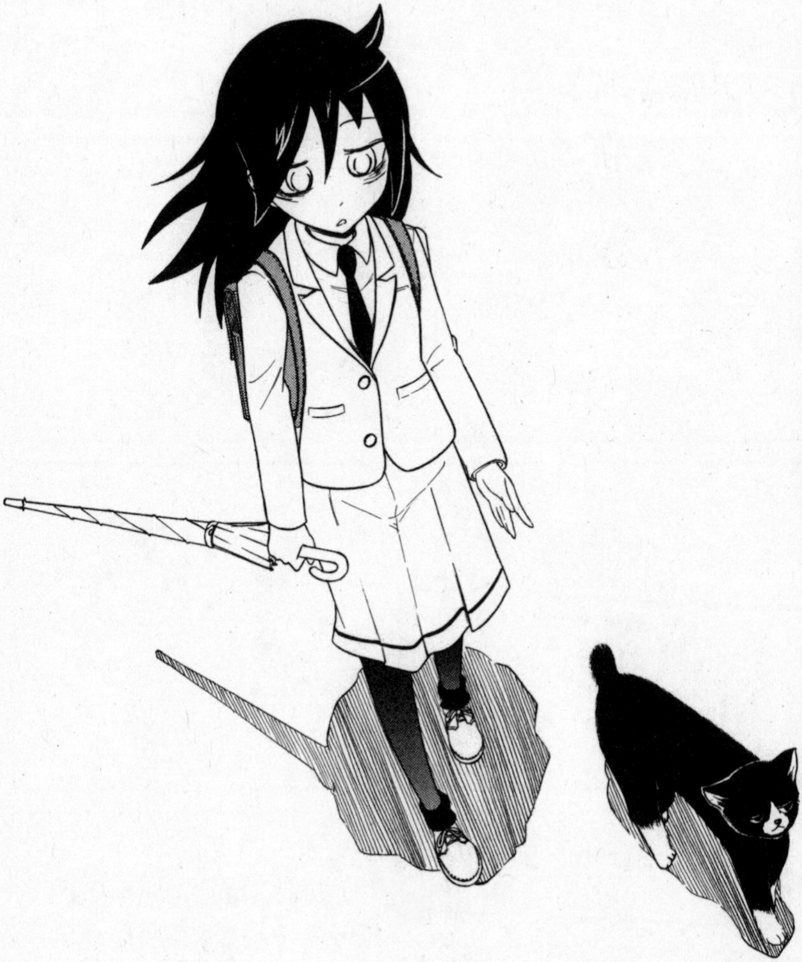

GOING TO SCHOOL ON A RAINY DAY

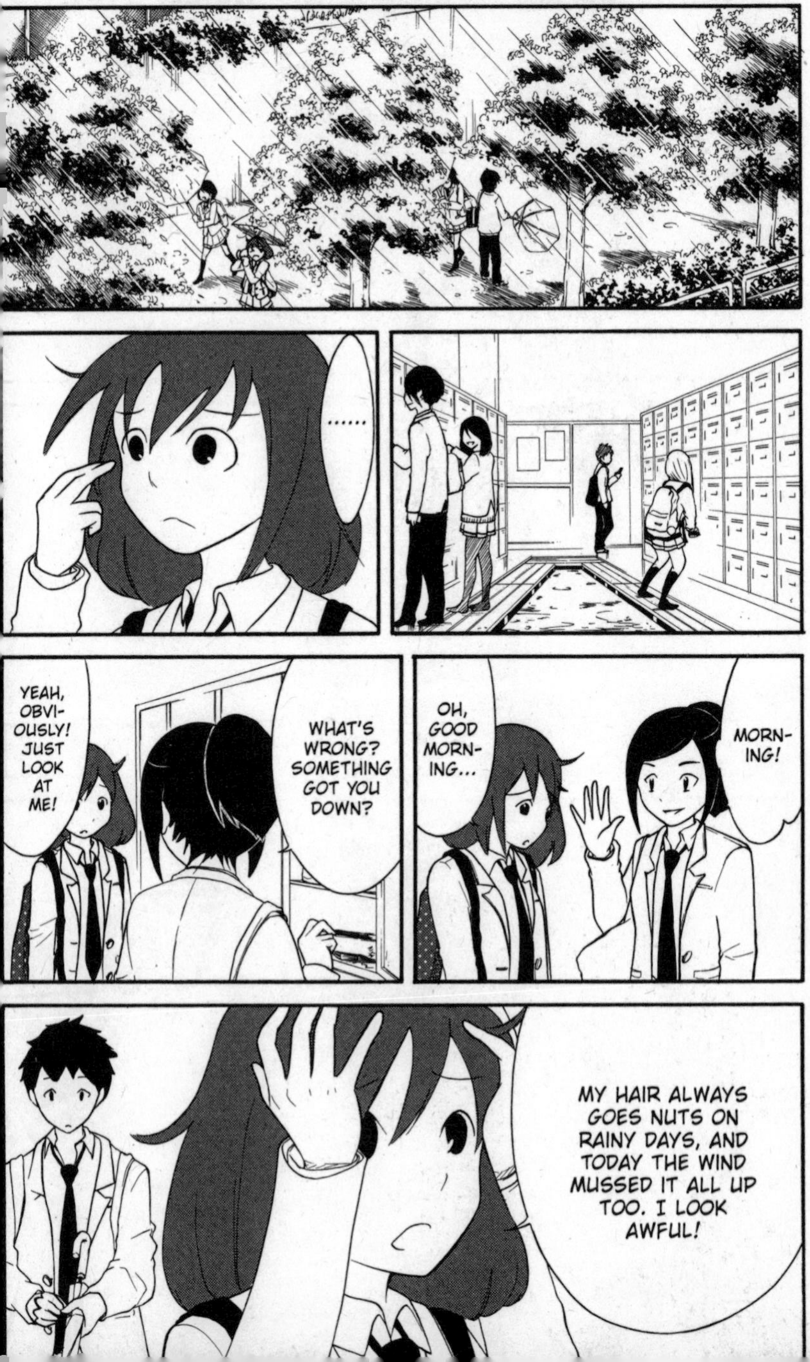
......
MORNING!
OH, GOOD MORNING...
WHAT'S WRONG? SOMETHING GOT YOU DOWN?
YEAH, OBVIOUSLY! JUST LOOK AT ME!
MY HAIR ALWAYS GOES NUTS ON RAINY DAYS, AND TODAY THE WIND MUSSED IT ALL UP TOO. I LOOK AWFUL!

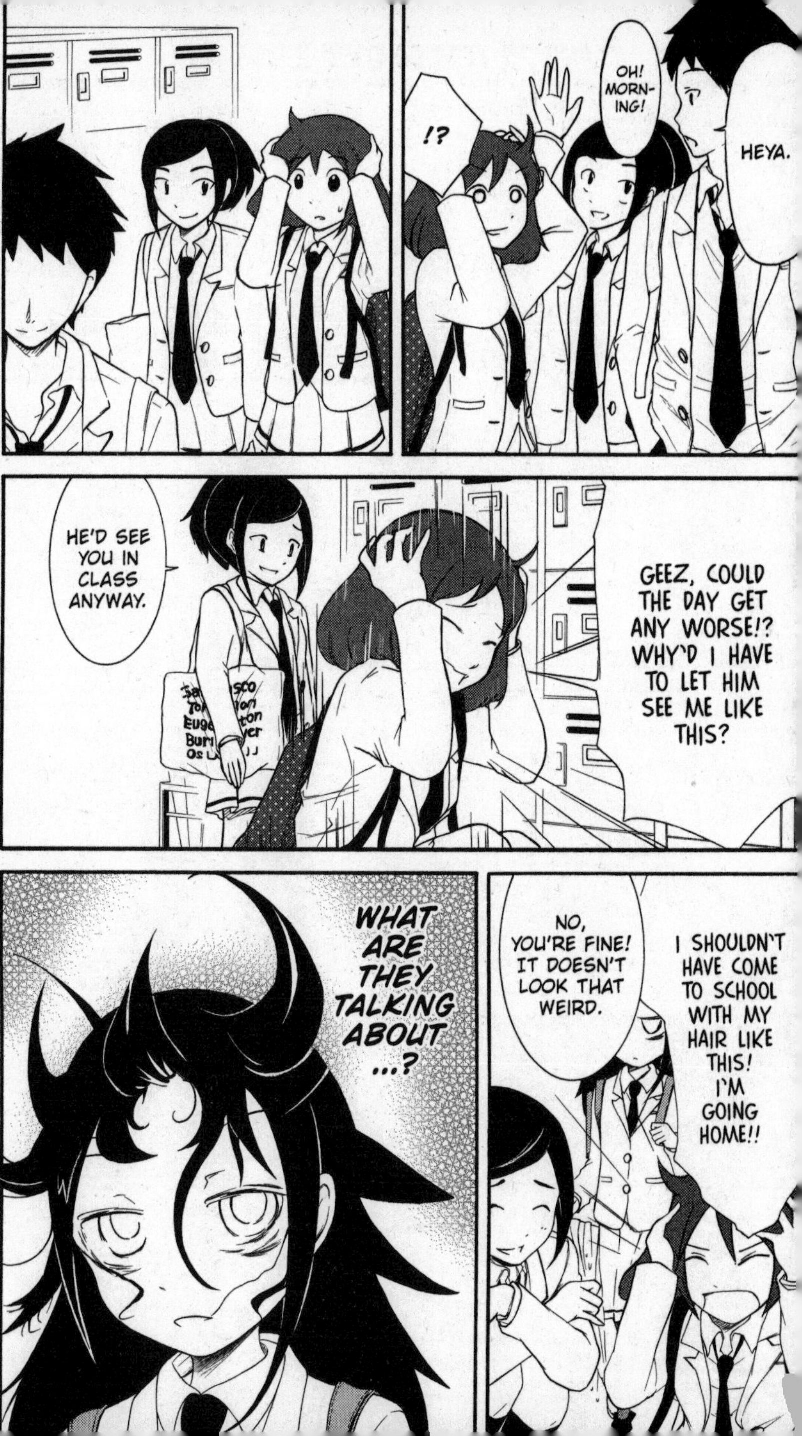
OH! MORNING!
HEYA.
!?
GEEZ, COULD THE DAY GET ANY WORSE!? WHY'D I HAVE TO LET HIM SEE ME LIKE THIS?
HE'D SEE YOU IN CLASS ANYWAY.
I SHOULDN'T HAVE COME TO SCHOOL WITH MY HAIR LIKE THIS! I'M GOING HOME!!
NO, YOU'RE FINE! IT DOESN'T LOOK THAT WEIRD.
WHAT ARE THEY TALKING ABOUT ...?

PSYCH QUIZ

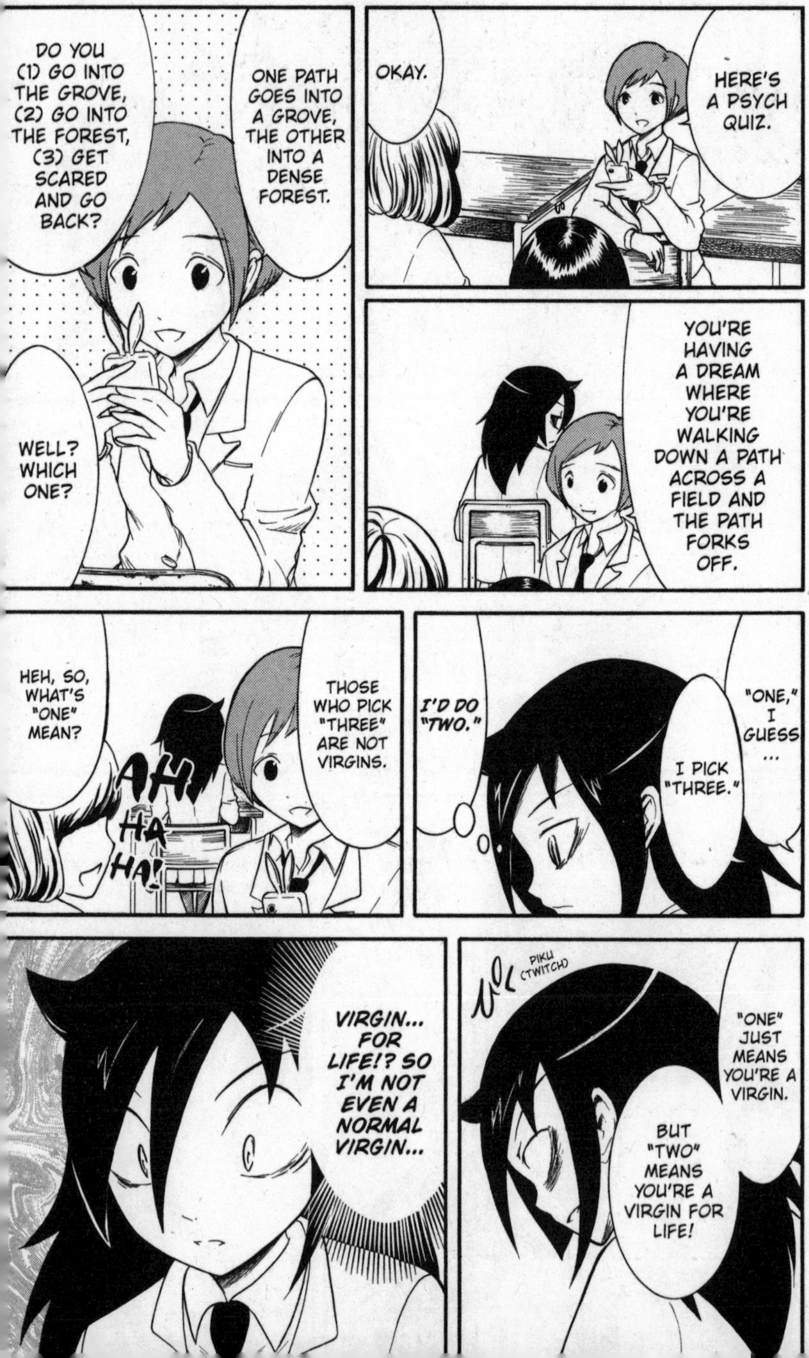
HERE'S A PSYCH QUIZ.
OKAY.
YOU'RE HAVING A DREAM WHERE YOU'RE WALKING DOWN A PATH ACROSS A FIELD AND THE PATH FORKS OFF.
ONE PATH GOES INTO A GROVE, THE OTHER INTO A DENSE FOREST.
DO YOU (1) GO INTO THE GROVE, (2) GO INTO THE FOREST, (3) GET SCARED AND GO BACK?
WELL? WHICH ONE?
"ONE," I GUESS...
I PICK "THREE."
I'D DO "TWO."
THOSE WHO PICK "THREE" ARE NOT VIRGINS.
HEH, SO, WHAT'S "ONE" MEAN?
AH HA HA!
PIKU (TWITCH)
"ONE" JUST MEANS YOU'RE A VIRGIN.
BUT "TWO" MEANS YOU'RE A VIRGIN FOR LIFE!
VIRGIN... FOR LIFE!? SO I'M NOT EVEN A NORMAL VIRGIN...

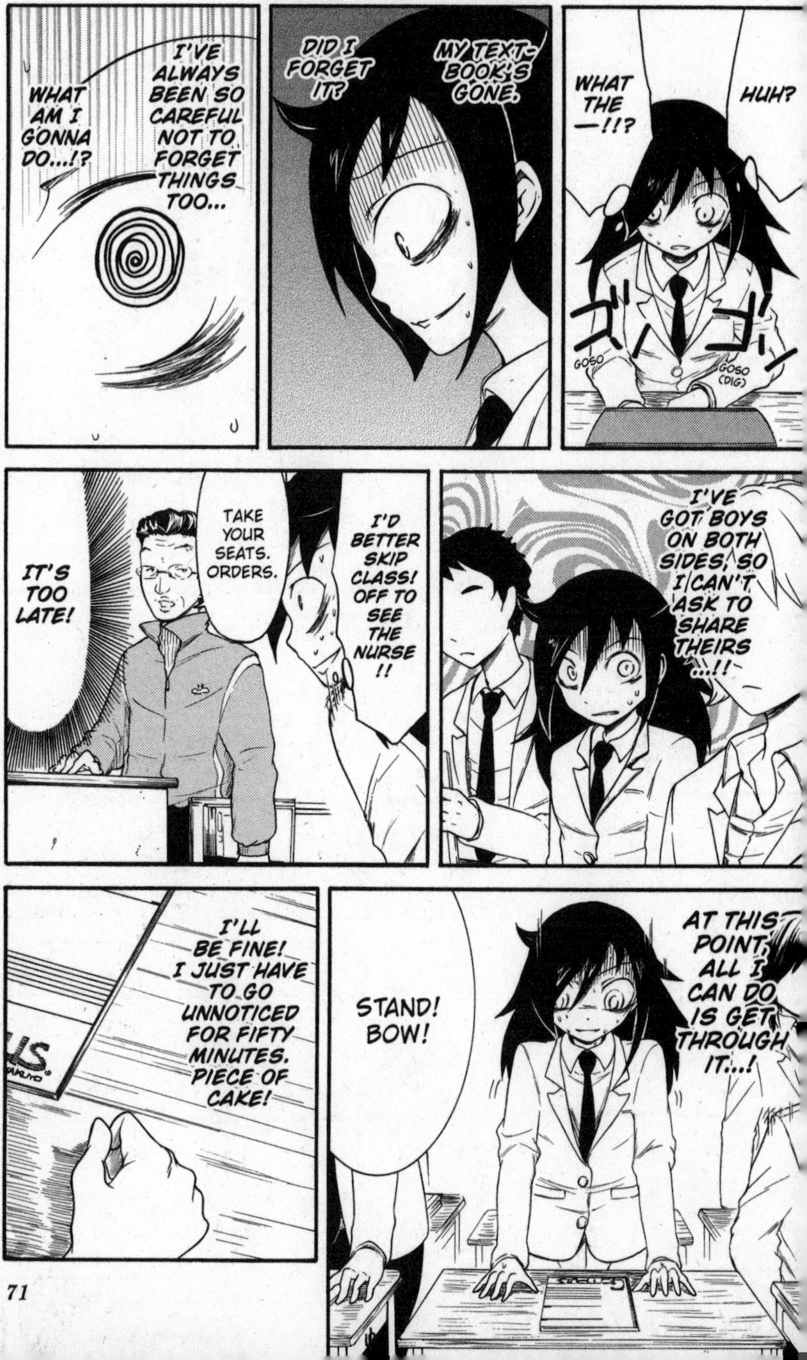
HUH?
WHAT THE—!!?
GOSO
GOSO (DIG)
MY TEXTBOOK'S GONE.
DID I FORGET IT?
I'VE ALWAYS BEEN SO CAREFUL NOT TO FORGET THINGS TOO...
WHAT AM I GONNA DO...!?
I'VE GOT BOYS ON BOTH SIDES, SO I CAN'T ASK TO SHARE THEIRS...!!
I'D BETTER SKIP CLASS! OFF TO SEE THE NURSE!!
TAKE YOUR SEATS. ORDERS.
IT'S TOO LATE!
AT THIS POINT, ALL I CAN DO IS GET THROUGH IT...!
STAND! BOW!
I'LL BE FINE! I JUST HAVE TO GO UNNOTICED FOR FIFTY MINUTES. PIECE OF CAKE!

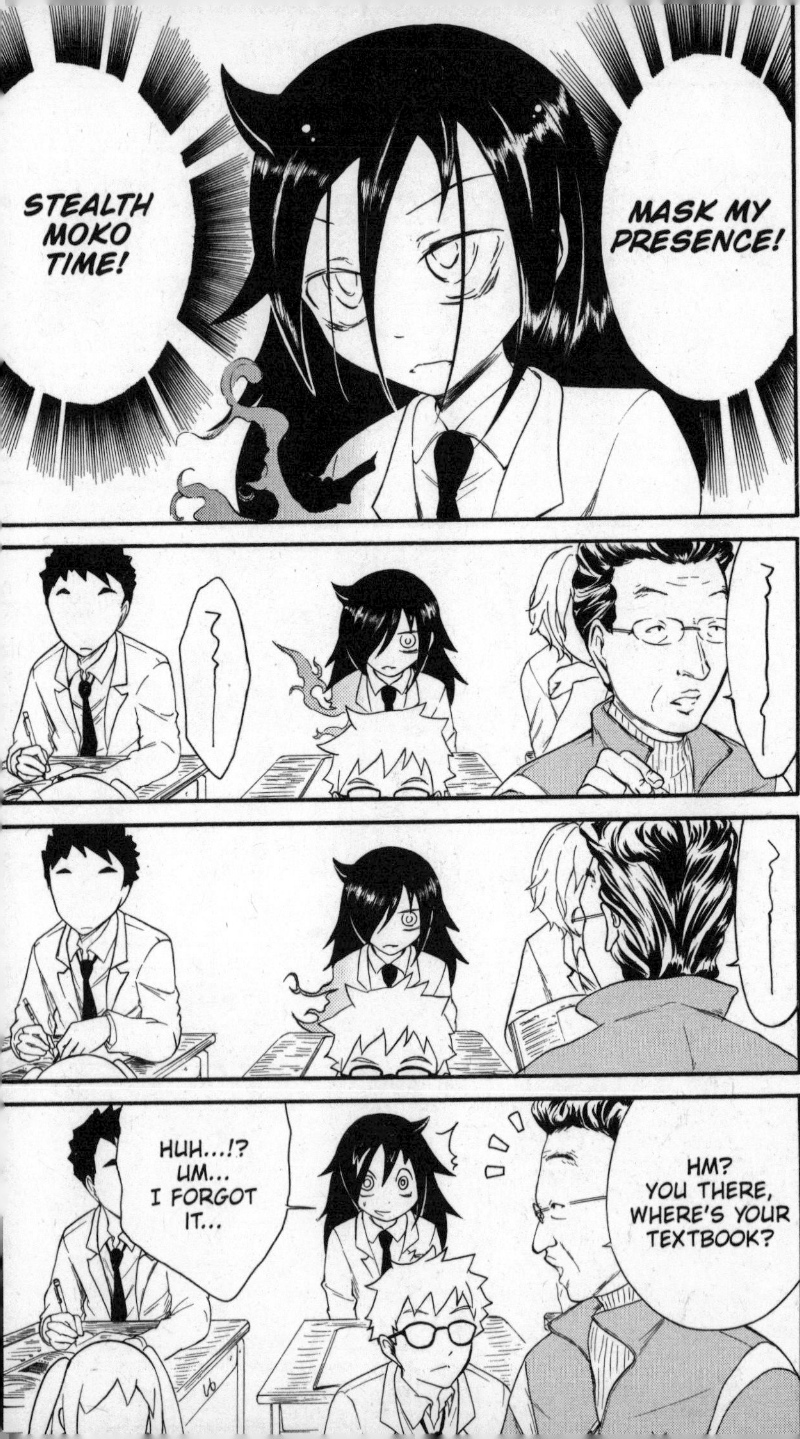
MASK MY PRESENCE!
STEALTH MOKO TIME!
HM? YOU THERE, WHERE'S YOUR TEXTBOOK?
HUH...!? UM... I FORGOT IT...

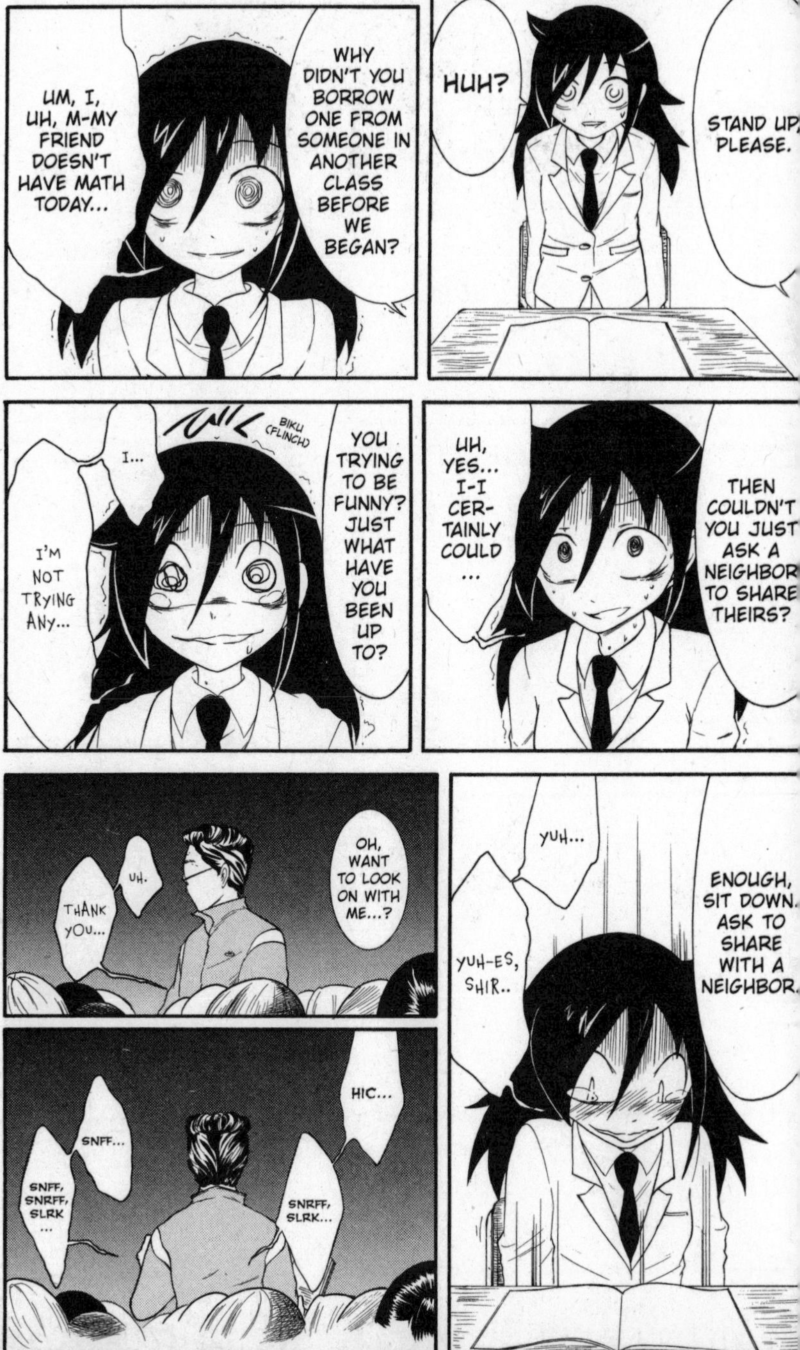
STAND UP, PLEASE.
HUH?
WHY DIDN'T YOU BORROW ONE FROM SOMEONE IN ANOTHER CLASS BEFORE WE BEGAN?
UM, I, UH, M-MY FRIEND DOESN'T HAVE MATH TODAY...
THEN COULDN'T YOU JUST ASK A NEIGHBOR TO SHARE THEIRS?
UH, YES... I-I CER-TAINLY COULD ...
YOU TRYING TO BE FUNNY? JUST WHAT HAVE YOU BEEN UP TO?
BIKU (FLINCH)
I...
I'M NOT TRYING ANY...
ENOUGH, SIT DOWN. ASK TO SHARE WITH A NEIGHBOR.
YUH...
YUH-ES, SHIR..
OH, WANT TO LOOK ON WITH ME...?
UH.
THANK YOU...
HIC...
SNRFF, SLRK...
SNFF...
SNFF, SNRFF, SLRK ...

THE UMBRELLA

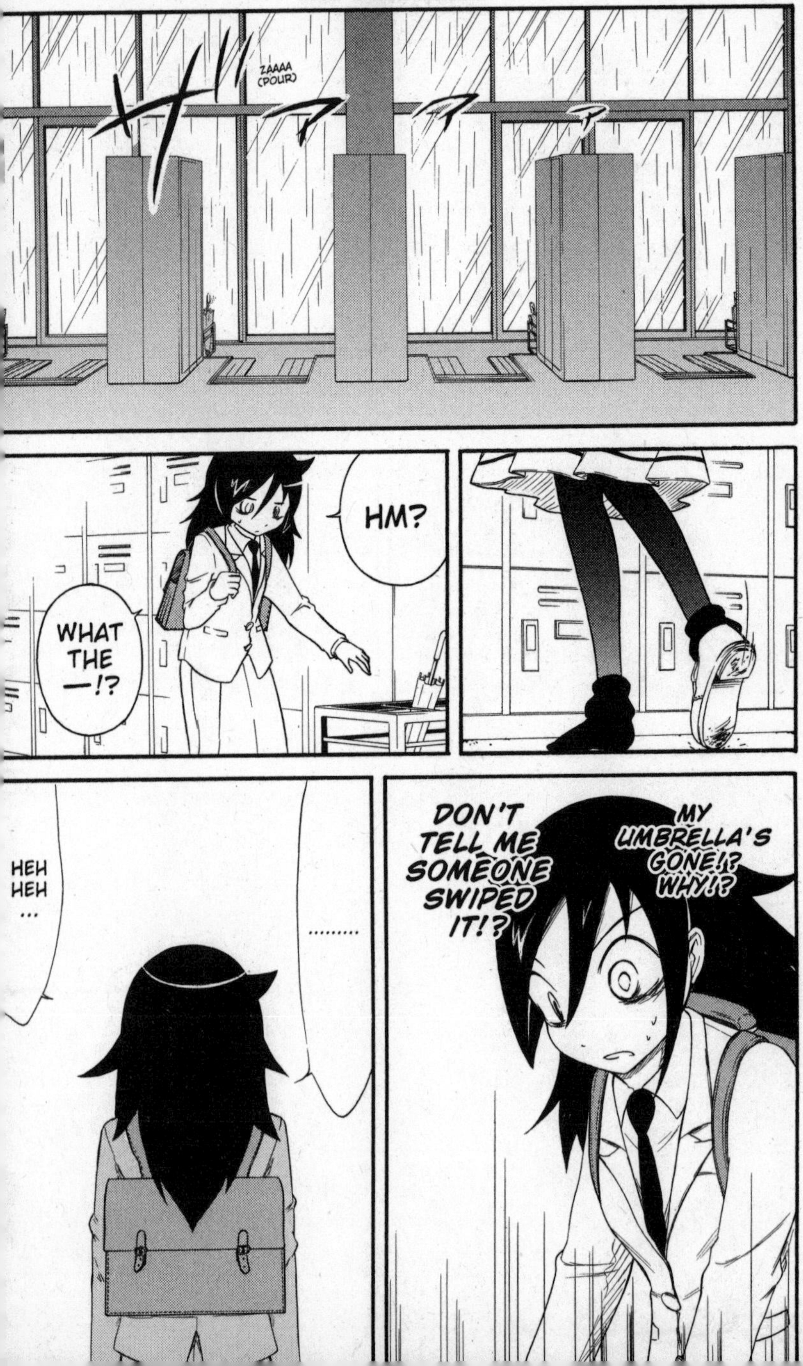
ZAAAA
(POUR)
HM?
WHAT THE—!?
MY UMBRELLA'S GONE!? WHY!?
DON'T TELL ME SOMEONE SWIPED IT!?
....
HEH HEH ...

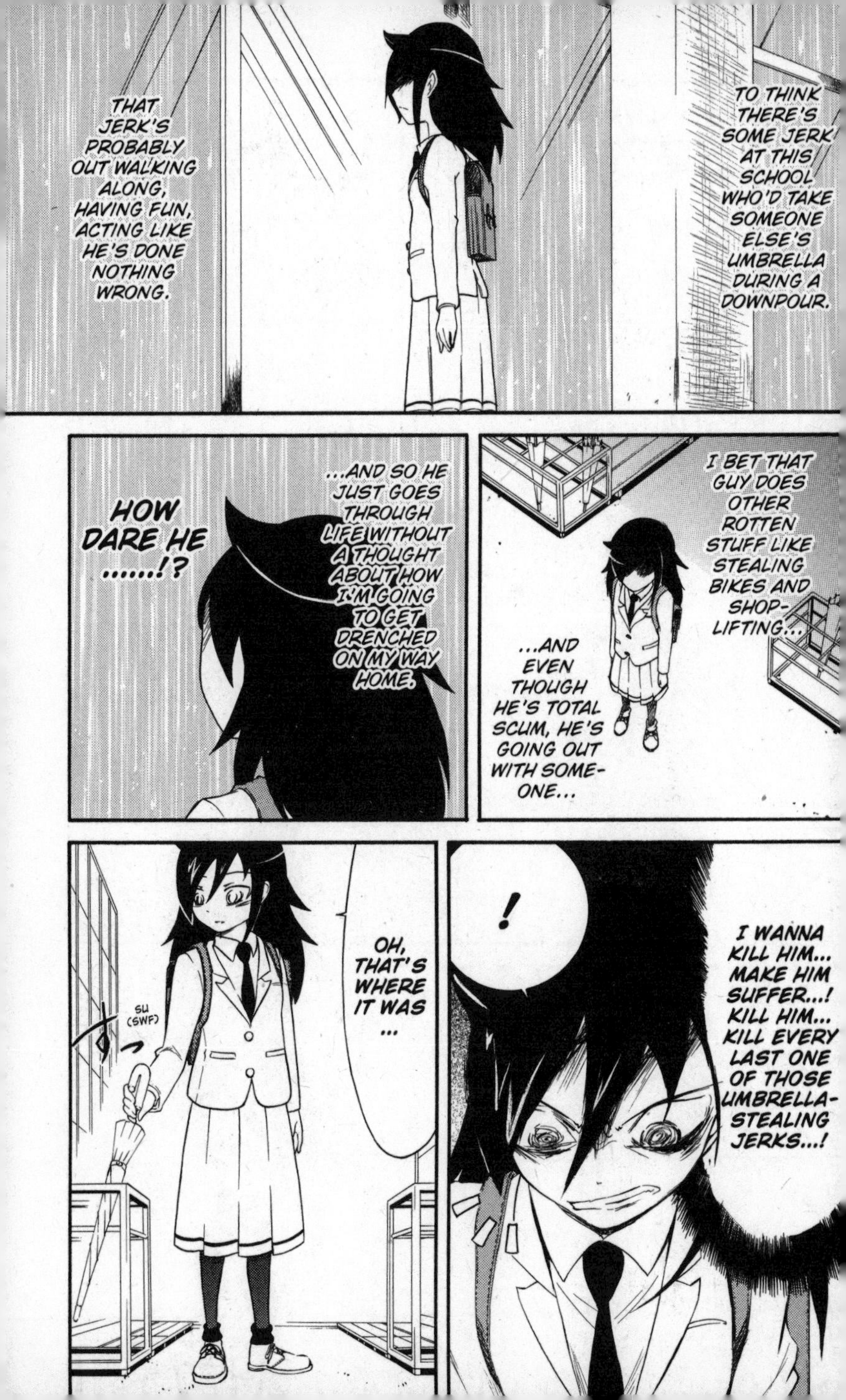
TO THINK THERE'S SOME JERK AT THIS SCHOOL WHO'D TAKE SOMEONE ELSE'S UMBRELLA DURING A DOWNPOUR.
THAT JERK'S PROBABLY OUT WALKING ALONG, HAVING FUN, ACTING LIKE HE'S DONE NOTHING WRONG.
I BET THAT GUY DOES OTHER ROTTEN STUFF LIKE STEALING BIKES AND SHOP-LIFTING...
...AND EVEN THOUGH HE'S TOTAL SCUM, HE'S GOING OUT WITH SOME-ONE...
...AND SO HE JUST GOES THROUGH LIFE WITHOUT A THOUGHT ABOUT HOW I'M GOING TO GET DRENCHED ON MY WAY HOME.
HOW DARE HE ......!?
!
I WANNA KILL HIM... MAKE HIM SUFFER...! KILL HIM... KILL EVERY LAST ONE OF THOSE UMBRELLA-STEALING JERKS...!
OH, THAT'S WHERE IT WAS ...
SU (SWF)

THE WAY HOME

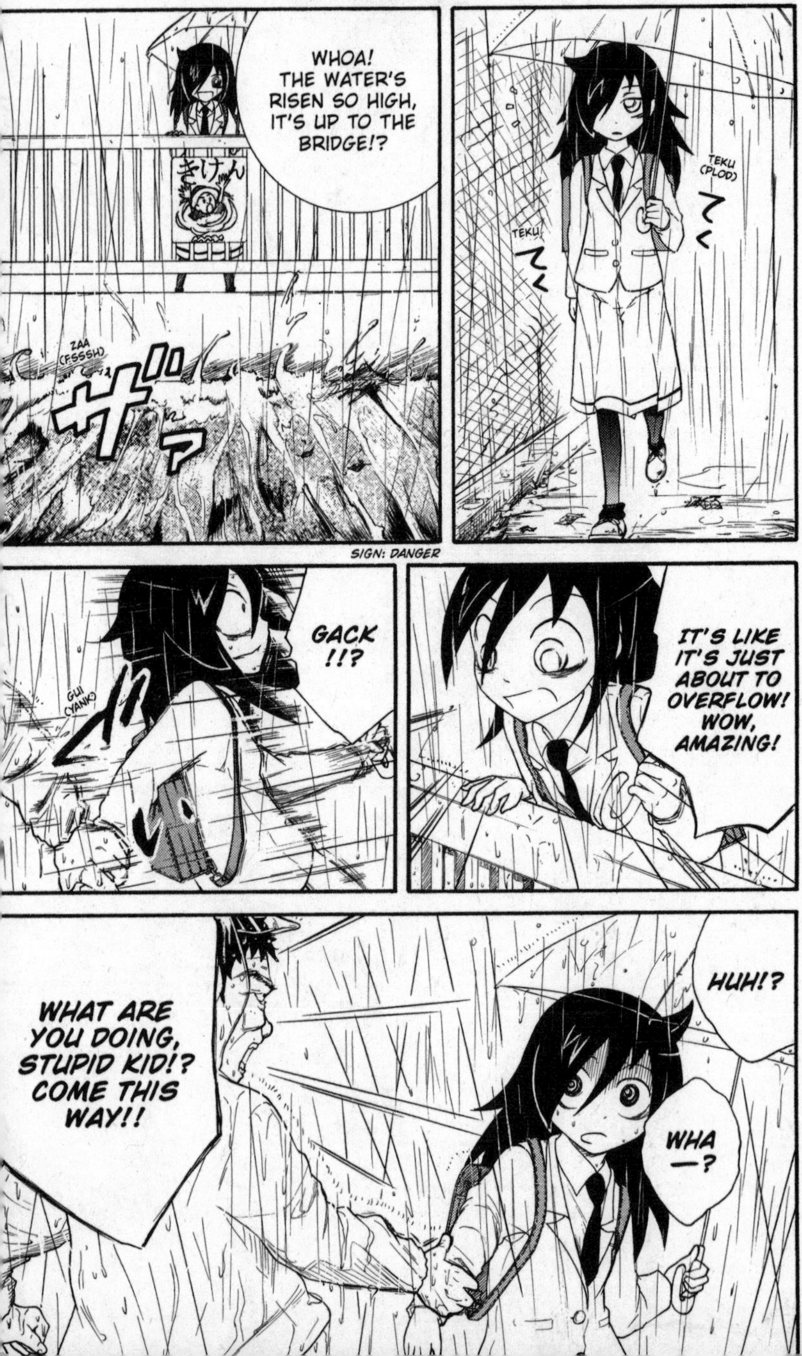
TEKU (PLOD)
TEKU
WHOA! THE WATER'S RISEN SO HIGH, IT'S UP TO THE BRIDGE!?
きけん
ZAA (FSSSH)
SIGN: DANGER
IT'S LIKE IT'S JUST ABOUT TO OVERFLOW! WOW, AMAZING!
GACK !!?
GUI (YANK)
HUH!?
WHA —?
WHAT ARE YOU DOING, STUPID KID!? COME THIS WAY!!

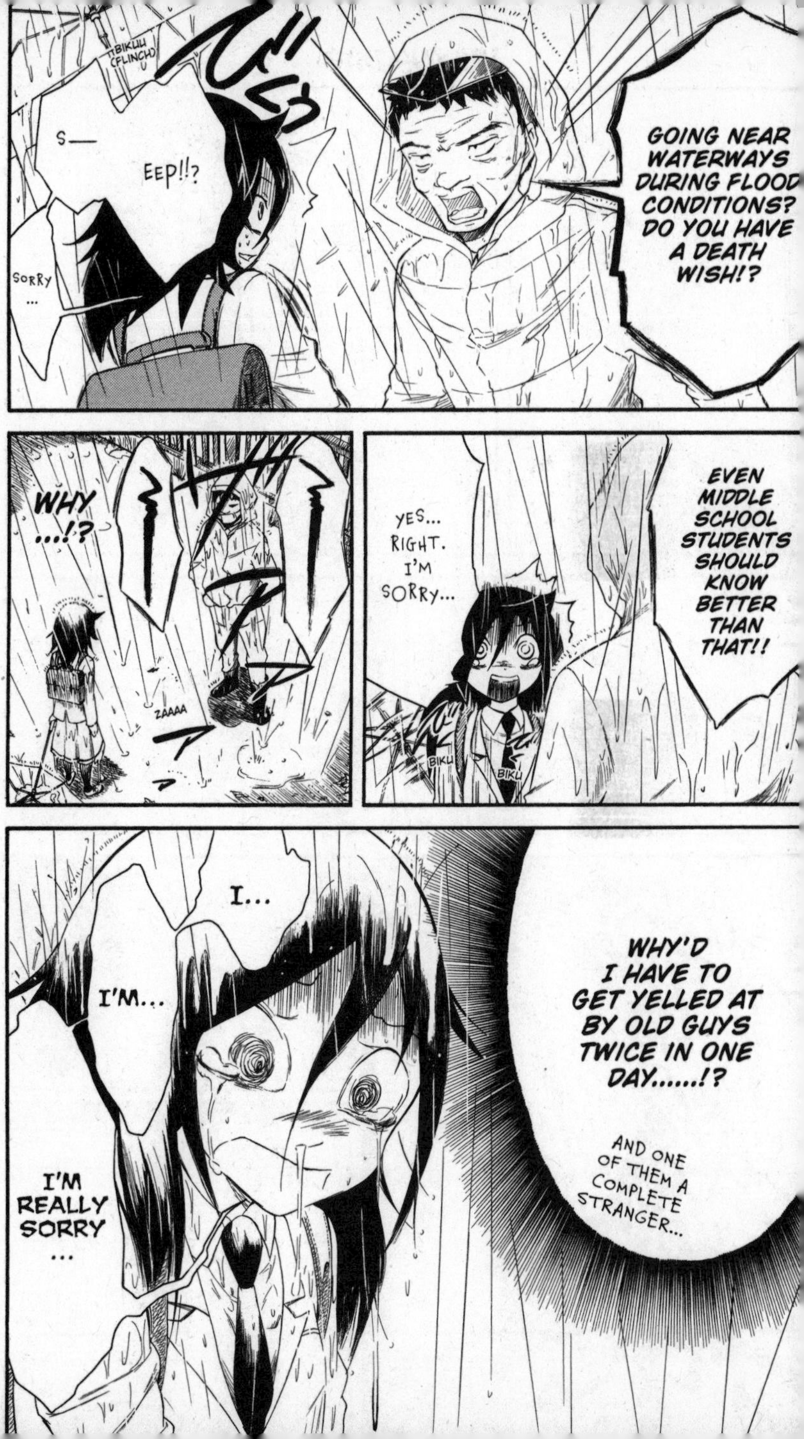
GOING NEAR WATERWAYS DURING FLOOD CONDITIONS? DO YOU HAVE A DEATH WISH!?
BIKUU (FLINCH)
S—
EEP!!?
SORRY ...
EVEN MIDDLE SCHOOL STUDENTS SHOULD KNOW BETTER THAN THAT!!
YES... RIGHT. I'M SORRY...
BIKU
BIKU
WHY ...!?
ZAAAA
WHY'D I HAVE TO GET YELLED AT BY OLD GUYS TWICE IN ONE DAY......!?
AND ONE OF THEM A COMPLETE STRANGER...
I...
I'M...
I'M REALLY SORRY ...

WHICH ONE?

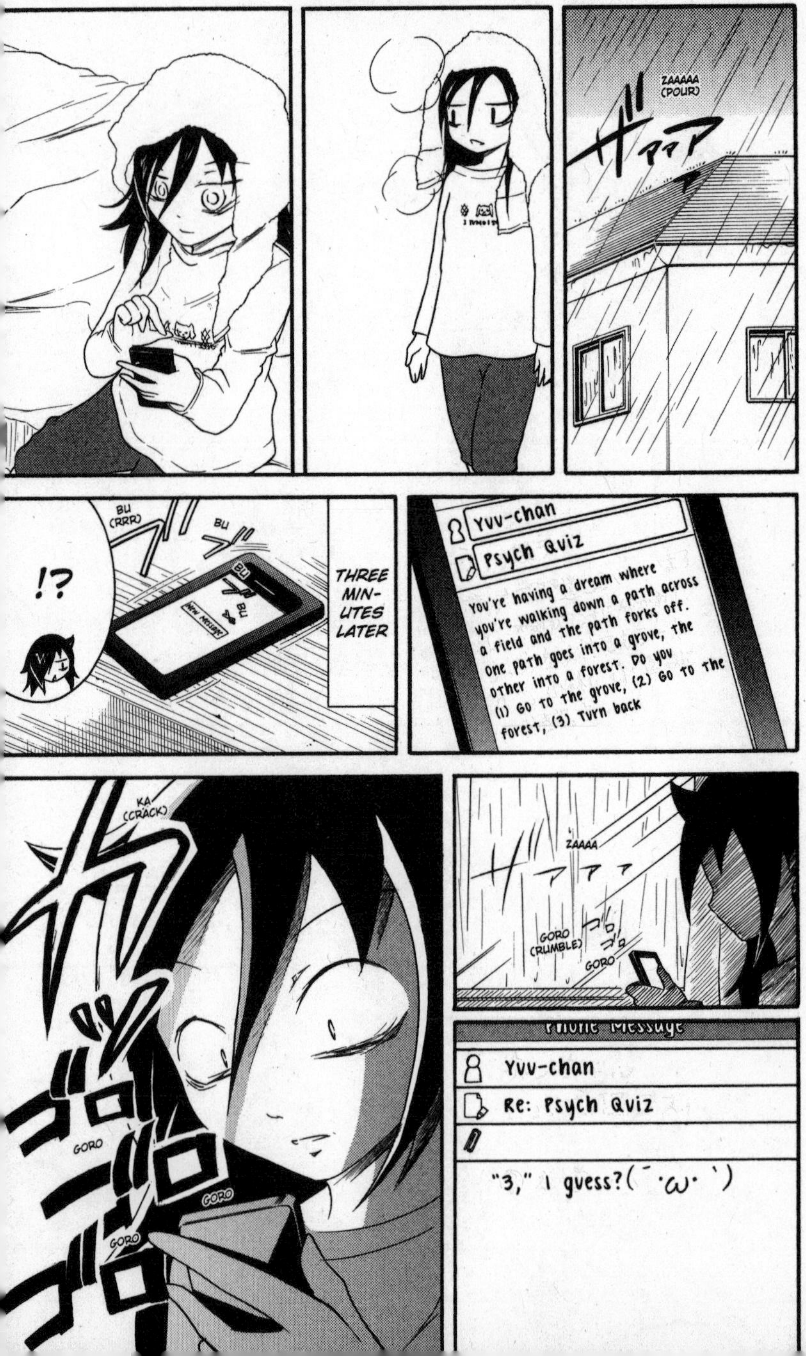
ZAAAAA (POUR)
Yuu-chan
Psych Quiz
You're having a dream where you're walking down a path across a field and the path forks off. One path goes into a grove, the other into a forest. Do you (1) Go to the grove, (2) Go to the forest, (3) Turn back
THREE MIN-UTES LATER
BU (RRR)
BU
BU
BU
!?
ZAAAA
GORO (RUMBLE)
GORO
Yuu-chan
Re: Psych Quiz
"3," I guess?(´・ω・`)
KA (CRACK)
GORO
GORO
GORO

No Matter How I Look at It, It's You Guys' Fault I'm Not Popular!

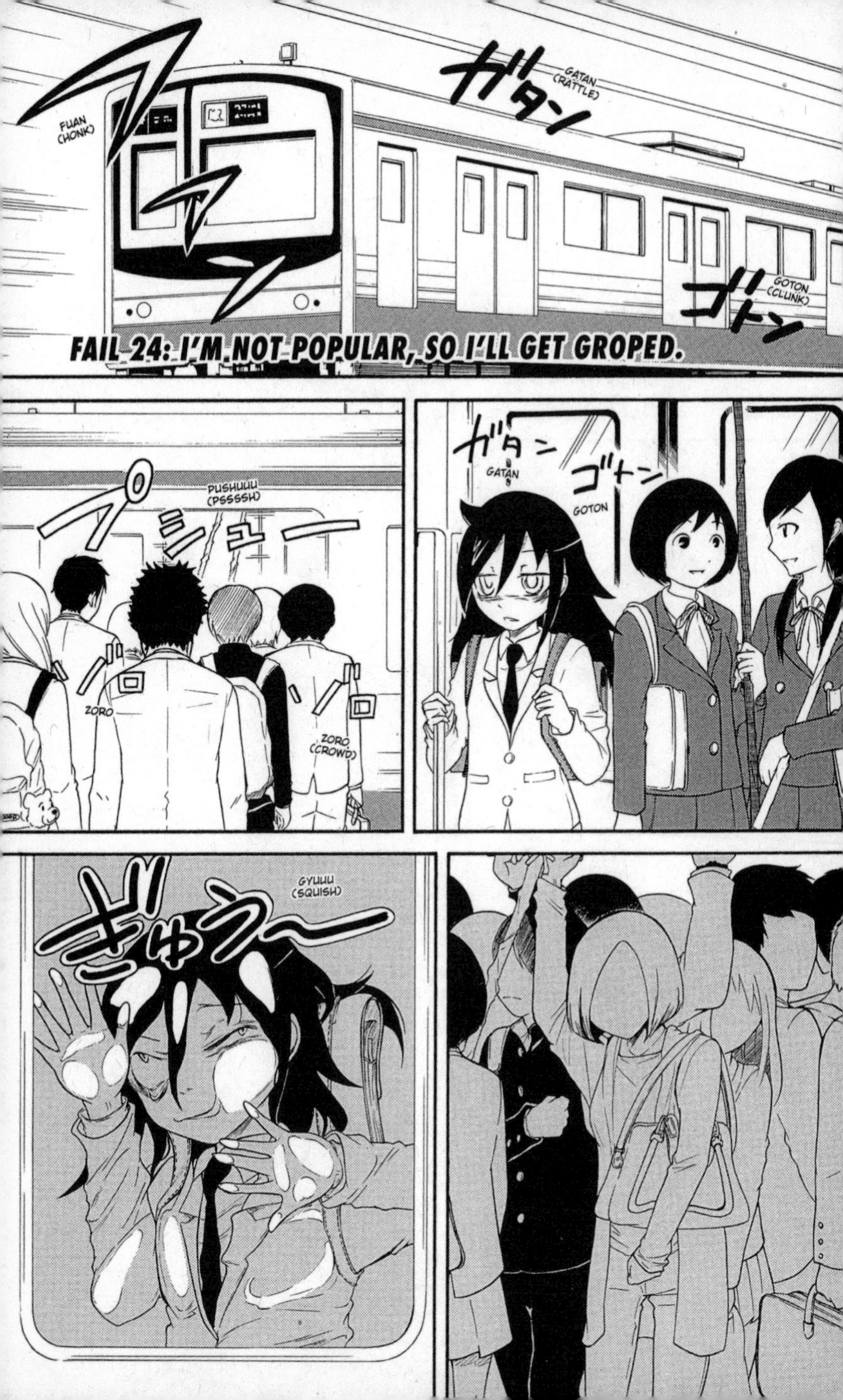
GATAN (RATTLE)
FUAN (HONK)
GOTON (CLUNK)
FAIL 24: I'M NOT POPULAR, SO I'LL GET GROPED.
GATAN
GOTON
PUSHUUU (PSSSSH)
ZORO
ZORO (CROWD)
GYUUU (SQUISH)

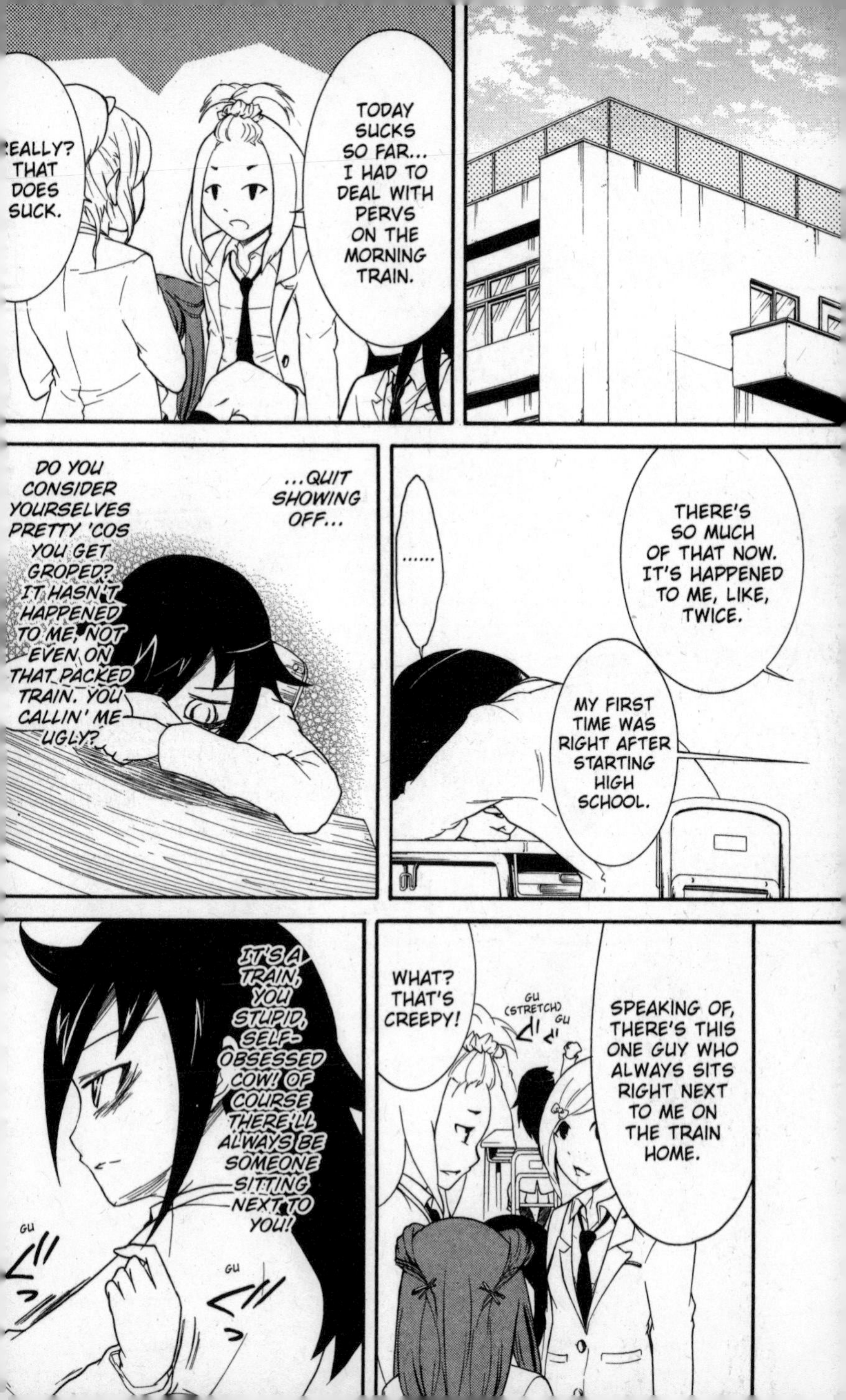
TODAY SUCKS SO FAR... I HAD TO DEAL WITH PERVS ON THE MORNING TRAIN.
REALLY? THAT DOES SUCK.
THERE'S SO MUCH OF THAT NOW. IT'S HAPPENED TO ME, LIKE, TWICE.
......
MY FIRST TIME WAS RIGHT AFTER STARTING HIGH SCHOOL.
...QUIT SHOWING OFF...
DO YOU CONSIDER YOURSELVES PRETTY 'COS YOU GET GROPED? IT HASN'T HAPPENED TO ME, NOT EVEN ON THAT PACKED TRAIN. YOU CALLIN' ME UGLY?
SPEAKING OF, THERE'S THIS ONE GUY WHO ALWAYS SITS RIGHT NEXT TO ME ON THE TRAIN HOME.
GU (STRETCH) GU
WHAT? THAT'S CREEPY!
IT'S A TRAIN, YOU STUPID, SELF-OBSESSED COW! OF COURSE THERE'LL ALWAYS BE SOMEONE SITTING NEXT TO YOU!
GU
GU

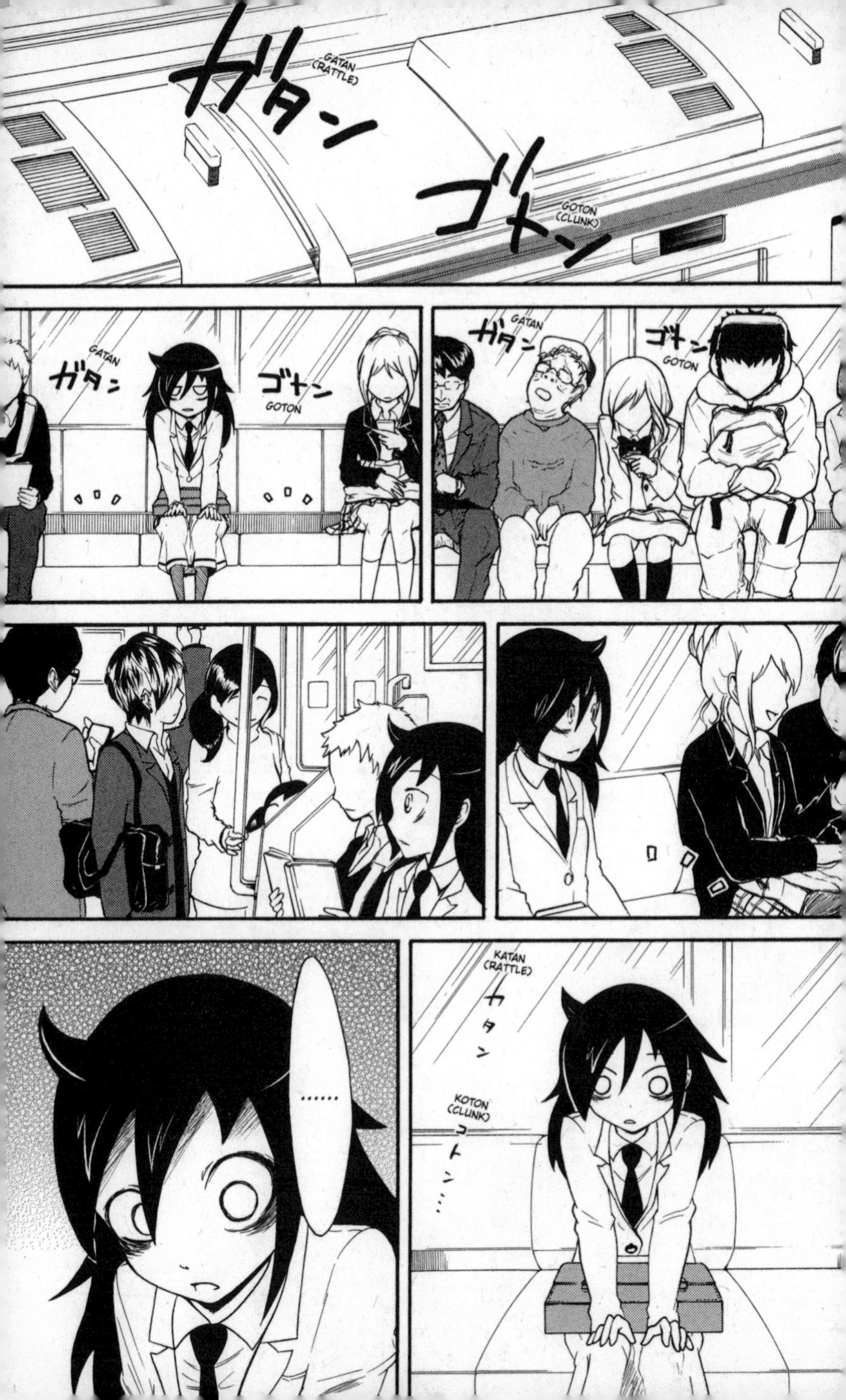

ガタン
GATAN (RATTLE)
ゴトン
GOTON (CLUNK)
ゴトン
GOTON
ガタン
GATAN
ゴトン
GOTON
ガタン
GATAN
KATAN (RATTLE)
カタン
KOTON (CLUNK)
コトン...
......

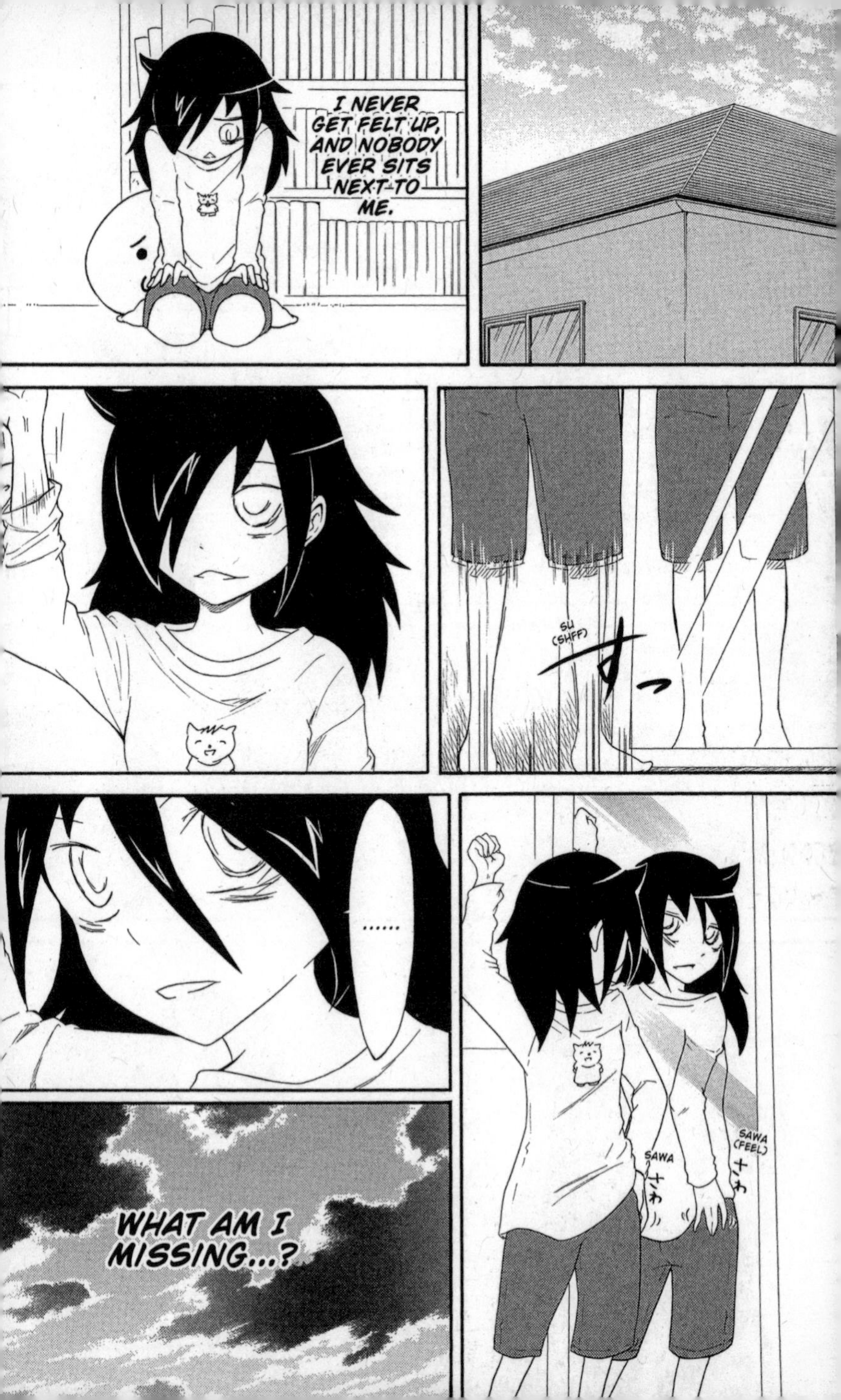
I NEVER GET FELT UP, AND NOBODY EVER SITS NEXT TO ME.
SU (SHFF)
すっ
SAWA (FEEL)
さわ
SAWA
さわ
......
WHAT AM I MISSING...?

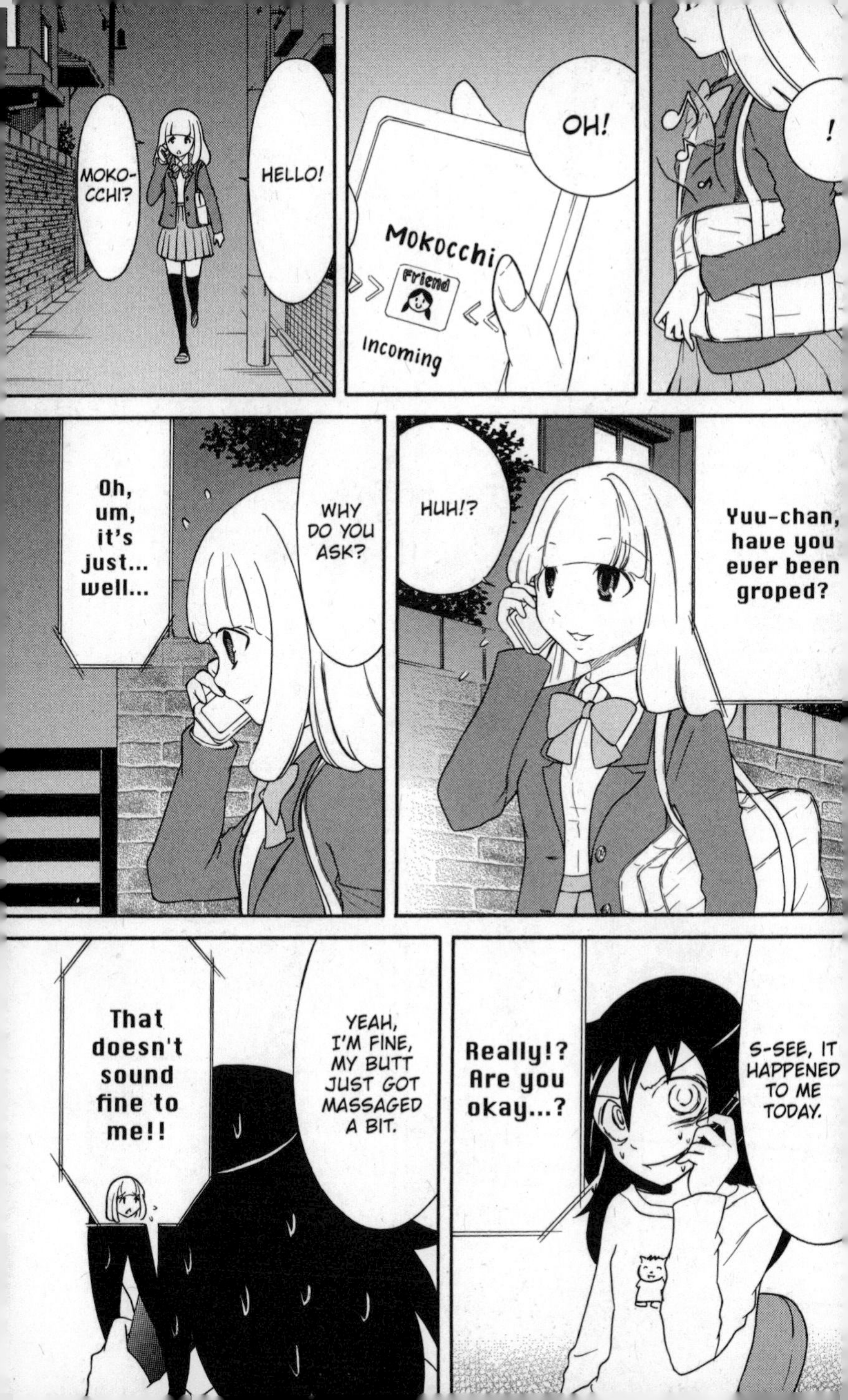
!
OH!
Mokocchi
Friend
Incoming
HELLO!
MOKO-CCHI?
Yuu-chan, have you ever been groped?
HUH!?
WHY DO YOU ASK?
Oh, um, it's just... well...
S-SEE, IT HAPPENED TO ME TODAY.
Really!? Are you okay...?
YEAH, I'M FINE, MY BUTT JUST GOT MASSAGED A BIT.
That doesn't sound fine to me!!

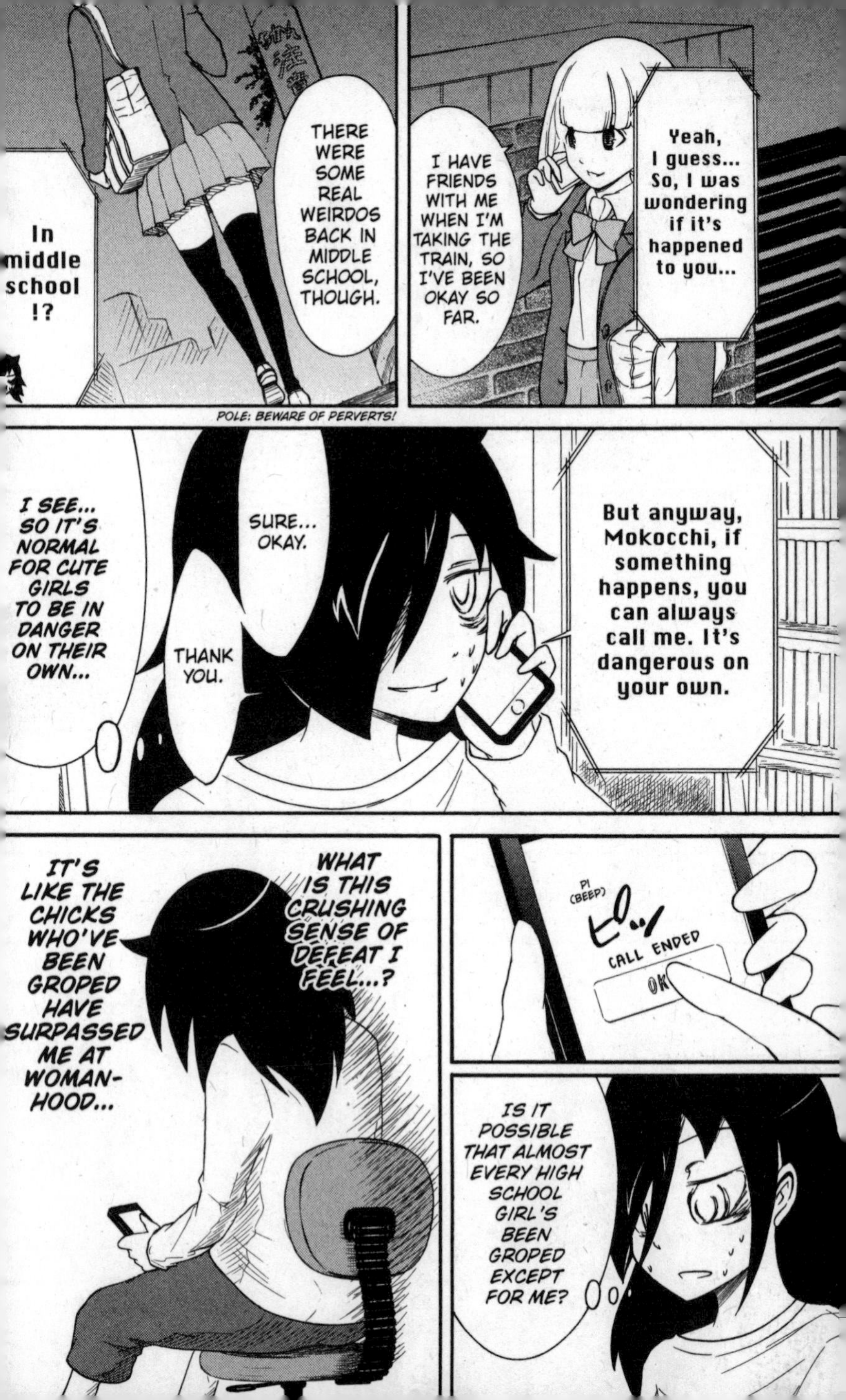
Yeah, I guess... So, I was wondering if it's happened to you...
I HAVE FRIENDS WITH ME WHEN I'M TAKING THE TRAIN, SO I'VE BEEN OKAY SO FAR.
THERE WERE SOME REAL WEIRDOS BACK IN MIDDLE SCHOOL, THOUGH.
In middle school!?
POLE: BEWARE OF PERVERTS!
But anyway, Mokocchi, if something happens, you can always call me. It's dangerous on your own.
SURE... OKAY.
THANK YOU.
I SEE... SO IT'S NORMAL FOR CUTE GIRLS TO BE IN DANGER ON THEIR OWN...
PI (BEEP)
CALL ENDED
OK
IS IT POSSIBLE THAT ALMOST EVERY HIGH SCHOOL GIRL'S BEEN GROPED EXCEPT FOR ME?
WHAT IS THIS CRUSHING SENSE OF DEFEAT I FEEL...?
IT'S LIKE THE CHICKS WHO'VE BEEN GROPED HAVE SURPASSED ME AT WOMAN-HOOD...

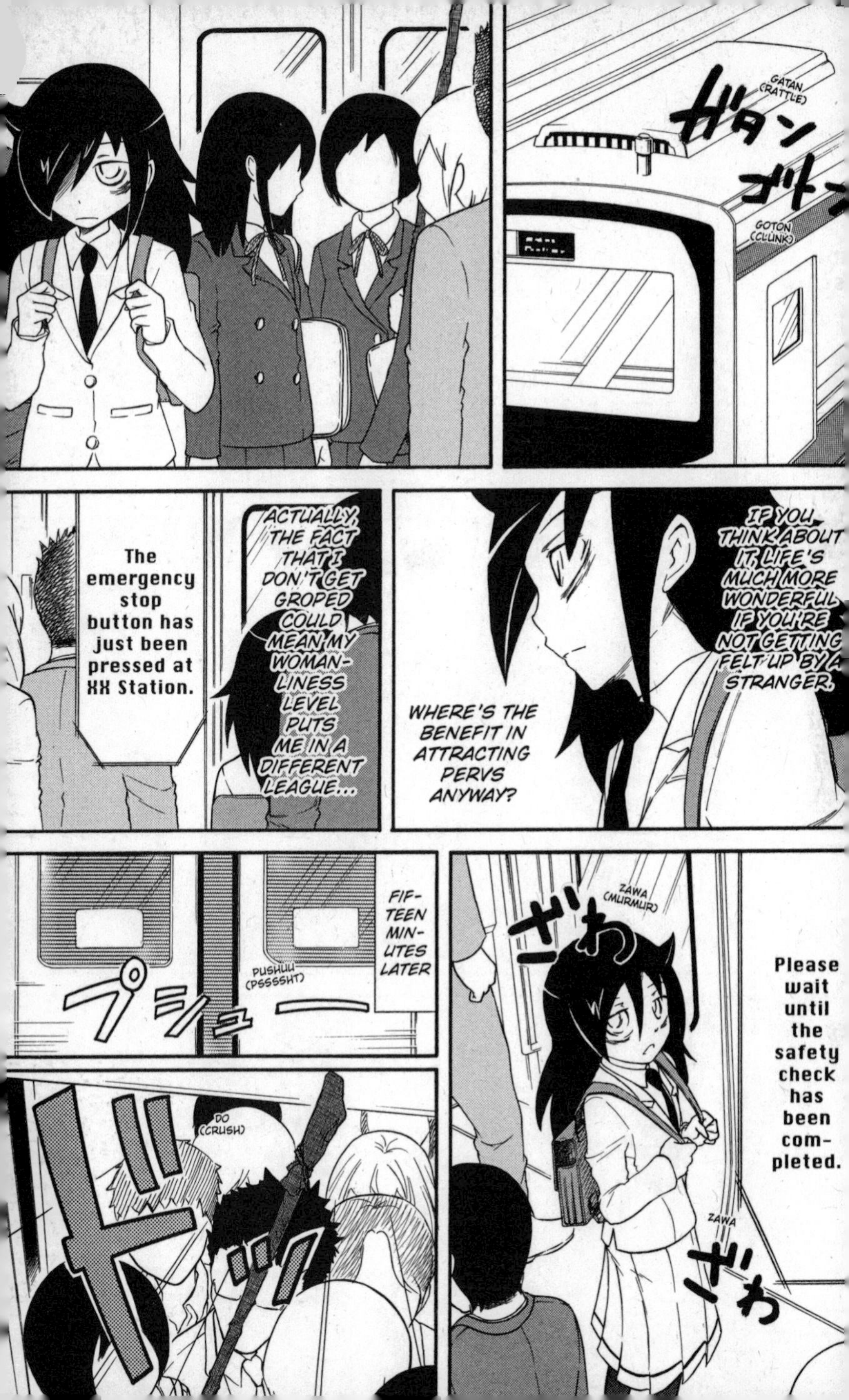
GATAN (RATTLE)
GOTON (CLUNK)
IF YOU THINK ABOUT IT, LIFE'S MUCH MORE WONDERFUL IF YOU'RE NOT GETTING FELT UP BY A STRANGER.
WHERE'S THE BENEFIT IN ATTRACTING PERVS ANYWAY?
ACTUALLY, THE FACT THAT I DON'T GET GROPED COULD MEAN MY WOMANLINESS LEVEL PUTS ME IN A DIFFERENT LEAGUE...
The emergency stop button has just been pressed at XX Station.
ZAWA (MURMUR)
Please wait until the safety check has been completed.
ZAWA
FIFTEEN MINUTES LATER
PUSHUU (PSSSSHT)
DO (CRUSH)

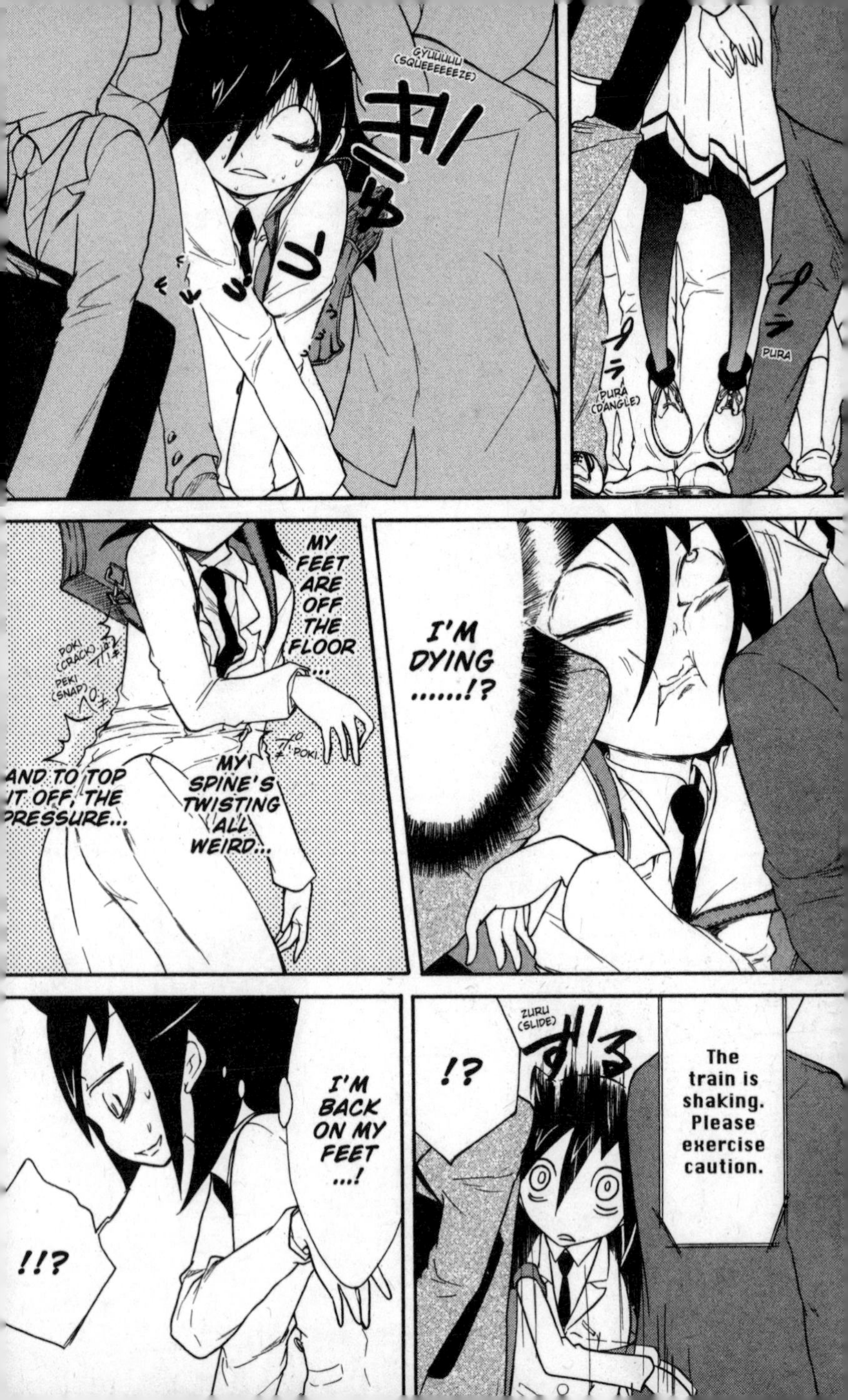

PURA
PURA (DANGLE)
GYUUUUU (SQUEEEEEEZE)
I'M DYING ......!?
MY FEET ARE OFF THE FLOOR...
POKI (CRACK)
PEKI (SNAP)
POKI
MY SPINE'S TWISTING ALL WEIRD...
AND TO TOP IT OFF, THE PRESSURE...
The train is shaking. Please exercise caution.
ZURU (SLIDE)
!?
I'M BACK ON MY FEET ...!
!!?

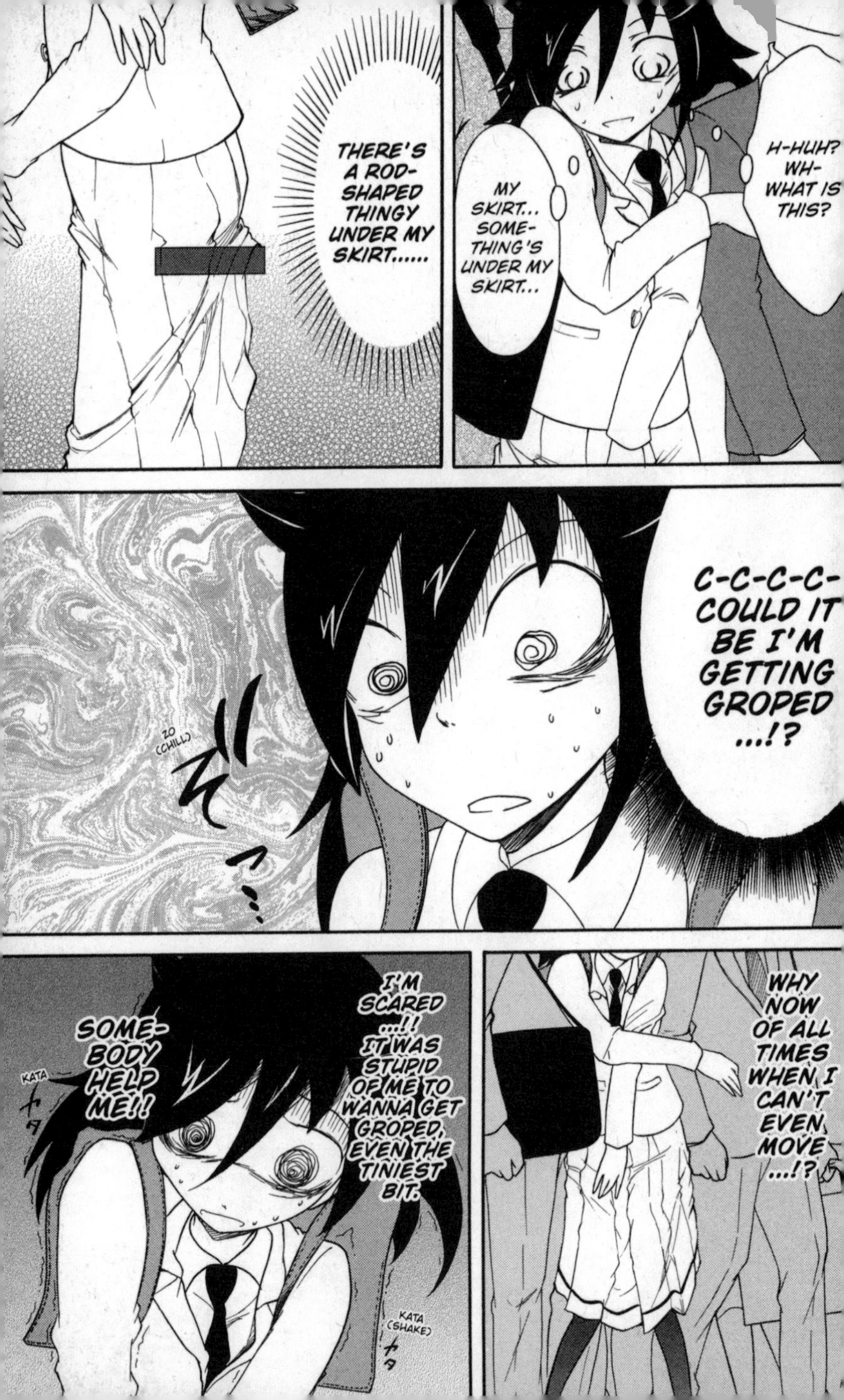
H-HUH? WH-WHAT IS THIS?
MY SKIRT... SOME-THING'S UNDER MY SKIRT...
THERE'S A ROD-SHAPED THINGY UNDER MY SKIRT......
C-C-C-C-COULD IT BE I'M GETTING GROPED ...!?
ZO (CHILL)
WHY NOW OF ALL TIMES WHEN I CAN'T EVEN MOVE ...!?
I'M SCARED ...!! IT WAS STUPID OF ME TO WANNA GET GROPED, EVEN THE TINIEST BIT.
SOME-BODY HELP ME!!
KATA
KATA (SHAKE)

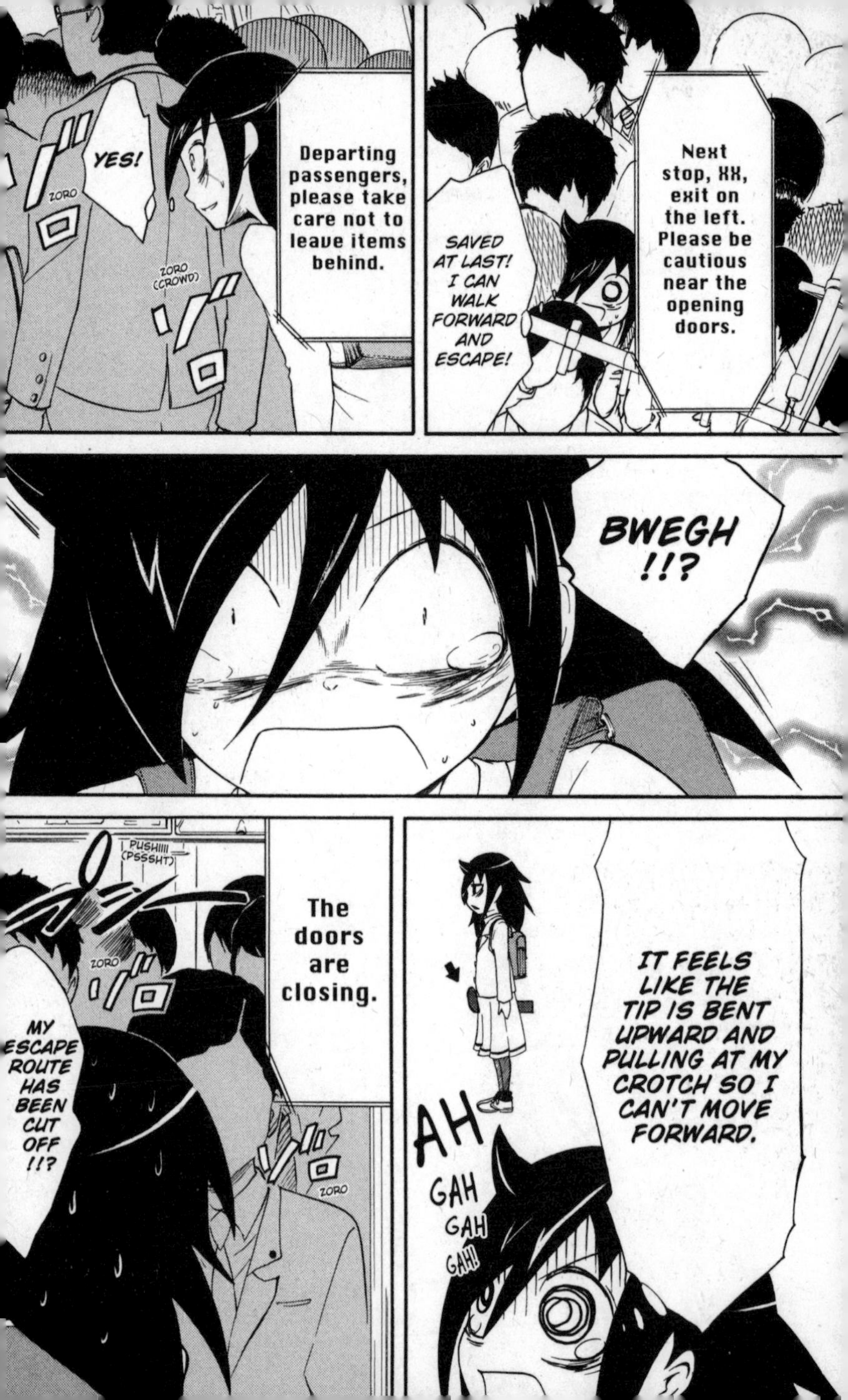
Next stop, XX, exit on the left. Please be cautious near the opening doors.
SAVED AT LAST! I CAN WALK FORWARD AND ESCAPE!
Departing passengers, please take care not to leave items behind.
YES!
ZORO
ZORO (CROWD)
BWEGH !!?
IT FEELS LIKE THE TIP IS BENT UPWARD AND PULLING AT MY CROTCH SO I CAN'T MOVE FORWARD.
AH
GAH GAH GAH!
The doors are closing.
PUSHIIII (PSSSHT)
ZORO
MY ESCAPE ROUTE HAS BEEN CUT OFF !!?
ZORO

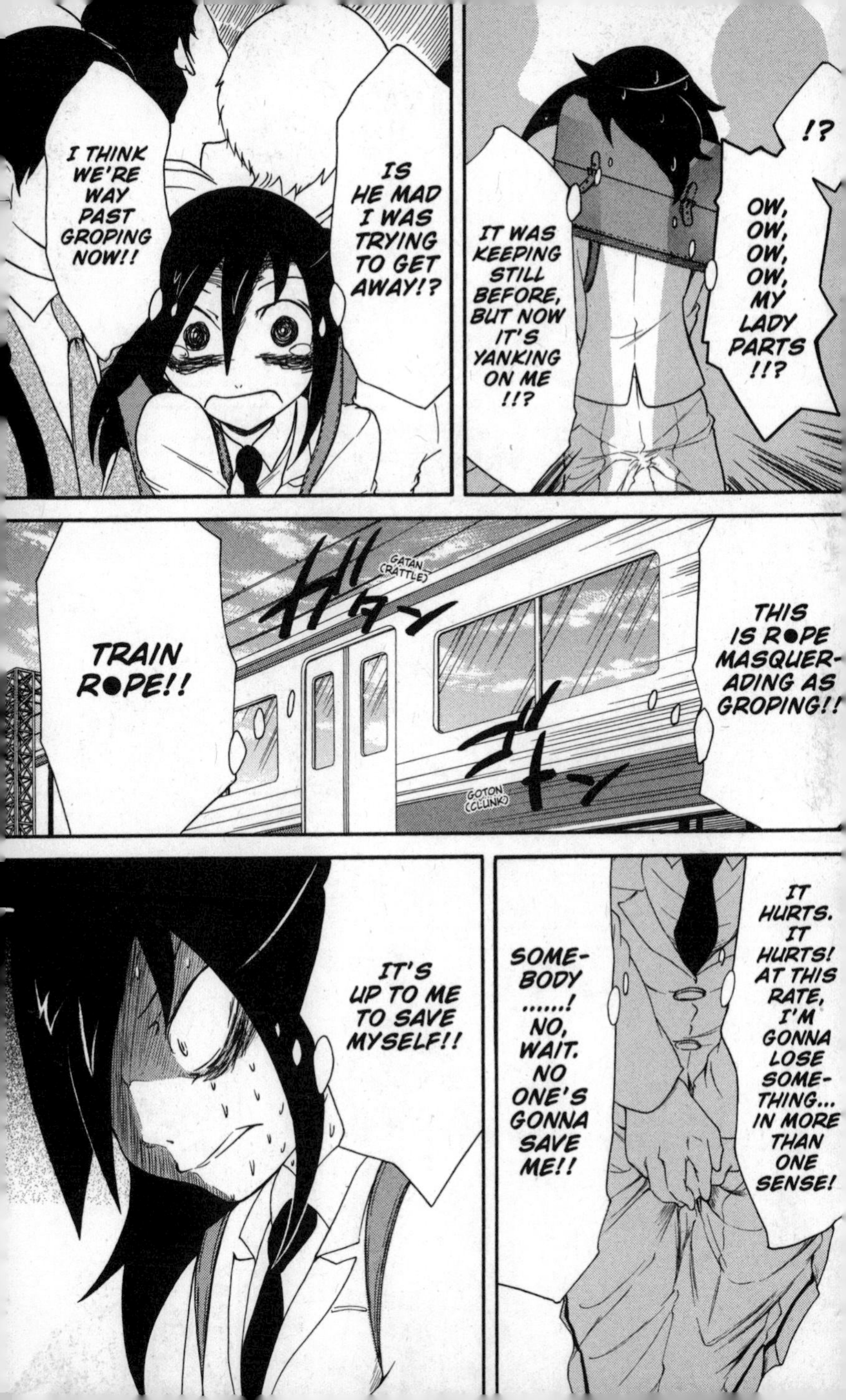
!?
OW, OW, OW, OW, MY LADY PARTS!!?
IT WAS KEEPING STILL BEFORE, BUT NOW IT'S YANKING ON ME!!?
IS HE MAD I WAS TRYING TO GET AWAY!?
I THINK WE'RE WAY PAST GROPING NOW!!
THIS IS R●PE MASQUERADING AS GROPING!!
GATAN (RATTLE)
TRAIN R●PE!!
GOTON (CLUNK)
IT HURTS. IT HURTS! AT THIS RATE, I'M GONNA LOSE SOMETHING... IN MORE THAN ONE SENSE!
SOMEBODY ......! NO, WAIT. NO ONE'S GONNA SAVE ME!!
IT'S UP TO ME TO SAVE MYSELF!!

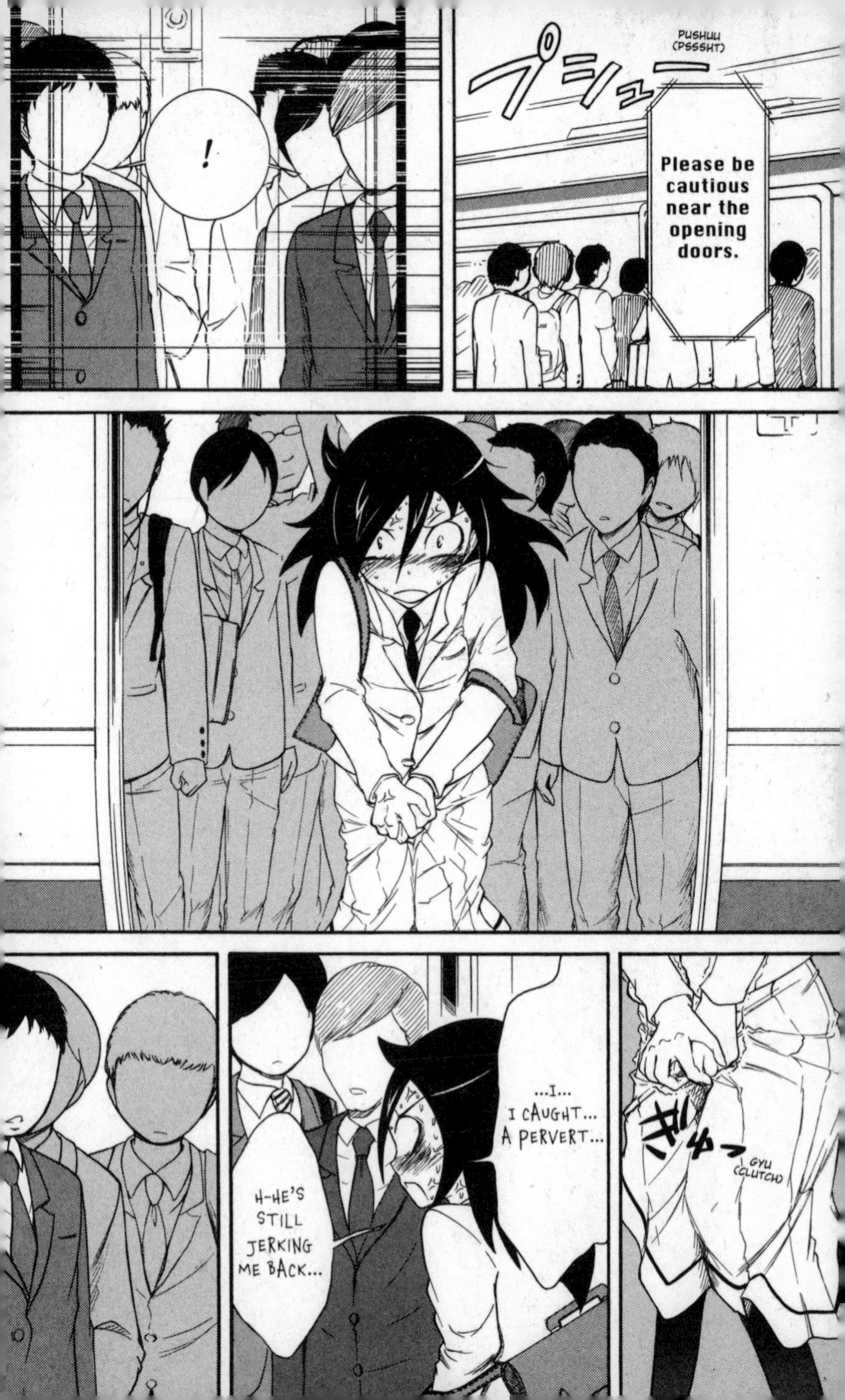
プシュー
PUSHUU (PSSSHT)
Please be cautious near the opening doors.
!
ぎゅっ
GYU (CLUTCH)
...I... I CAUGHT... A PERVERT...
H-HE'S STILL JERKING ME BACK...

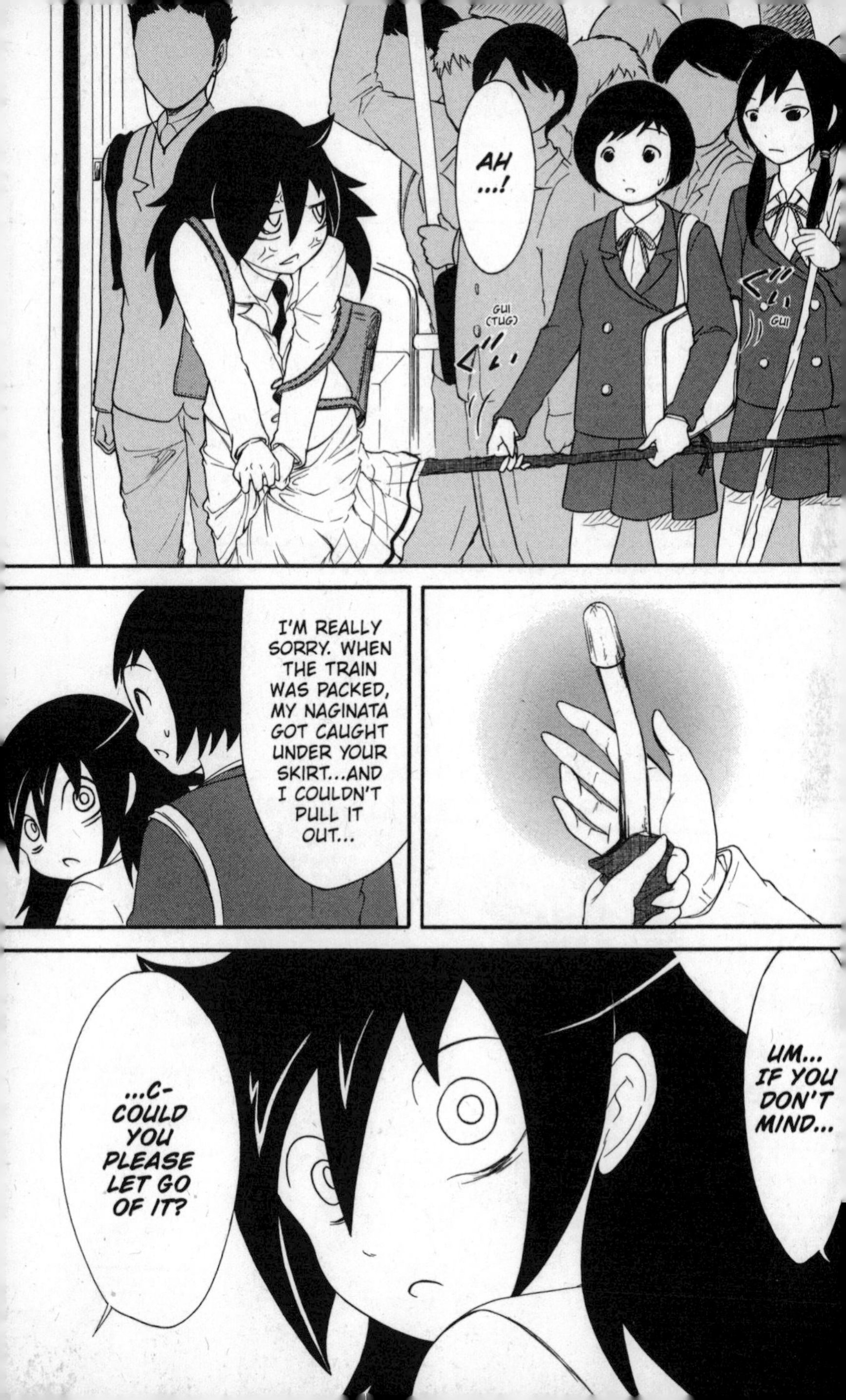
AH ...!
GUI
GUI (TUG)
I'M REALLY SORRY. WHEN THE TRAIN WAS PACKED, MY NAGINATA GOT CAUGHT UNDER YOUR SKIRT...AND I COULDN'T PULL IT OUT...
UM... IF YOU DON'T MIND...
...C-COULD YOU PLEASE LET GO OF IT?

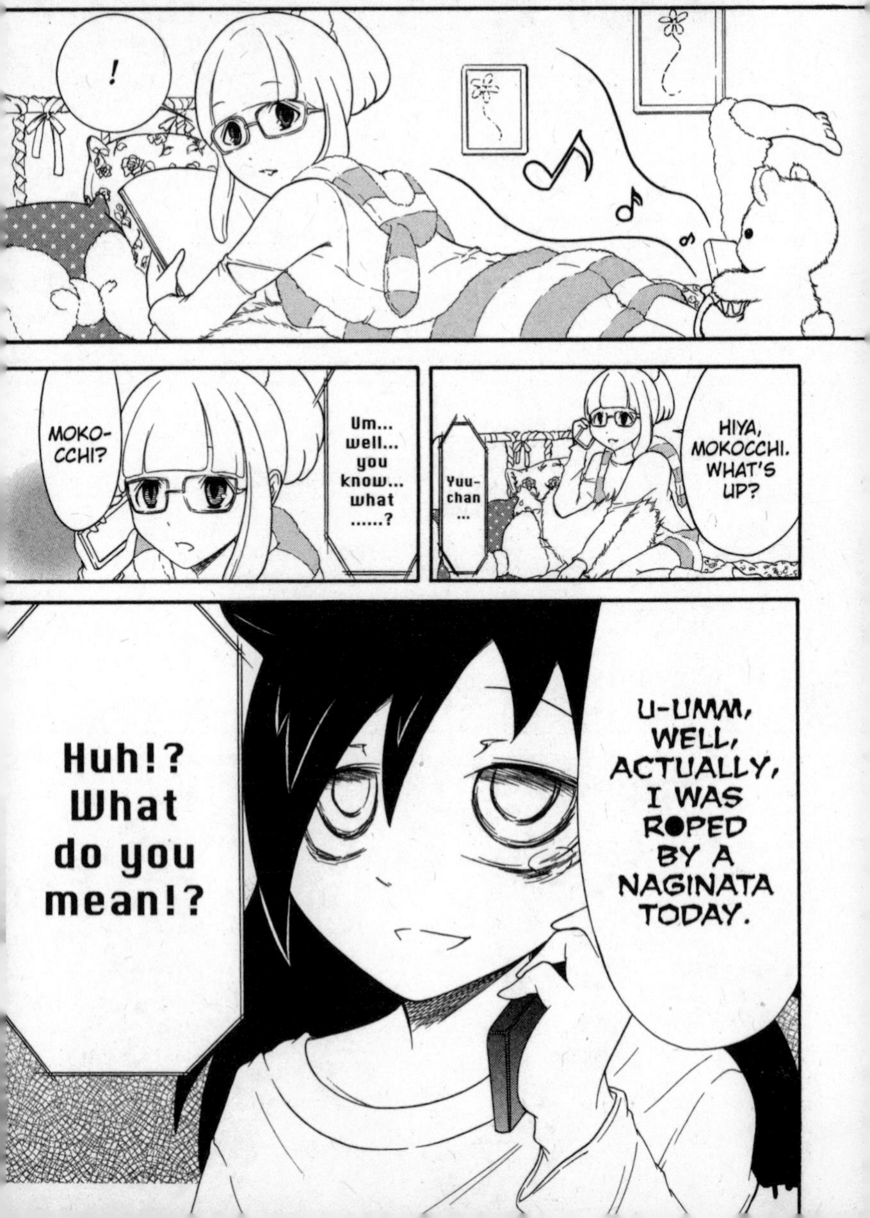
!
HIYA, MOKOCCHI. WHAT'S UP?
Yuu-chan ...
Um... well... you know... what ......?
MOKO-CCHI?
U-UMM, WELL, ACTUALLY, I WAS ROPED BY A NAGINATA TODAY.
Huh!? What do you mean!?

No Matter How I Look at It, It's You Guys' Fault I'm Not Popular!

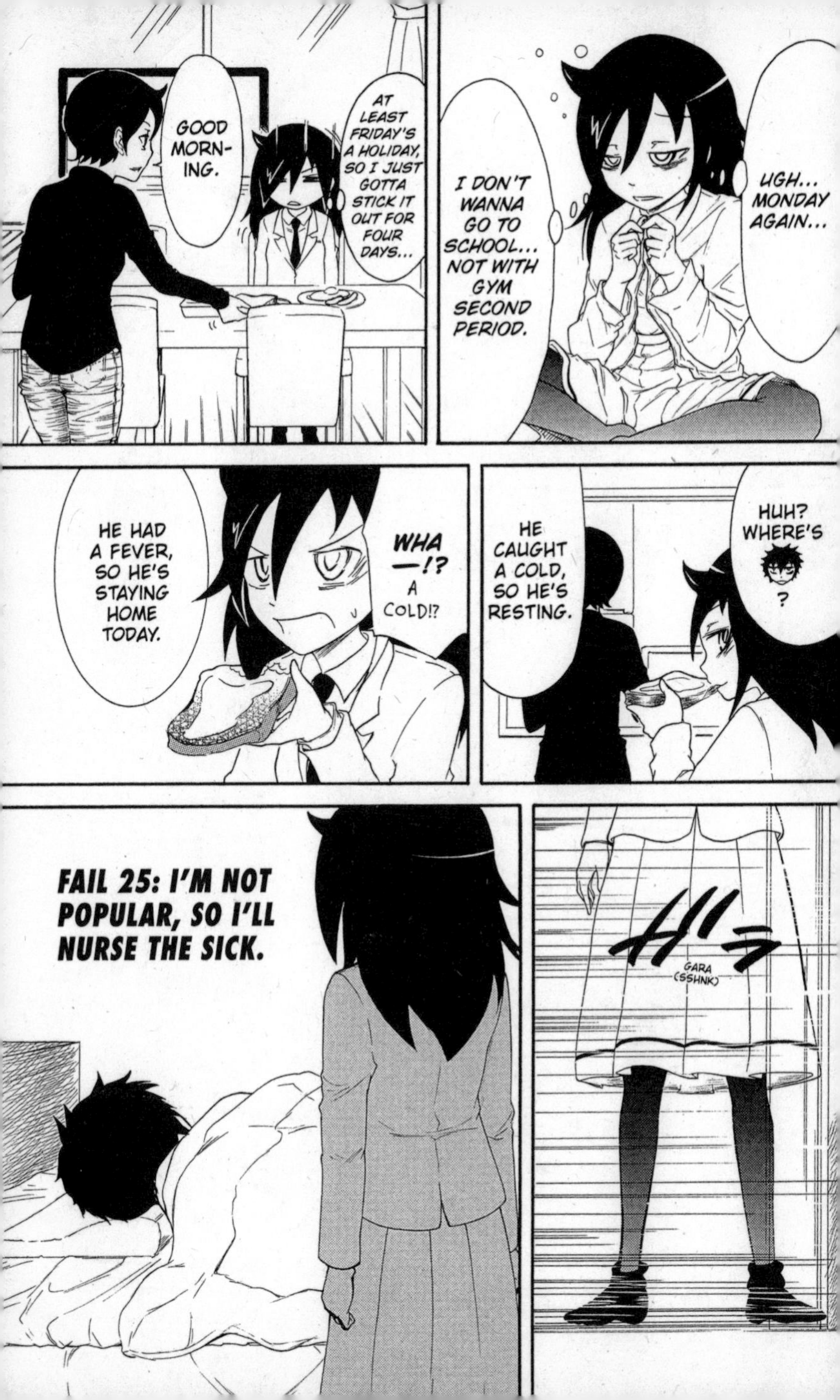
UGH... MONDAY AGAIN...
I DON'T WANNA GO TO SCHOOL... NOT WITH GYM SECOND PERIOD.
AT LEAST FRIDAY'S A HOLIDAY, SO I JUST GOTTA STICK IT OUT FOR FOUR DAYS...
GOOD MORN-ING.
HUH? WHERE'S ?
HE CAUGHT A COLD, SO HE'S RESTING.
WHA—!? A COLD!?
HE HAD A FEVER, SO HE'S STAYING HOME TODAY.
GARA (SSHNK)
FAIL 25: I'M NOT POPULAR, SO I'LL NURSE THE SICK.

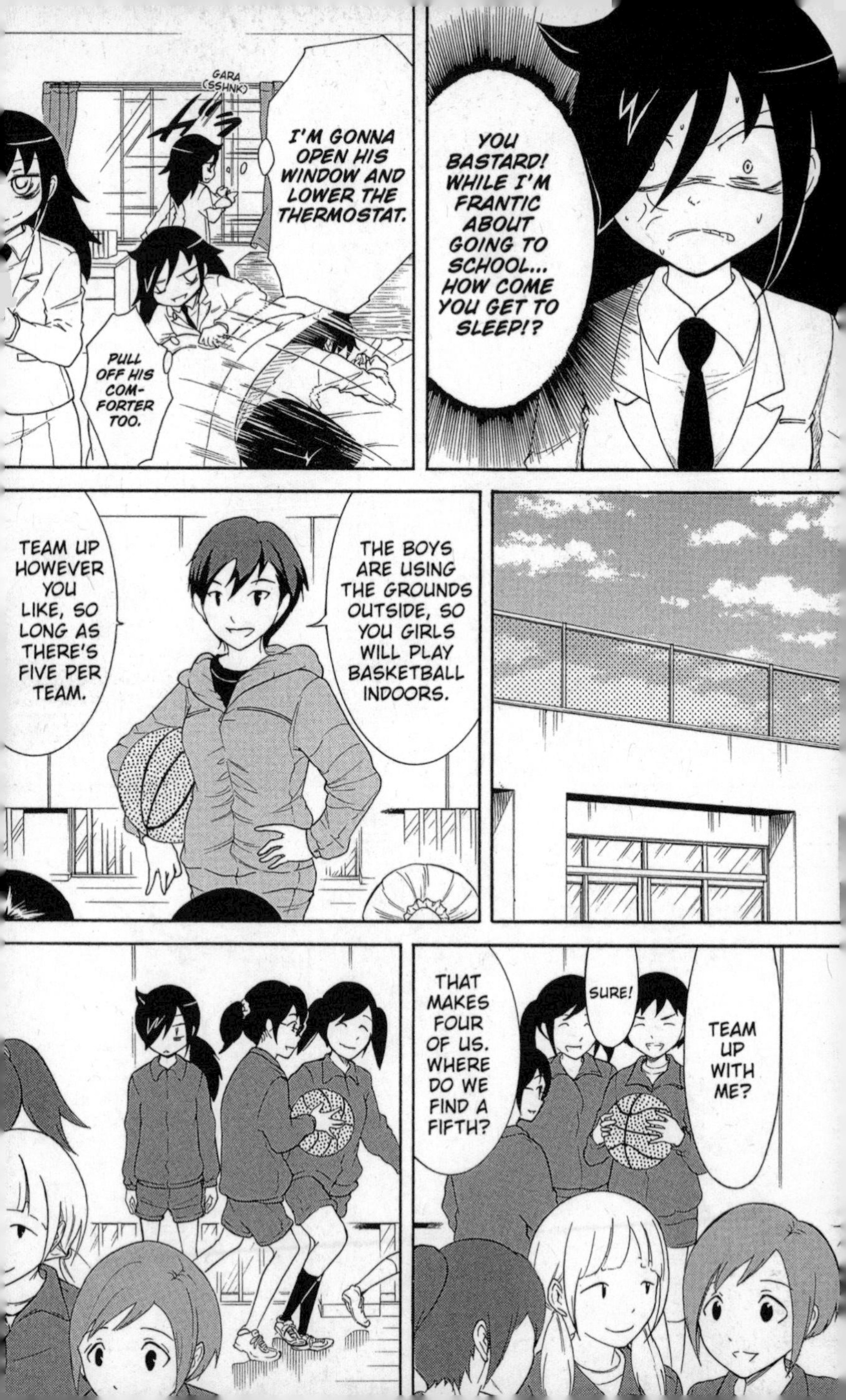
YOU BASTARD! WHILE I'M FRANTIC ABOUT GOING TO SCHOOL... HOW COME YOU GET TO SLEEP!?
I'M GONNA OPEN HIS WINDOW AND LOWER THE THERMOSTAT.
GARA (SSHNK)
PULL OFF HIS COM-FORTER TOO.
THE BOYS ARE USING THE GROUNDS OUTSIDE, SO YOU GIRLS WILL PLAY BASKETBALL INDOORS.
TEAM UP HOWEVER YOU LIKE, SO LONG AS THERE'S FIVE PER TEAM.
TEAM UP WITH ME?
SURE!
THAT MAKES FOUR OF US. WHERE DO WE FIND A FIFTH?

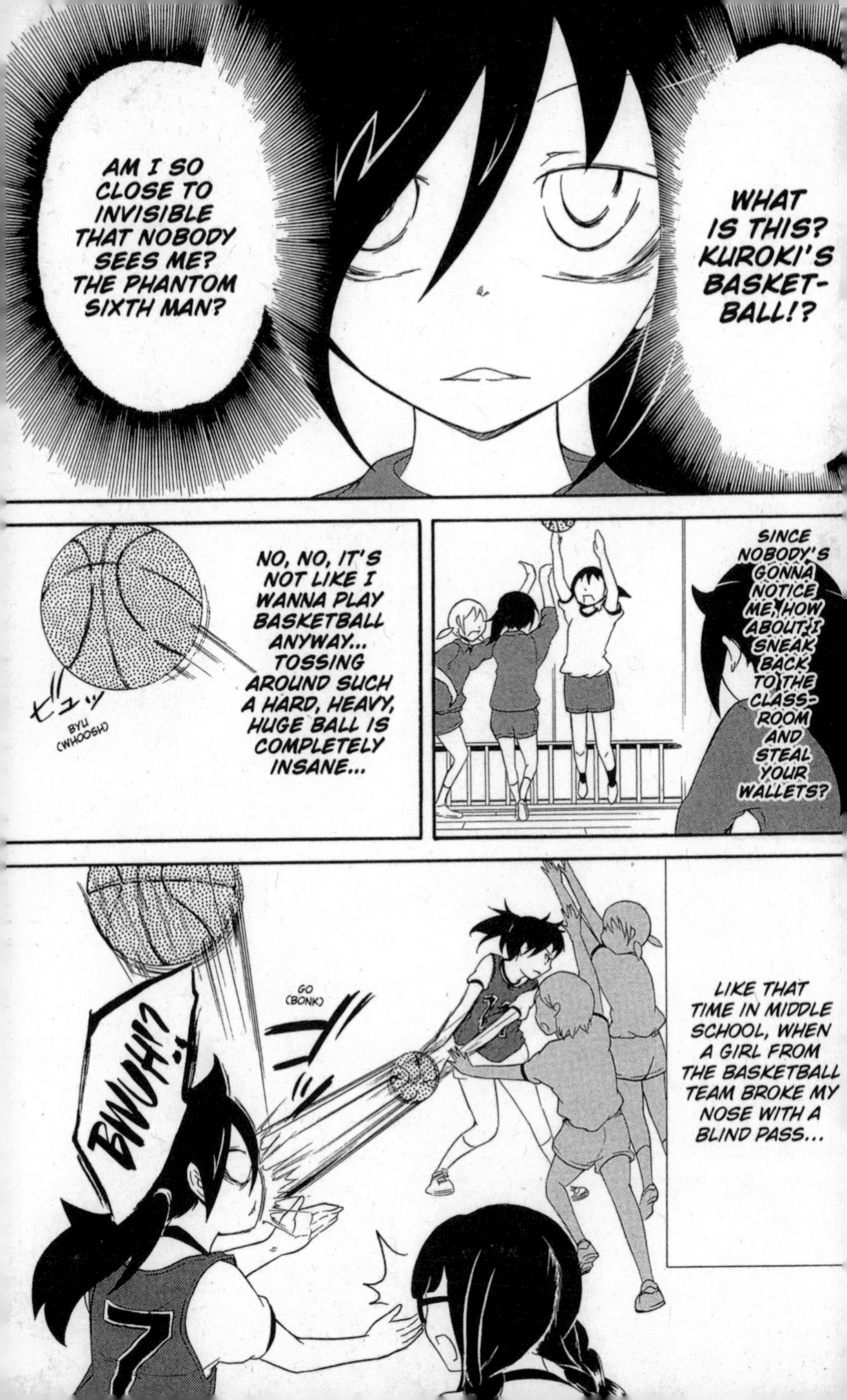
WHAT IS THIS? KUROKI'S BASKET-BALL!?
AM I SO CLOSE TO INVISIBLE THAT NOBODY SEES ME? THE PHANTOM SIXTH MAN?
SINCE NOBODY'S GONNA NOTICE ME, HOW ABOUT I SNEAK BACK TO THE CLASS-ROOM AND STEAL YOUR WALLETS?
NO, NO, IT'S NOT LIKE I WANNA PLAY BASKETBALL ANYWAY... TOSSING AROUND SUCH A HARD, HEAVY, HUGE BALL IS COMPLETELY INSANE...
ビュッ
BYU (WHOOSH)
LIKE THAT TIME IN MIDDLE SCHOOL, WHEN A GIRL FROM THE BASKETBALL TEAM BROKE MY NOSE WITH A BLIND PASS...
ゴ
GO (BONK)
BWUH!?

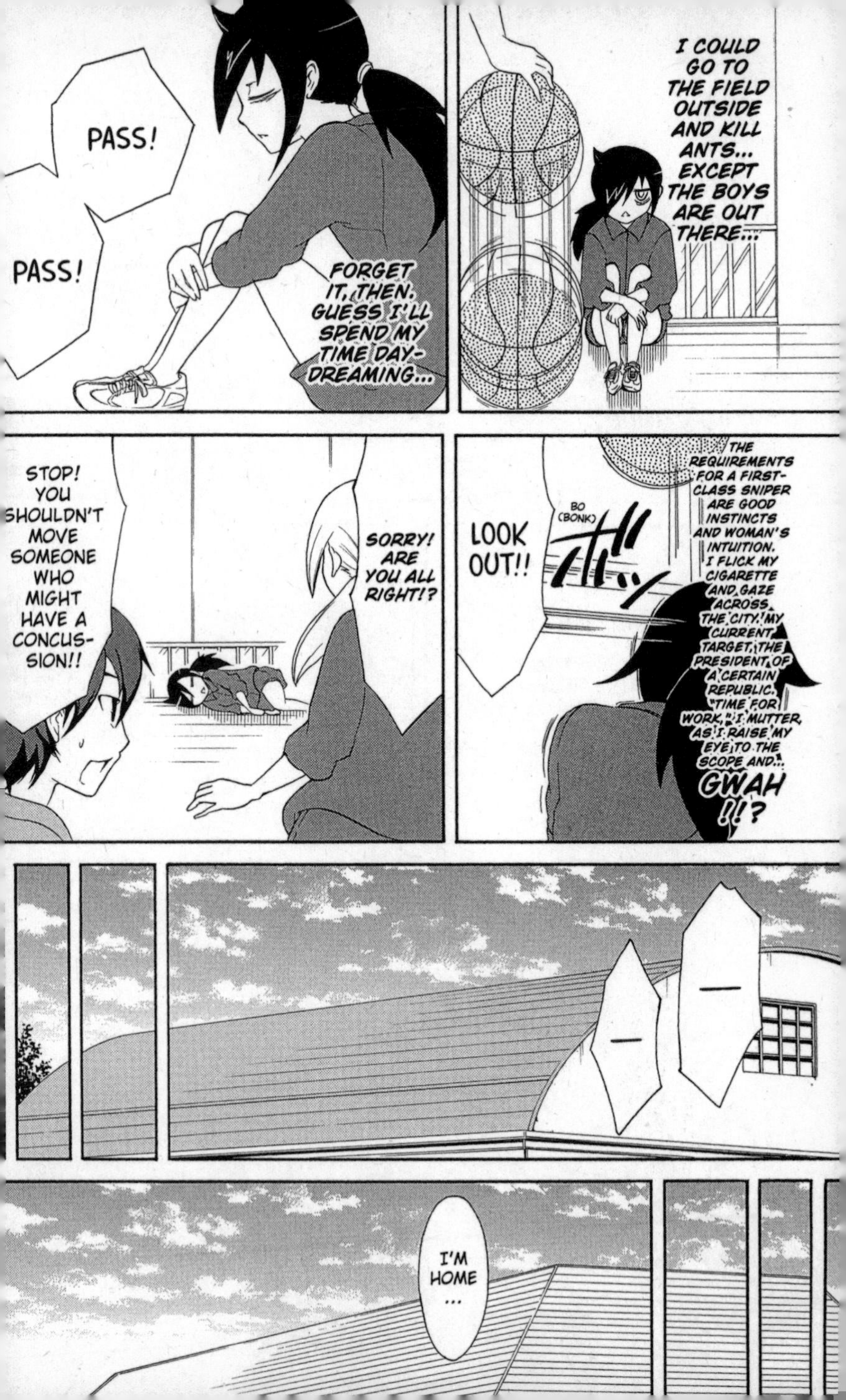

I COULD GO TO THE FIELD OUTSIDE AND KILL ANTS... EXCEPT THE BOYS ARE OUT THERE...
PASS!
PASS!
FORGET IT, THEN. GUESS I'LL SPEND MY TIME DAY-DREAMING...
THE REQUIREMENTS FOR A FIRST-CLASS SNIPER ARE GOOD INSTINCTS AND WOMAN'S INTUITION. I FLICK MY CIGARETTE AND GAZE ACROSS THE CITY. MY CURRENT TARGET: THE PRESIDENT OF A CERTAIN REPUBLIC. "TIME FOR WORK," I MUTTER, AS I RAISE MY EYE TO THE SCOPE AND... GWAH !!?
BO (BONK)
LOOK OUT!!
SORRY! ARE YOU ALL RIGHT!?
STOP! YOU SHOULDN'T MOVE SOMEONE WHO MIGHT HAVE A CONCUS-SION!!
I'M HOME ...

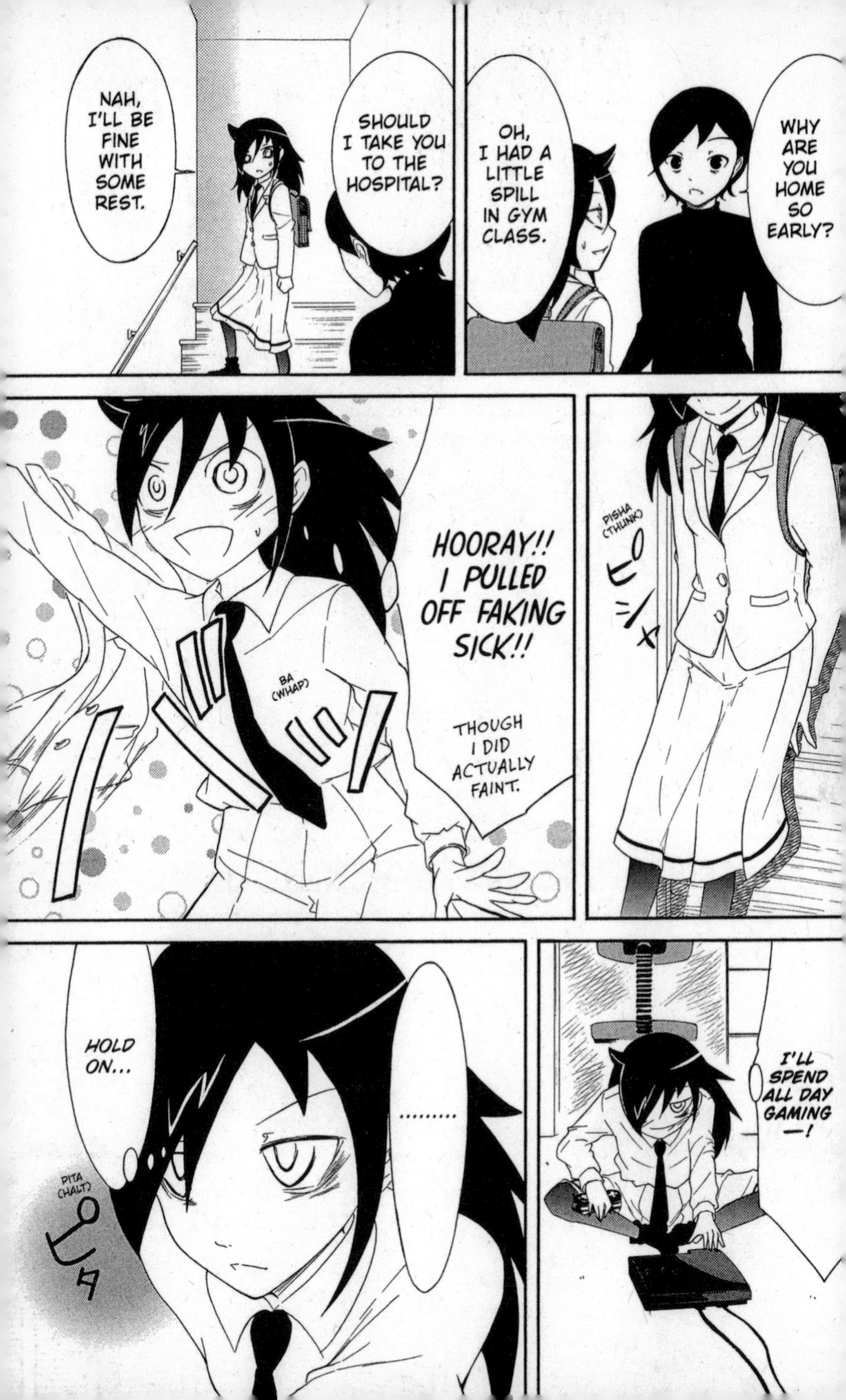
WHY ARE YOU HOME SO EARLY?
OH, I HAD A LITTLE SPILL IN GYM CLASS.
SHOULD I TAKE YOU TO THE HOSPITAL?
NAH, I'LL BE FINE WITH SOME REST.
PISHA (THUNK)
HOORAY!! I PULLED OFF FAKING SICK!!
THOUGH I DID ACTUALLY FAINT.
BA (WHAP)
I'LL SPEND ALL DAY GAMING—!
....
HOLD ON...
PITA (HALT)

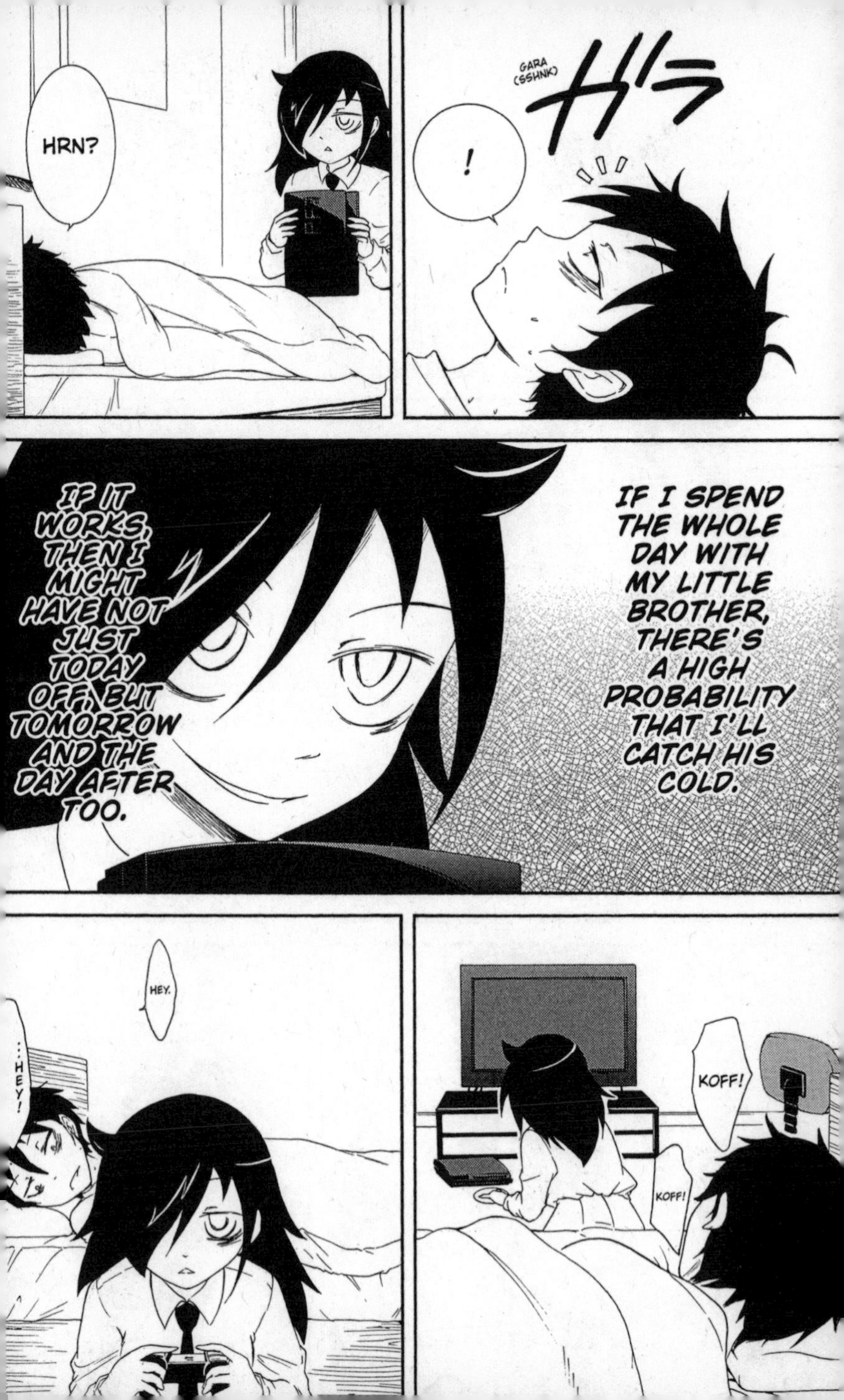
GARA (SSHNK)
ガラ
!
HRN?
IF I SPEND THE WHOLE DAY WITH MY LITTLE BROTHER, THERE'S A HIGH PROBABILITY THAT I'LL CATCH HIS COLD.
IF IT WORKS, THEN I MIGHT HAVE NOT JUST TODAY OFF, BUT TOMORROW AND THE DAY AFTER TOO.
KOFF!
KOFF!
HEY.
...HEY!

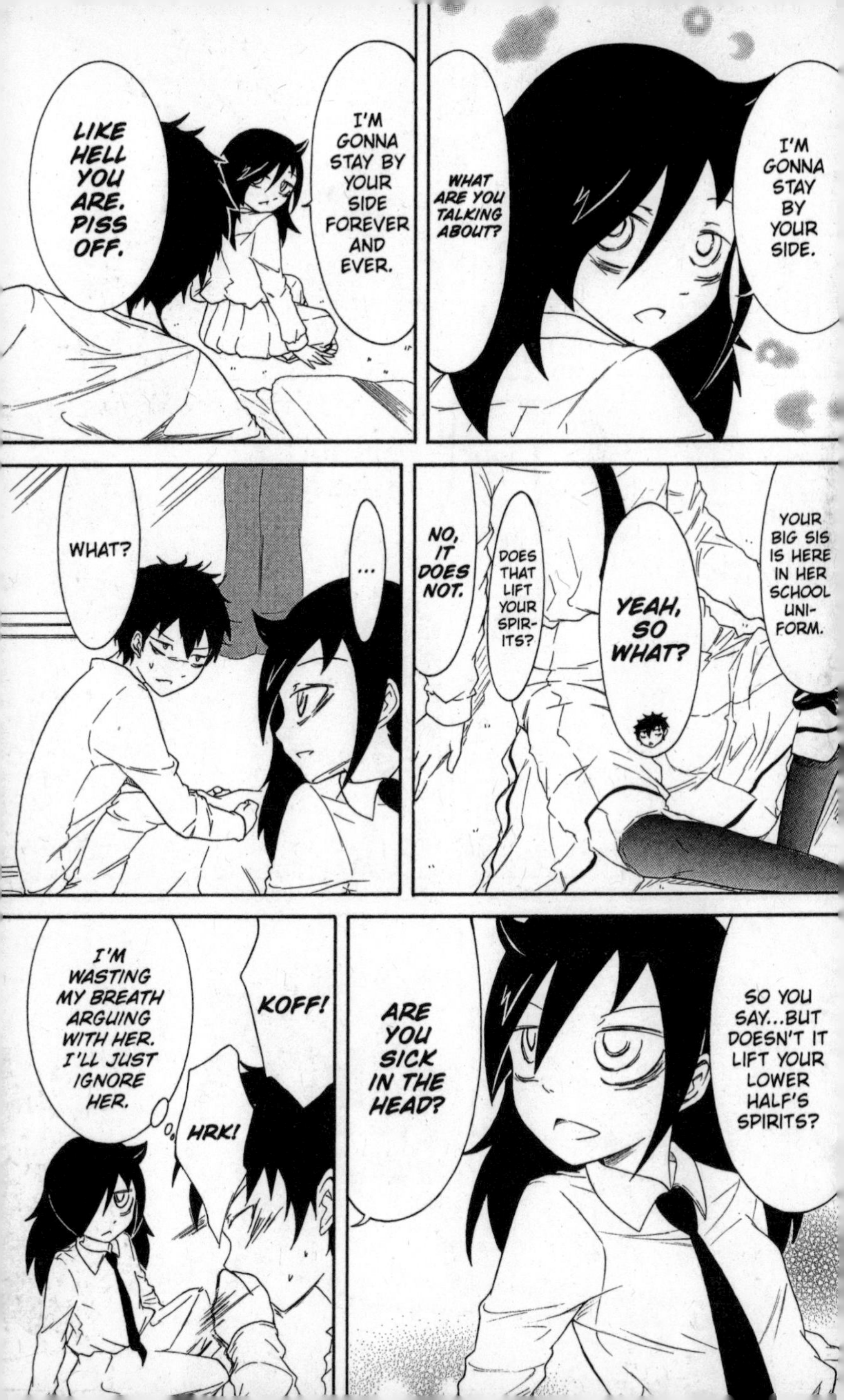
I'M GONNA STAY BY YOUR SIDE.
WHAT ARE YOU TALKING ABOUT?
I'M GONNA STAY BY YOUR SIDE FOREVER AND EVER.
LIKE HELL YOU ARE. PISS OFF.
YOUR BIG SIS IS HERE IN HER SCHOOL UNI-FORM.
YEAH, SO WHAT?
DOES THAT LIFT YOUR SPIR-ITS?
NO, IT DOES NOT.
...
WHAT?
SO YOU SAY...BUT DOESN'T IT LIFT YOUR LOWER HALF'S SPIRITS?
ARE YOU SICK IN THE HEAD?
KOFF!
HRK!
I'M WASTING MY BREATH ARGUING WITH HER. I'LL JUST IGNORE HER.

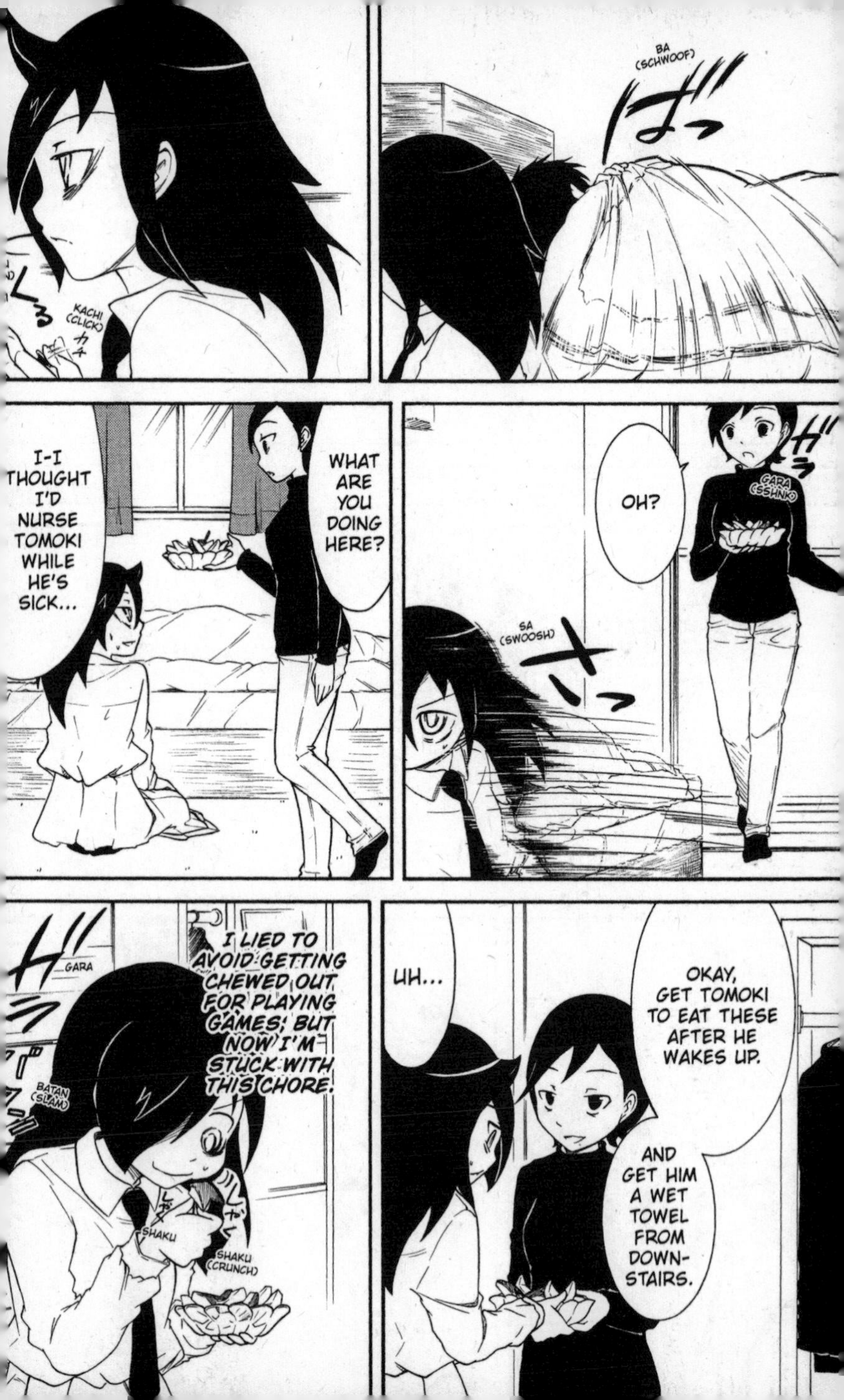
BA (SCHWOOF)
KACHI (CLICK)
GARA (SSHNK)
OH?
SA (SWOOSH)
WHAT ARE YOU DOING HERE?
I-I THOUGHT I'D NURSE TOMOKI WHILE HE'S SICK...
OKAY, GET TOMOKI TO EAT THESE AFTER HE WAKES UP.
AND GET HIM A WET TOWEL FROM DOWN-STAIRS.
UH...
GARA
BATAN (SLAM)
I LIED TO AVOID GETTING CHEWED OUT FOR PLAYING GAMES, BUT NOW I'M STUCK WITH THIS CHORE.
SHAKU
SHAKU (CRUNCH)

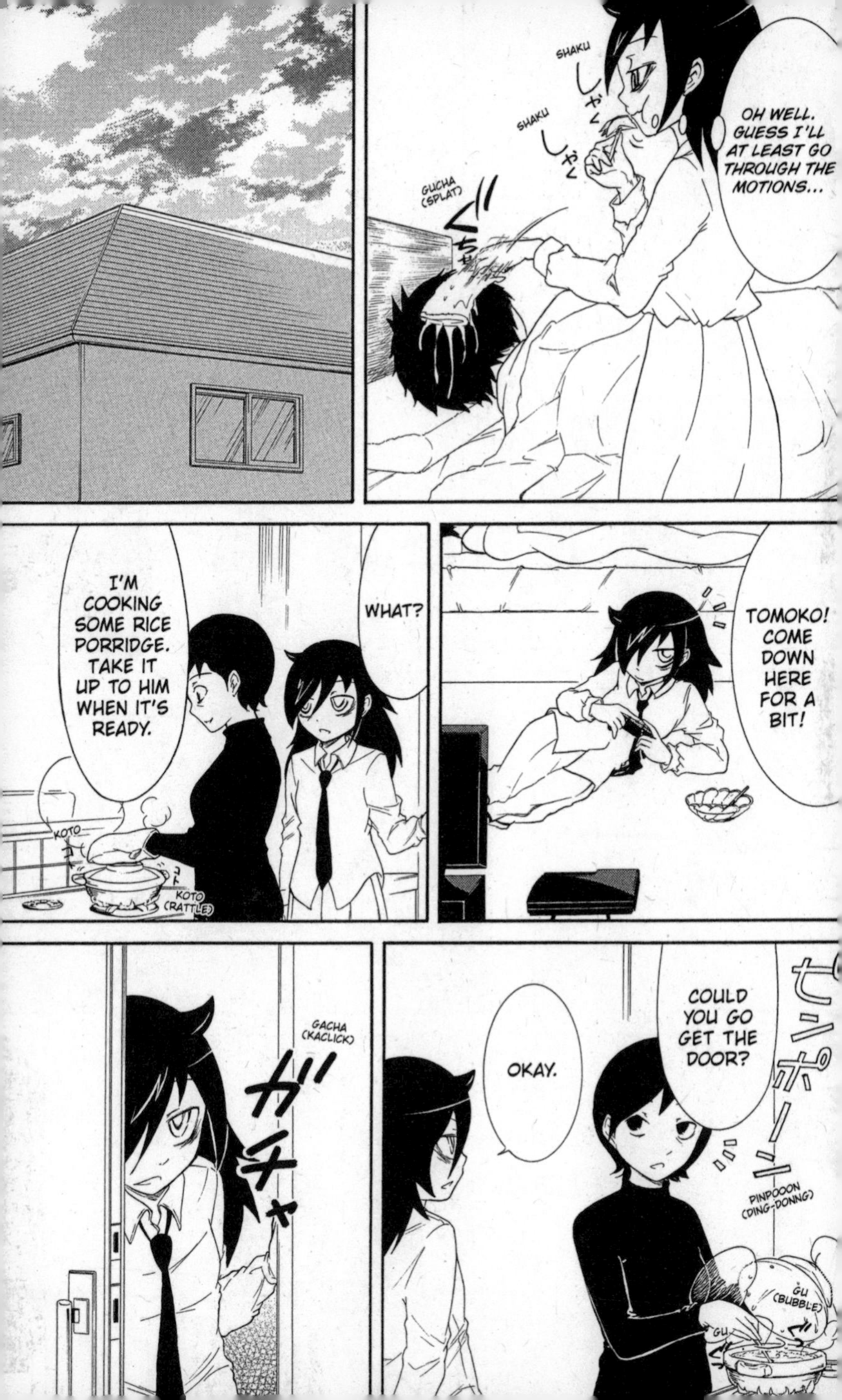
OH WELL. GUESS I'LL AT LEAST GO THROUGH THE MOTIONS...
SHAKU
SHAKU
GUCHA (SPLAT)
TOMOKO! COME DOWN HERE FOR A BIT!
WHAT?
I'M COOKING SOME RICE PORRIDGE. TAKE IT UP TO HIM WHEN IT'S READY.
KOTO
KOTO (RATTLE)
PINPOOON (DING-DONNG)
COULD YOU GO GET THE DOOR?
OKAY.
GU (BUBBLE)
GU
GACHA (KACLICK)

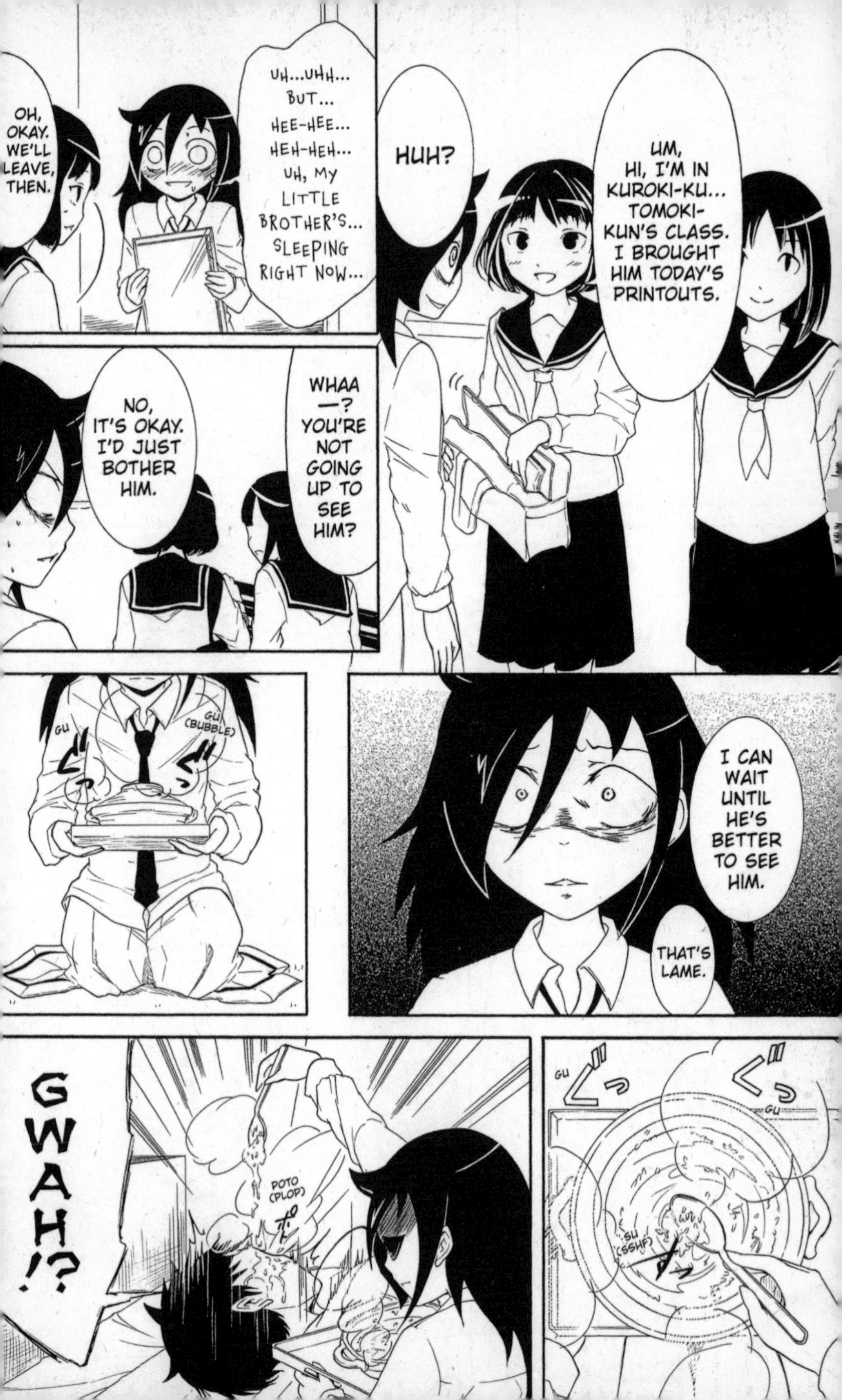
UM, HI, I'M IN KUROKI-KU... TOMOKI-KUN'S CLASS. I BROUGHT HIM TODAY'S PRINTOUTS.
HUH?
UH...UHH... BUT... HEE-HEE... HEH-HEH... UH, MY LITTLE BROTHER'S... SLEEPING RIGHT NOW...
OH, OKAY. WE'LL LEAVE, THEN.
WHAA—? YOU'RE NOT GOING UP TO SEE HIM?
NO, IT'S OKAY. I'D JUST BOTHER HIM.
I CAN WAIT UNTIL HE'S BETTER TO SEE HIM.
THAT'S LAME.
GU (BUBBLE)
GU
GU
GU
SU (SSHF)
POTO (PLOP)
GWAH!?

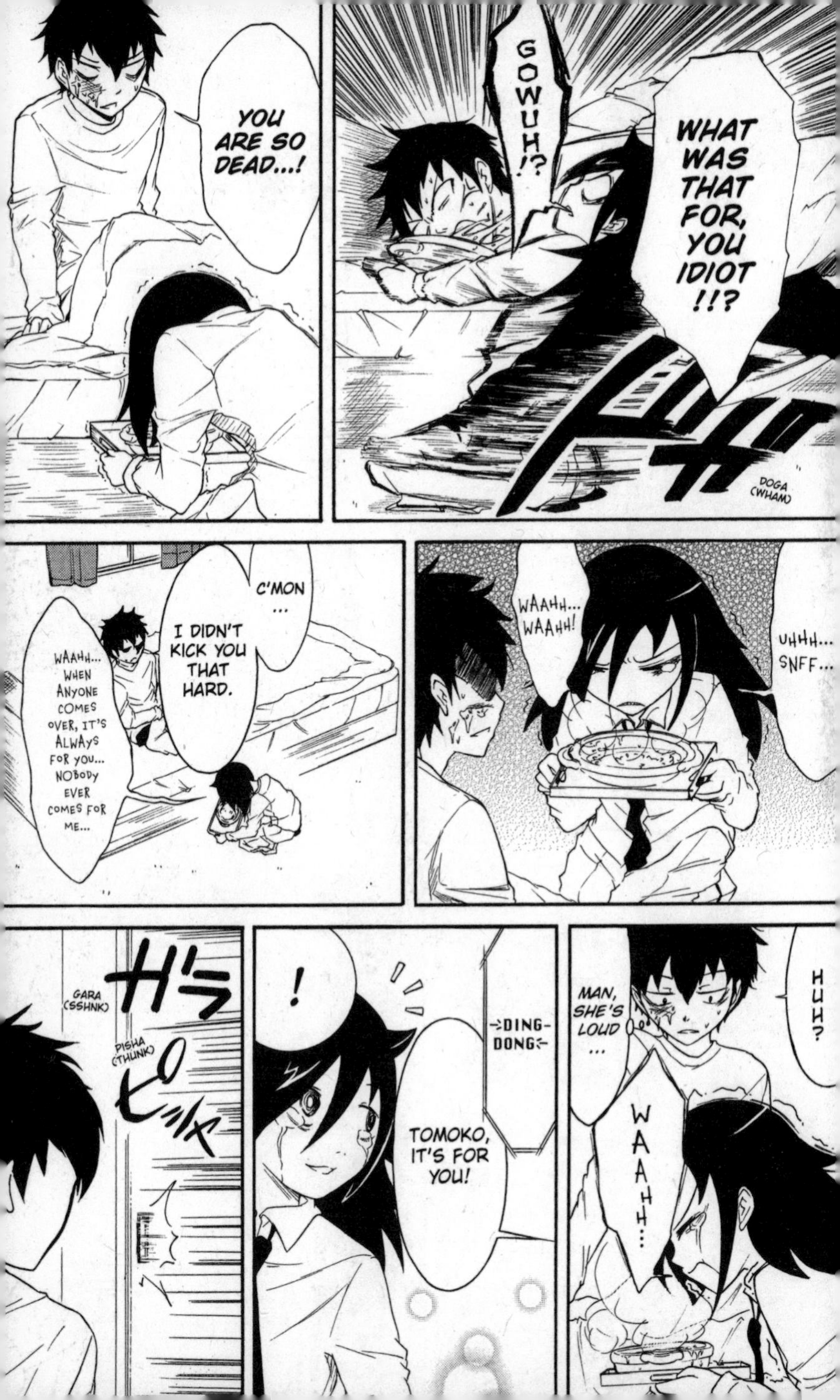

WHAT WAS THAT FOR, YOU IDIOT!!?
GOWUH!?
DOGA (WHAM)
YOU ARE SO DEAD...!
UHHH... SNFF...
WAAHH... WAAHH!
C'MON...
I DIDN'T KICK YOU THAT HARD.
WAAHH... WHEN ANYONE COMES OVER, IT'S ALWAYS FOR YOU... NOBODY EVER COMES FOR ME...
HUH?
MAN, SHE'S LOUD...
WAAHH...
DING-DONG
TOMOKO, IT'S FOR YOU!
!
GARA (SSHNK)
PISHA (THUNK)

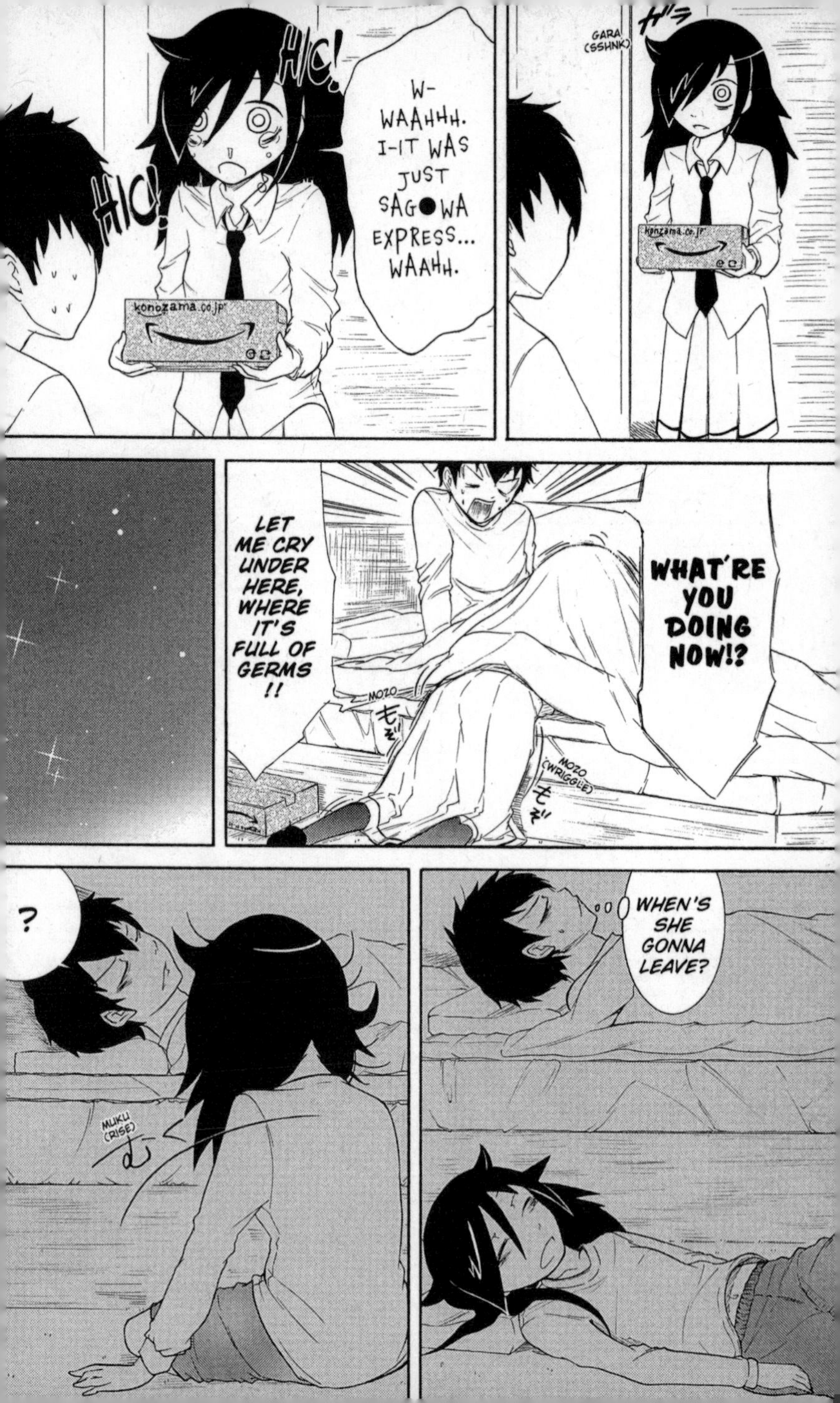
GARA (SSHNK)
konzama.co.jp
HIC!
HIC!
W- WAAHHH. I-IT WAS JUST SAG●WA EXPRESS... WAAHH.
konozama.co.jp
WHAT'RE YOU DOING NOW!?
LET ME CRY UNDER HERE, WHERE IT'S FULL OF GERMS!!
MOZO
MOZO (WRIGGLE)
WHEN'S SHE GONNA LEAVE?
?
MUKU (RISE)

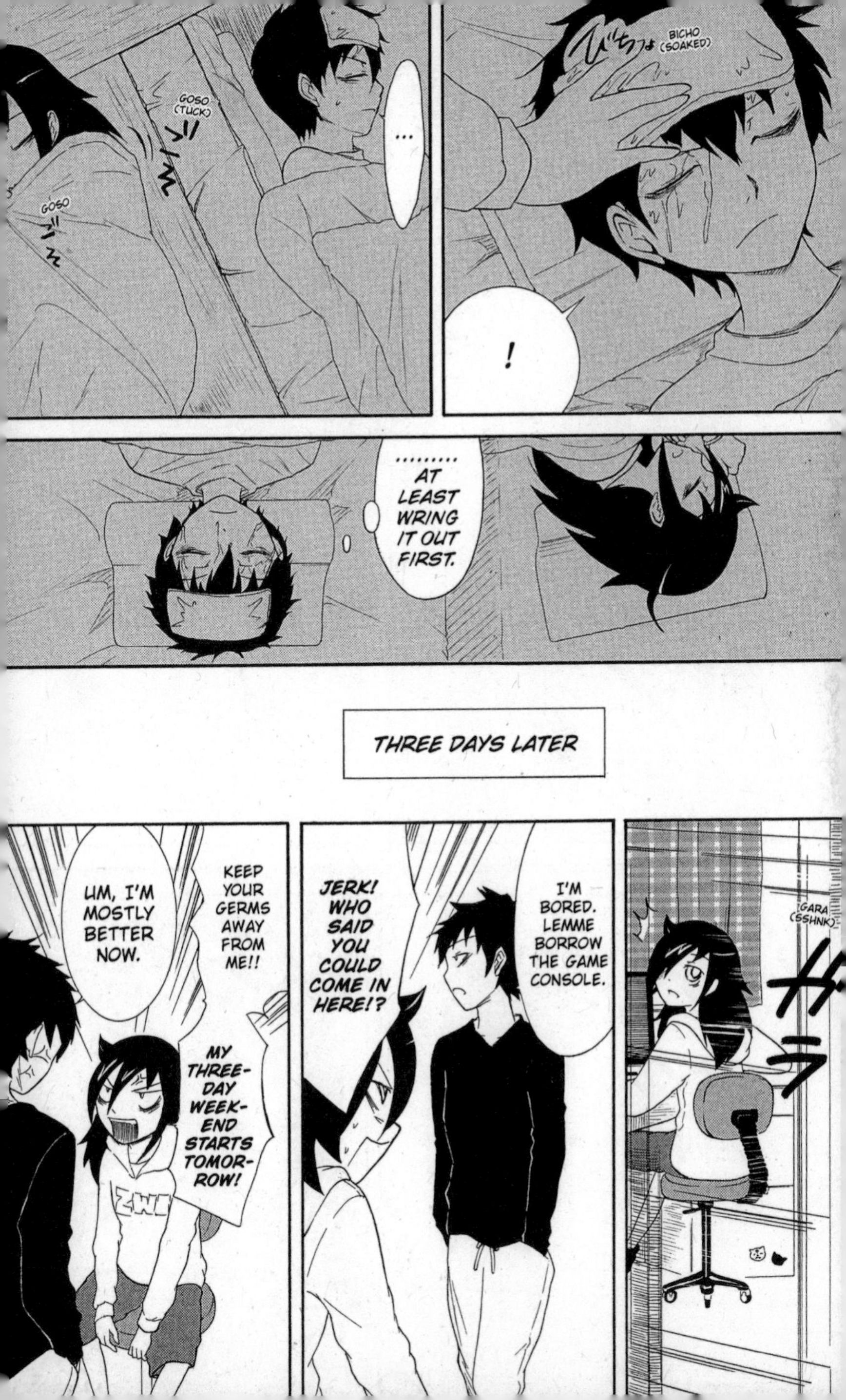
BICHO (SOAKED)
!
GOSO (TUCK)
GOSO
...
..........AT LEAST WRING IT OUT FIRST.
THREE DAYS LATER
GARA (SSHNK)
I'M BORED. LEMME BORROW THE GAME CONSOLE.
JERK! WHO SAID YOU COULD COME IN HERE!?
KEEP YOUR GERMS AWAY FROM ME!!
UM, I'M MOSTLY BETTER NOW.
MY THREE-DAY WEEK-END STARTS TOMOR-ROW!

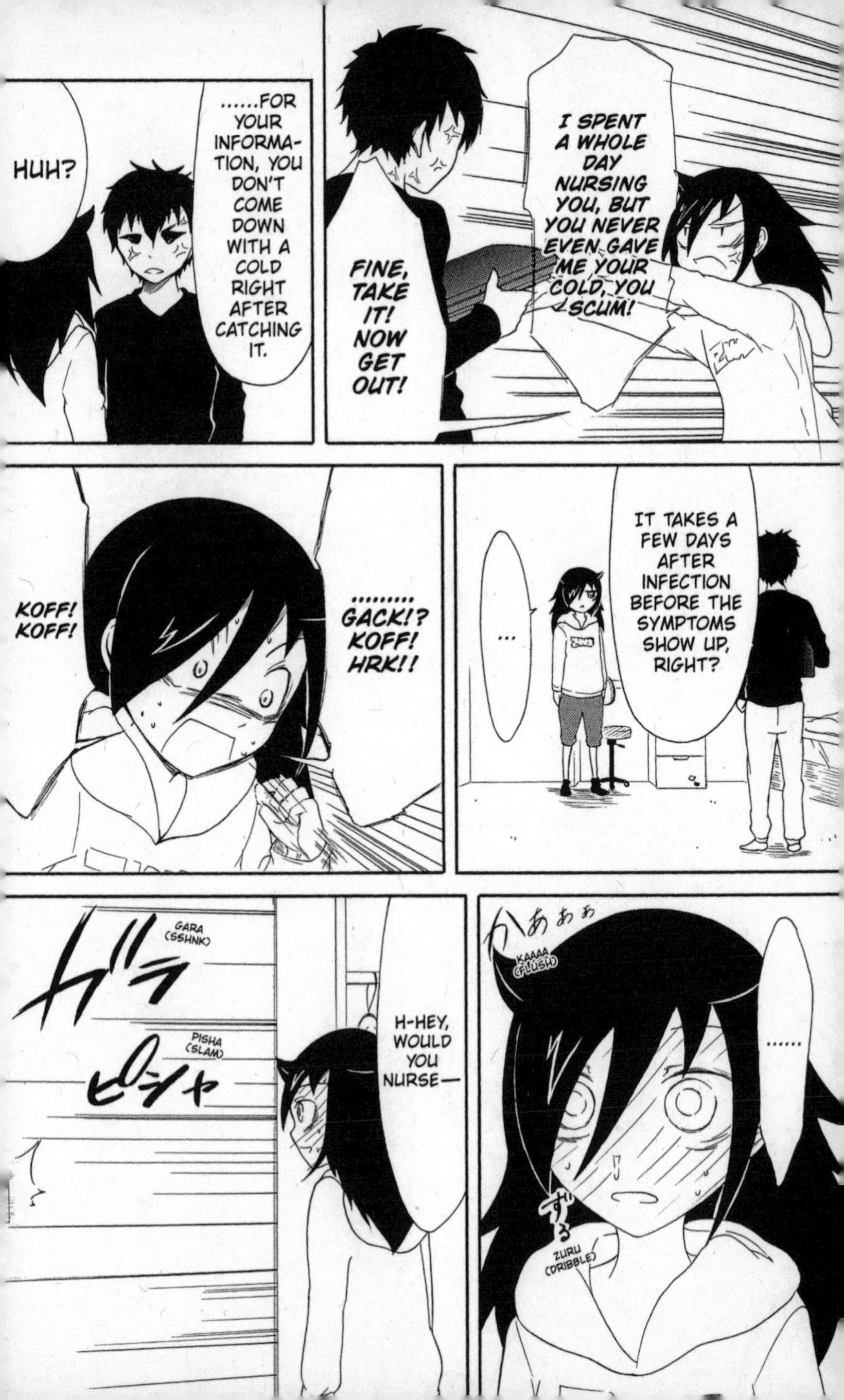
I SPENT A WHOLE DAY NURSING YOU, BUT YOU NEVER EVEN GAVE ME YOUR COLD, YOU SCUM!
FINE, TAKE IT! NOW GET OUT!
......FOR YOUR INFORMATION, YOU DON'T COME DOWN WITH A COLD RIGHT AFTER CATCHING IT.
HUH?
IT TAKES A FEW DAYS AFTER INFECTION BEFORE THE SYMPTOMS SHOW UP, RIGHT?
...
.... GACK!? KOFF! HRK!!
KOFF! KOFF!
KAAAA (FLUSH)
......
ずる
ZURU (DRIBBLE)
H-HEY, WOULD YOU NURSE—
ガラ
GARA (SSHNK)
ピシャ
PISHA (SLAM)

No Matter How I Look at It, It's You Guys' Fault I'm Not Popular!

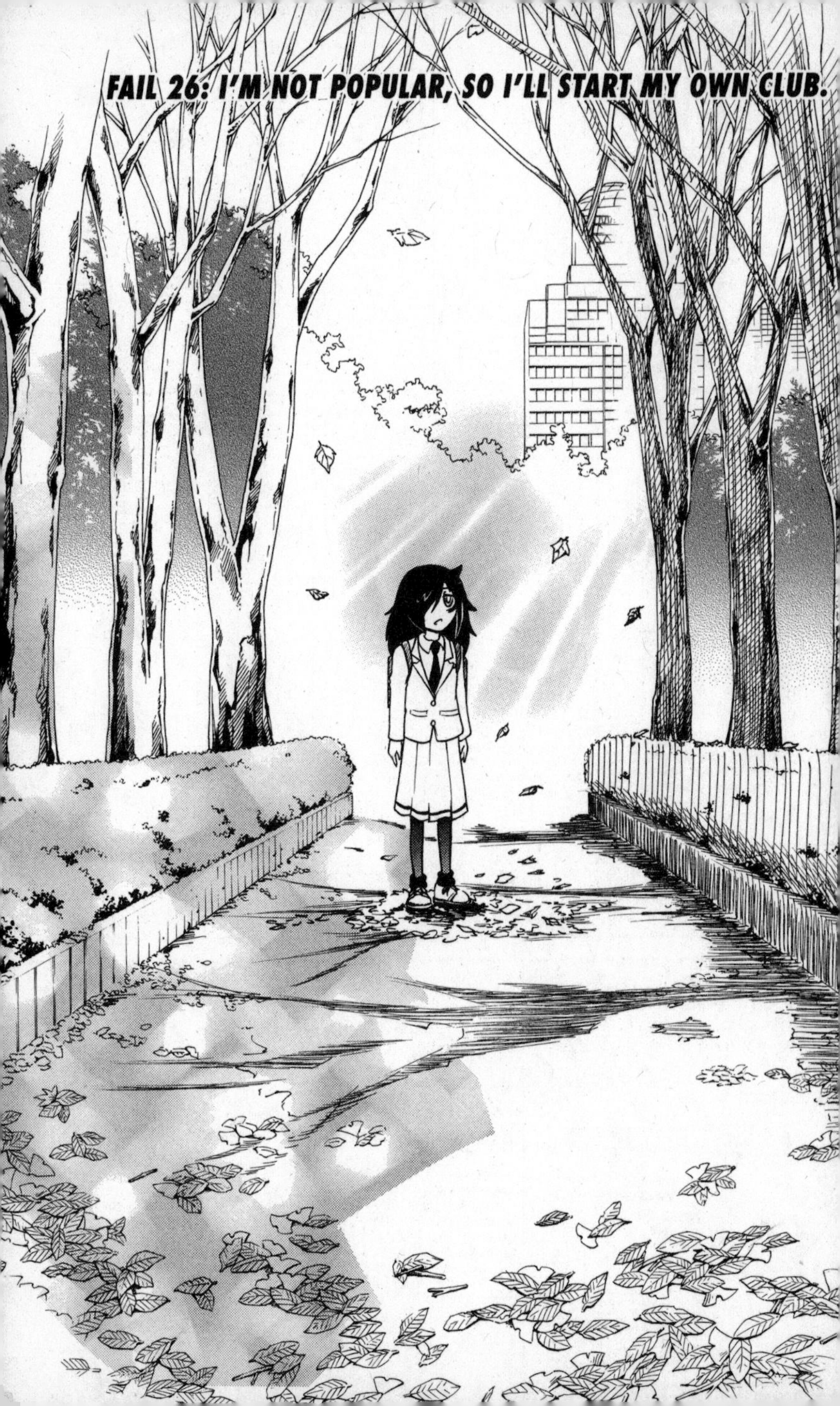
FAIL 26: I'M NOT POPULAR, SO I'LL START MY OWN CLUB.

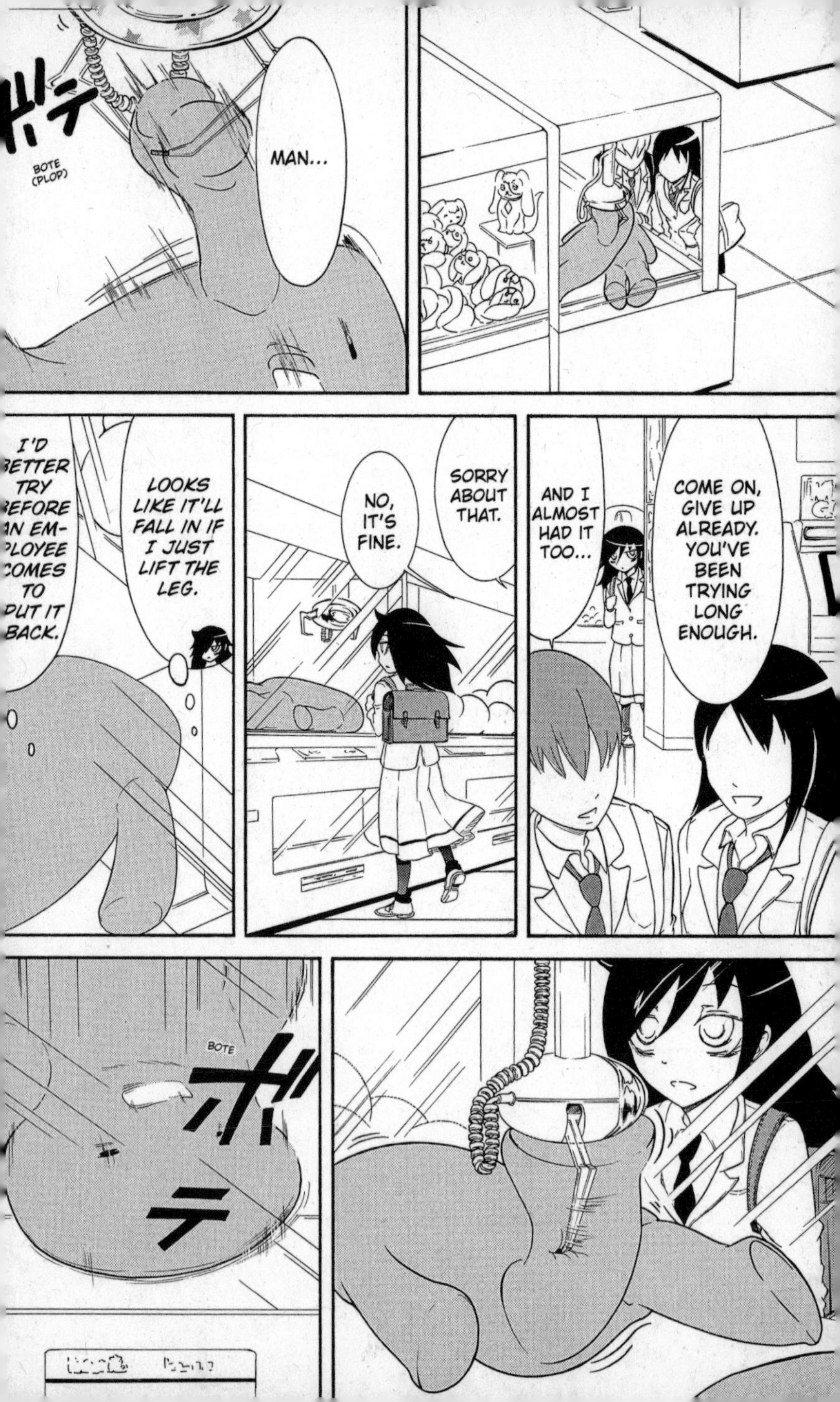
MAN...
BOTE
(PLOP)
COME ON, GIVE UP ALREADY. YOU'VE BEEN TRYING LONG ENOUGH.
AND I ALMOST HAD IT TOO...
SORRY ABOUT THAT.
NO, IT'S FINE.
LOOKS LIKE IT'LL FALL IN IF I JUST LIFT THE LEG.
I'D BETTER TRY BEFORE AN EM- PLOYEE COMES TO PUT IT BACK.
BOTE

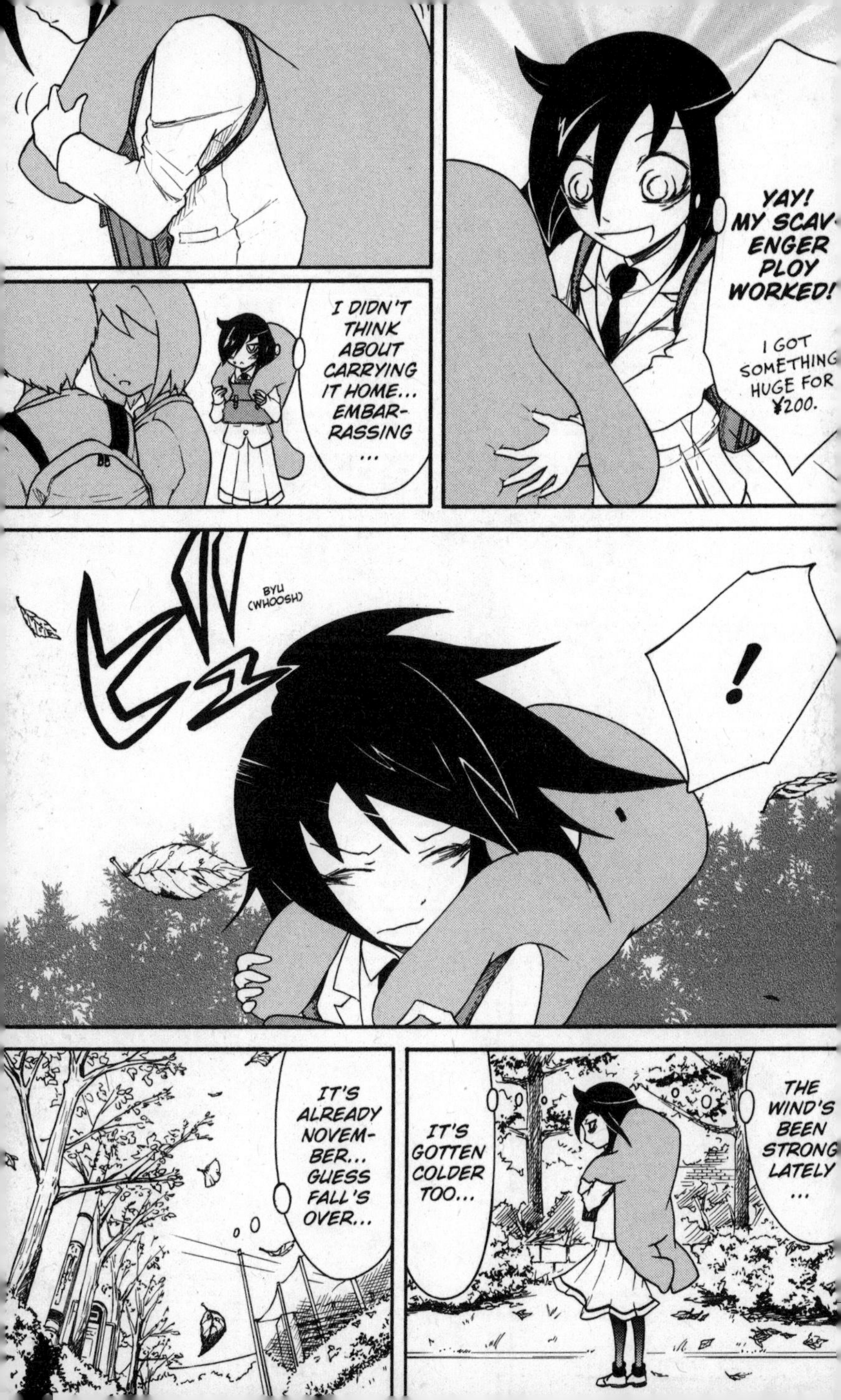

YAY! MY SCAV-ENGER PLOY WORKED!
I GOT SOMETHING HUGE FOR ¥200.
I DIDN'T THINK ABOUT CARRYING IT HOME... EMBAR-RASSING ...
!
BYU (WHOOSH)
THE WIND'S BEEN STRONG LATELY ...
IT'S GOTTEN COLDER TOO...
IT'S ALREADY NOVEM-BER... GUESS FALL'S OVER...

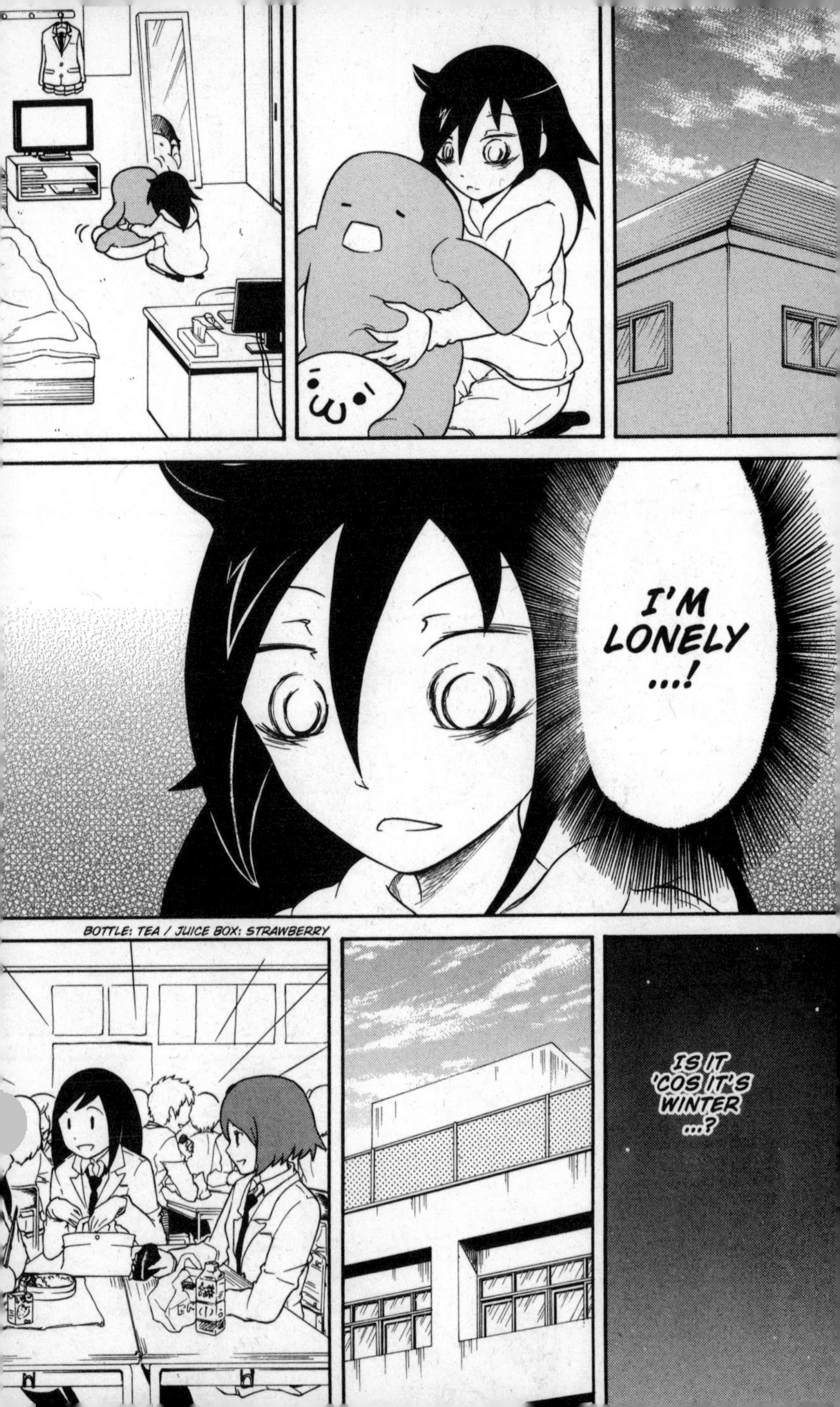
I'M LONELY ...!
IS IT 'COS IT'S WINTER ...?
BOTTLE: TEA / JUICE BOX: STRAWBERRY

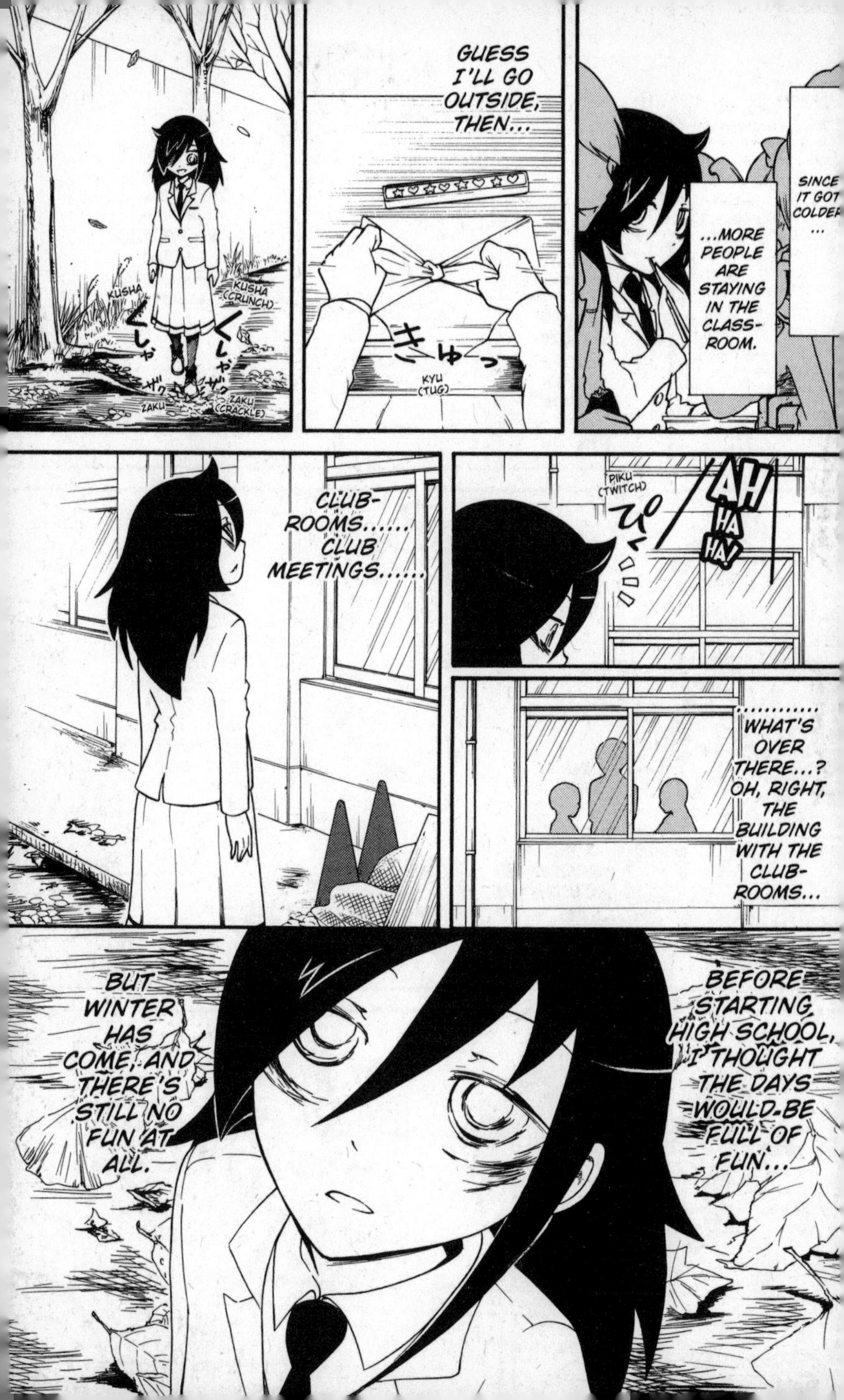
SINCE IT GOT COLDER...
...MORE PEOPLE ARE STAYING IN THE CLASS-ROOM.
GUESS I'LL GO OUTSIDE, THEN...
きゅっ
KYU (TUG)
くしゃ
KUSHA (CRUNCH)
くしゃ
KUSHA
ザク
ZAKU (CRACKLE)
ザク
ZAKU
PIKU (TWITCH)
ぴく
AH HA HA!
.... WHAT'S OVER THERE...? OH, RIGHT, THE BUILDING WITH THE CLUB-ROOMS...
CLUB-ROOMS...... CLUB MEETINGS......
BEFORE STARTING HIGH SCHOOL, I THOUGHT THE DAYS WOULD BE FULL OF FUN...
BUT WINTER HAS COME, AND THERE'S STILL NO FUN AT ALL.

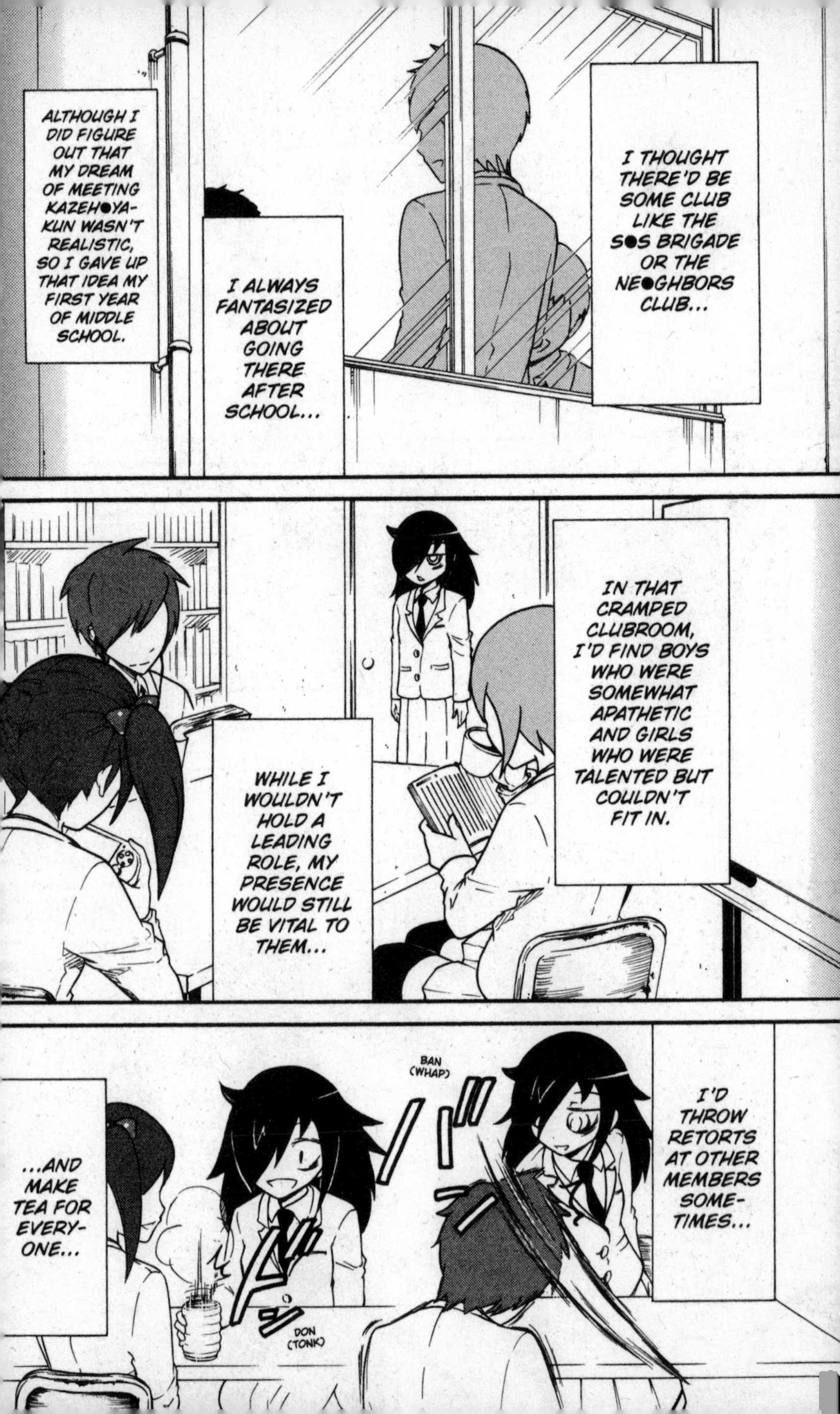
I THOUGHT THERE'D BE SOME CLUB LIKE THE S●S BRIGADE OR THE NE●GHBORS CLUB...
I ALWAYS FANTASIZED ABOUT GOING THERE AFTER SCHOOL...
ALTHOUGH I DID FIGURE OUT THAT MY DREAM OF MEETING KAZEH●YA-KUN WASN'T REALISTIC, SO I GAVE UP THAT IDEA MY FIRST YEAR OF MIDDLE SCHOOL.
IN THAT CRAMPED CLUBROOM, I'D FIND BOYS WHO WERE SOMEWHAT APATHETIC AND GIRLS WHO WERE TALENTED BUT COULDN'T FIT IN.
WHILE I WOULDN'T HOLD A LEADING ROLE, MY PRESENCE WOULD STILL BE VITAL TO THEM...
I'D THROW RETORTS AT OTHER MEMBERS SOME-TIMES...
BAN (WHAP)
DON (TONK)
...AND MAKE TEA FOR EVERY-ONE...

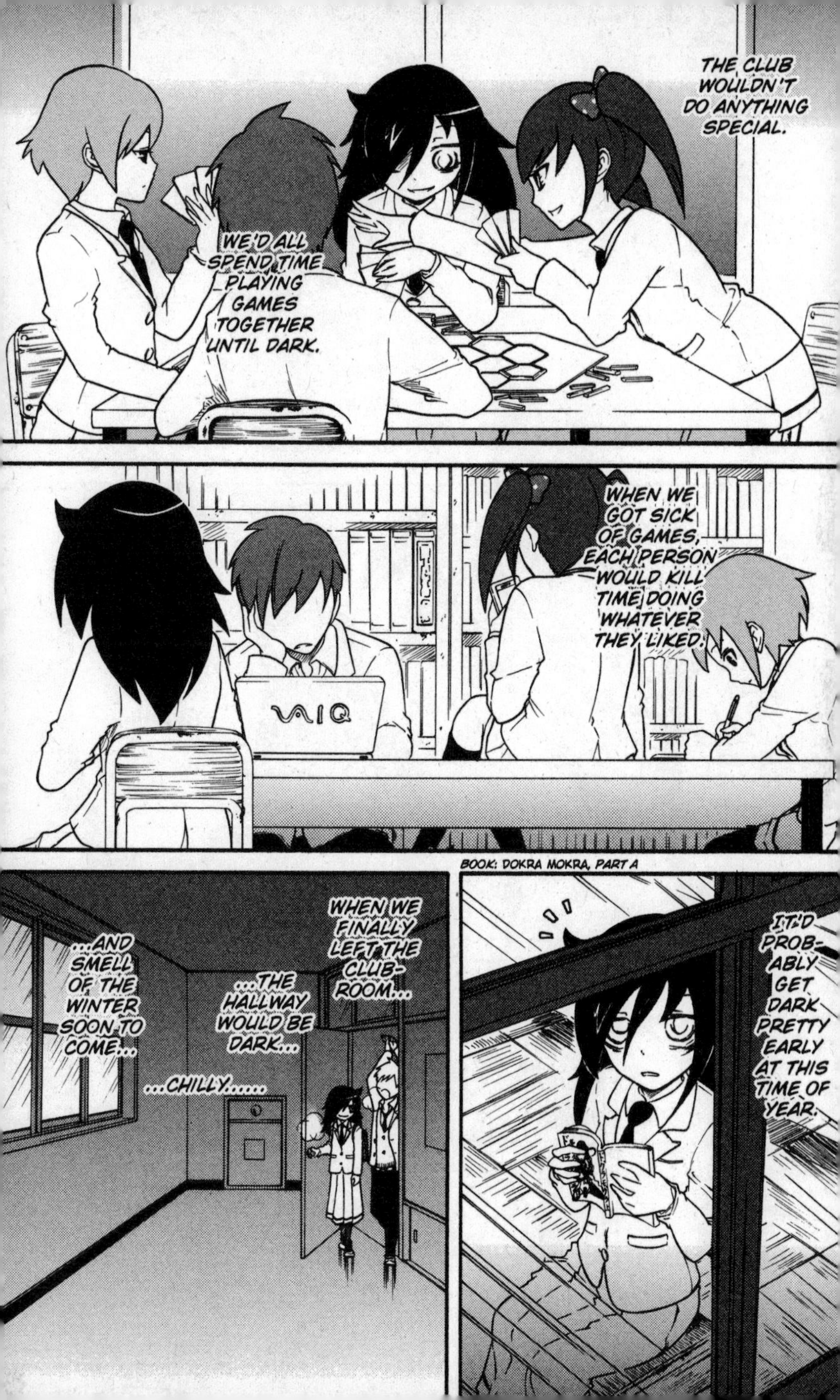

THE CLUB WOULDN'T DO ANYTHING SPECIAL.
WE'D ALL SPEND TIME PLAYING GAMES TOGETHER UNTIL DARK.
WHEN WE GOT SICK OF GAMES, EACH PERSON WOULD KILL TIME DOING WHATEVER THEY LIKED.
VAIO
BOOK: DOKRA MOKRA, PART A
IT'D PROBABLY GET DARK PRETTY EARLY AT THIS TIME OF YEAR.
WHEN WE FINALLY LEFT THE CLUB-ROOM...
...THE HALLWAY WOULD BE DARK...
...CHILLY......
...AND SMELL OF THE WINTER SOON TO COME...

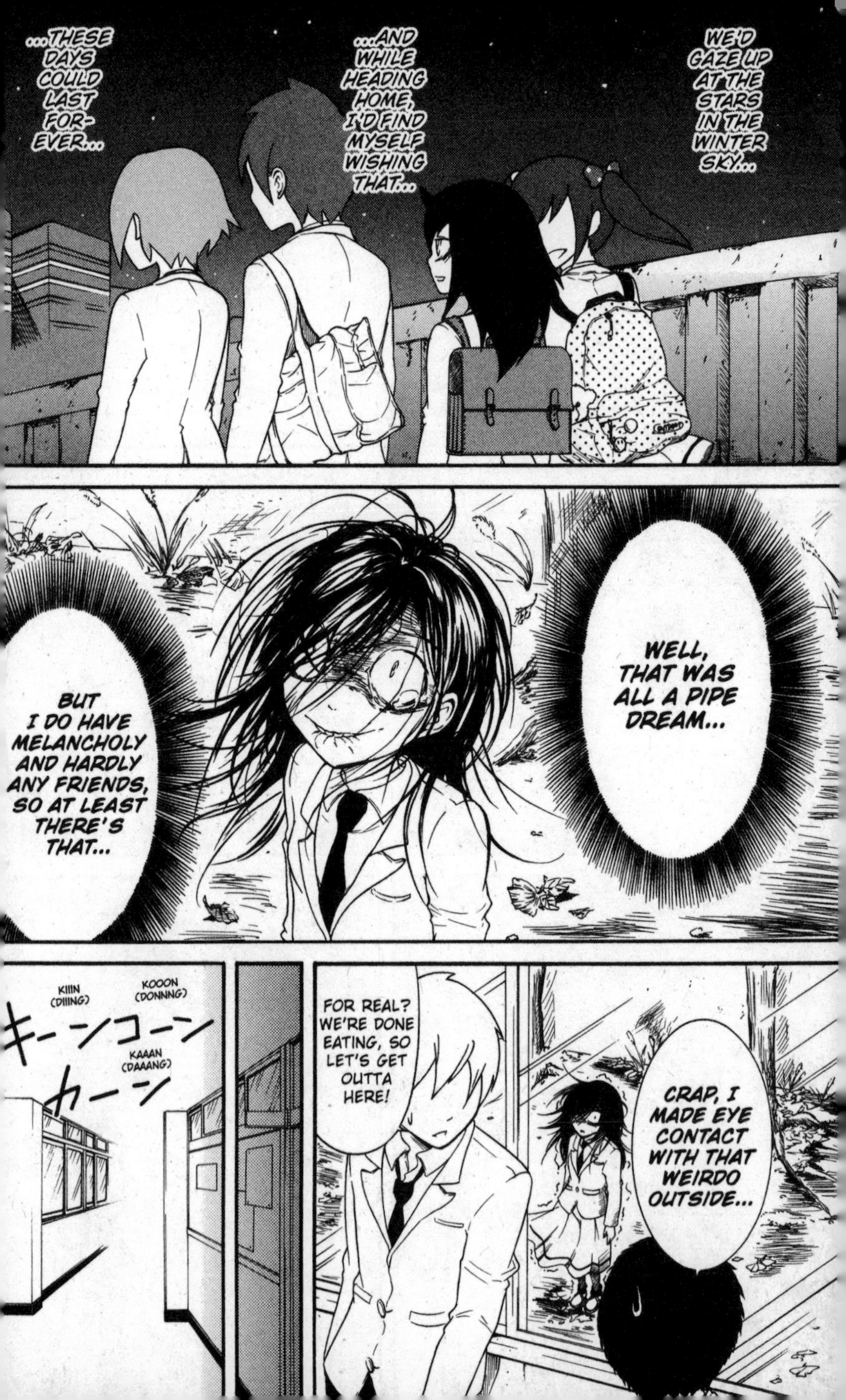
WE'D GAZE UP AT THE STARS IN THE WINTER SKY...
...AND WHILE HEADING HOME, I'D FIND MYSELF WISHING THAT...
...THESE DAYS COULD LAST FOR-EVER...
WELL, THAT WAS ALL A PIPE DREAM...
BUT I DO HAVE MELANCHOLY AND HARDLY ANY FRIENDS, SO AT LEAST THERE'S THAT...
CRAP, I MADE EYE CONTACT WITH THAT WEIRDO OUTSIDE...
FOR REAL? WE'RE DONE EATING, SO LET'S GET OUTTA HERE!
キーンコーン
KIIIN (DIIING)
KOOON (DONNNG)
カーン
KAAAN (DAAANG)

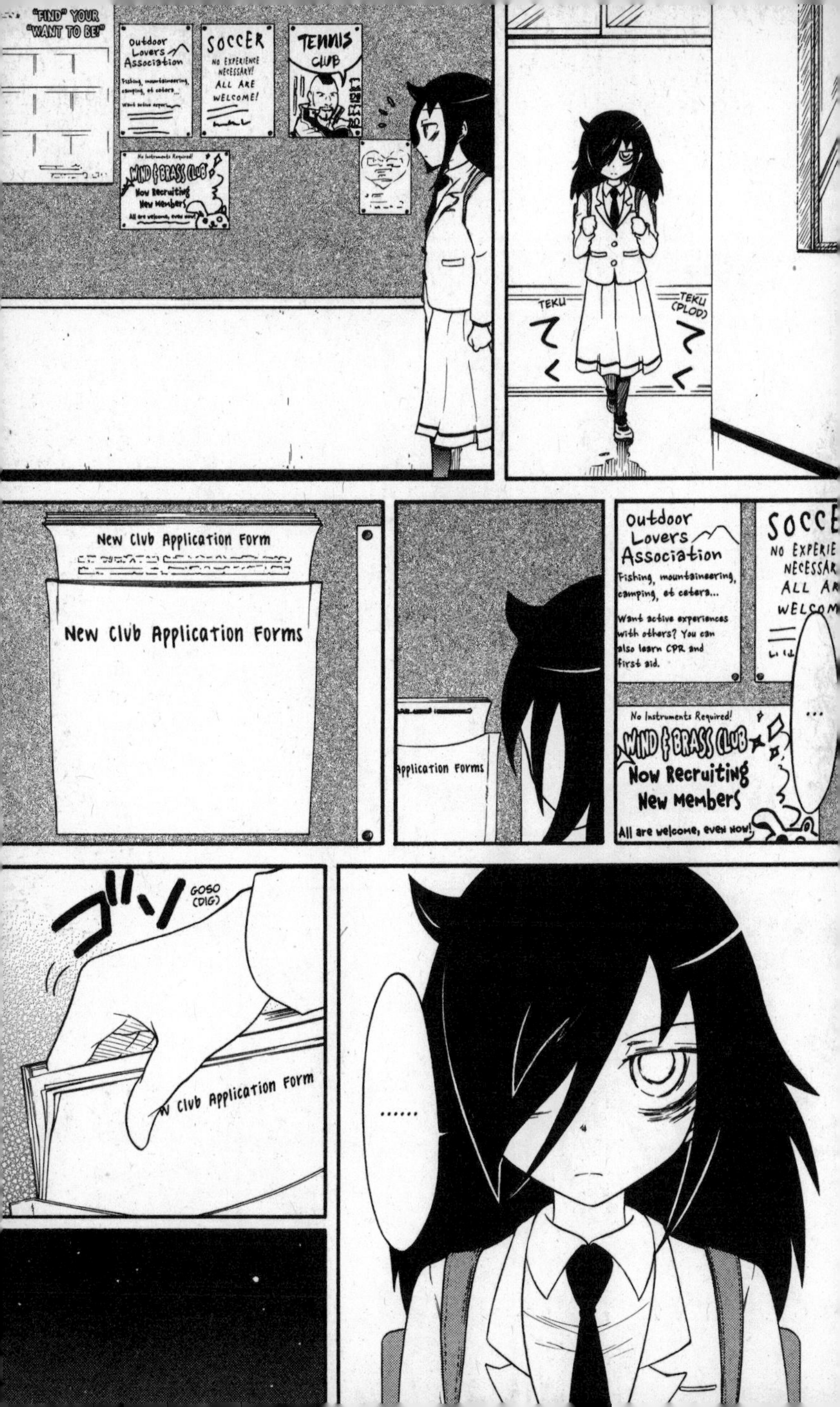

TEKU
TEKU (PLOD)
"FIND" YOUR "WANT TO BE!"
Outdoor Lovers Association
Fishing, mountaineering, camping, et cetera...
SOCCER
NO EXPERIENCE NECESSARY!
ALL ARE WELCOME!
TENNIS CLUB
No Instruments Required!
WIND & BRASS CLUB
Now Recruiting New Members
All are welcome, even now!
Outdoor Lovers Association
Fishing, mountaineering, camping, et cetera...
Want active experiences with others? You can also learn CPR and first aid.
No Instruments Required!
WIND & BRASS CLUB
Now Recruiting New Members
All are welcome, even now!
...
Application Forms
New Club Application Form
New Club Application Forms
......
ゴソ
GOSO (DIG)
Club Application Form

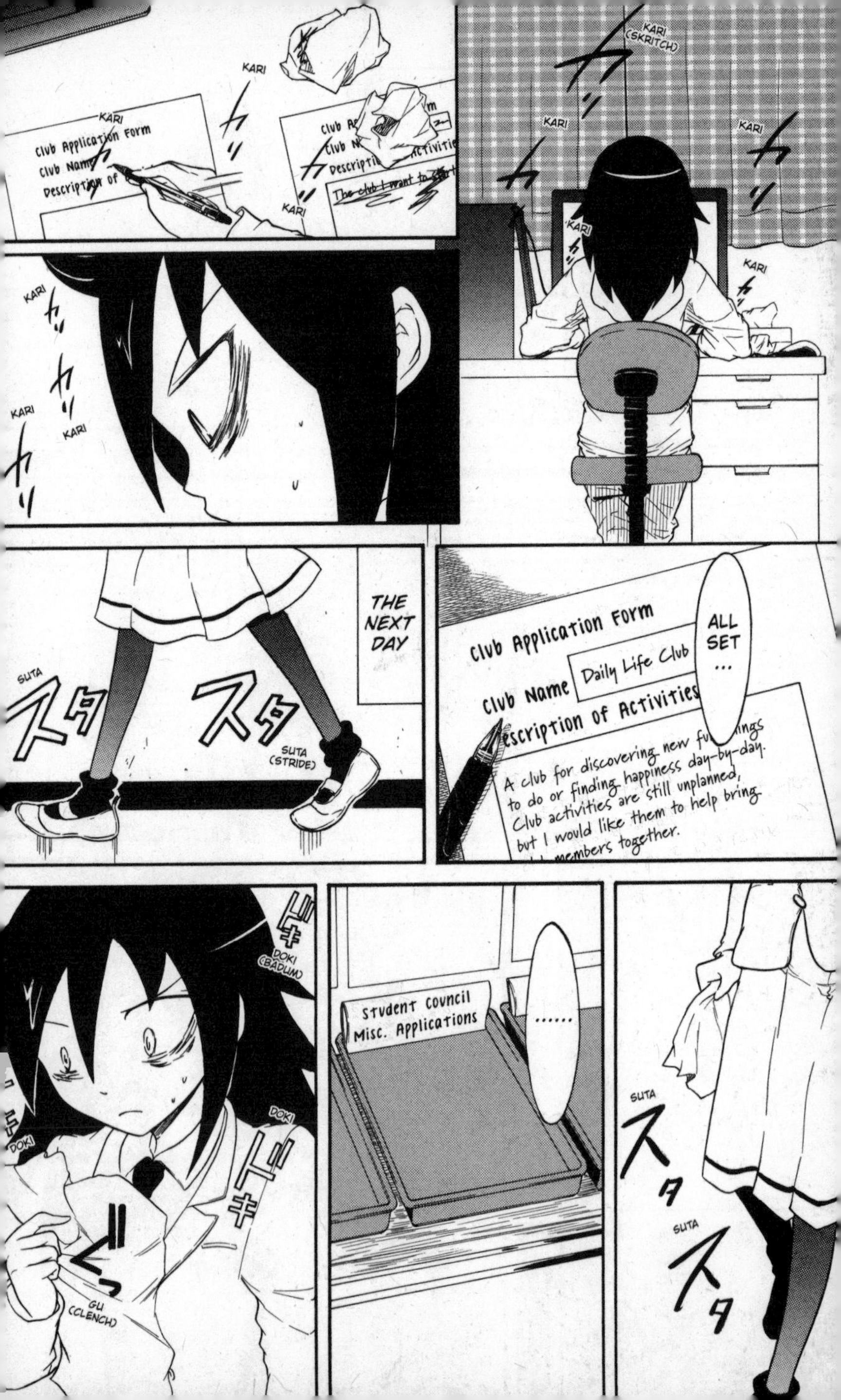
KARI (SKRITCH)
KARI
KARI
KARI
KARI
KARI
Club Application Form
Club Name
Description of
KARI
KARI
The club I want to start
KARI
KARI
KARI
KARI
Club Application Form
Club Name
Daily Life Club
Description of Activities
A club for discovering new fun things to do or finding happiness day-by-day. Club activities are still unplanned, but I would like them to help bring members together.
ALL SET ...
THE NEXT DAY
SUTA (STRIDE)
SUTA
SUTA
SUTA
Student Council Misc. Applications
......
DOKI (BADUM)
DOKI
DOKI
GU (CLENCH)

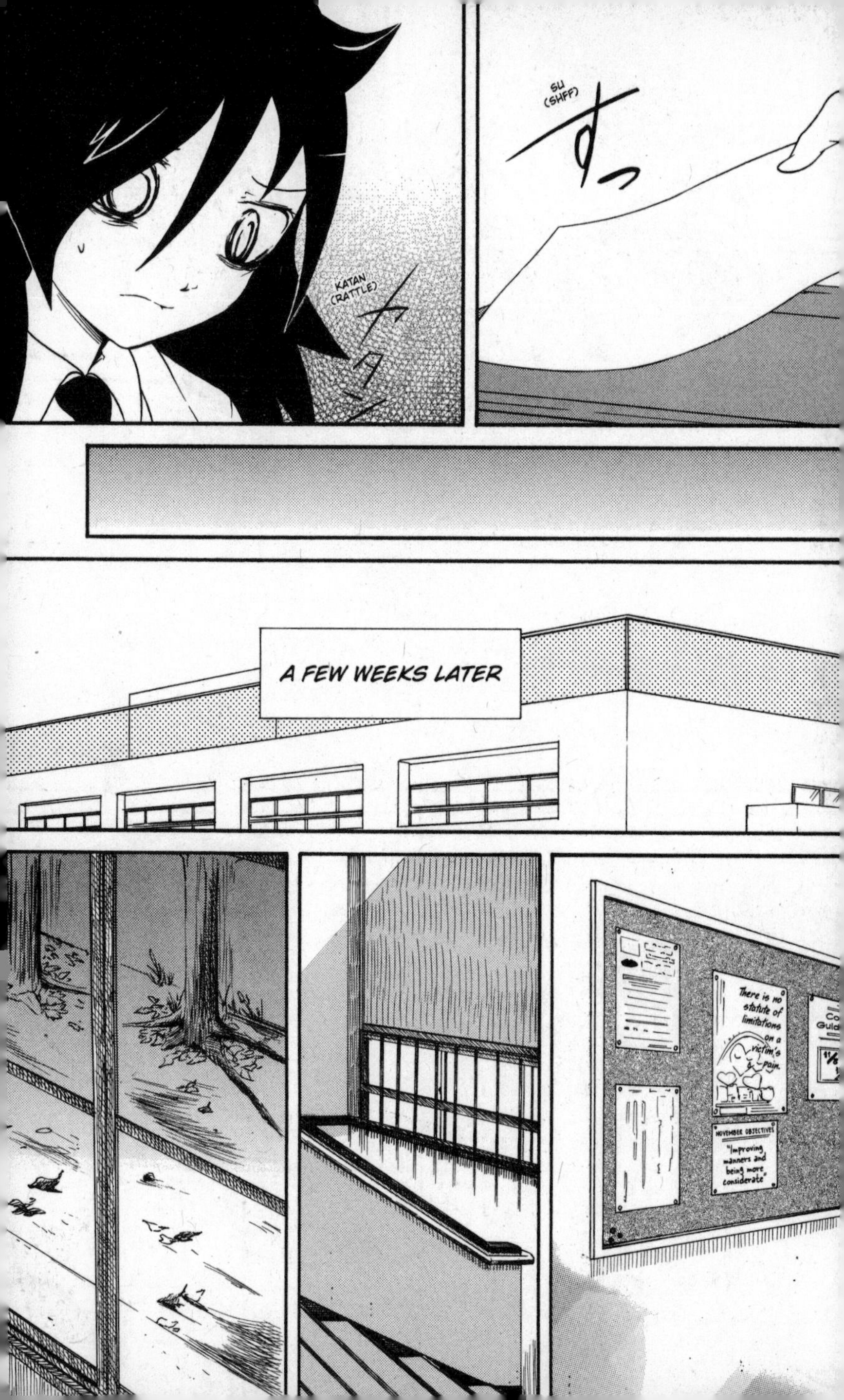
SU (SHFF)
すっ
KATAN (RATTLE)
カタン
A FEW WEEKS LATER
There is no statute of limitations on a victim's pain.
NOVEMBER OBJECTIVES
"Improving manners and being more considerate"

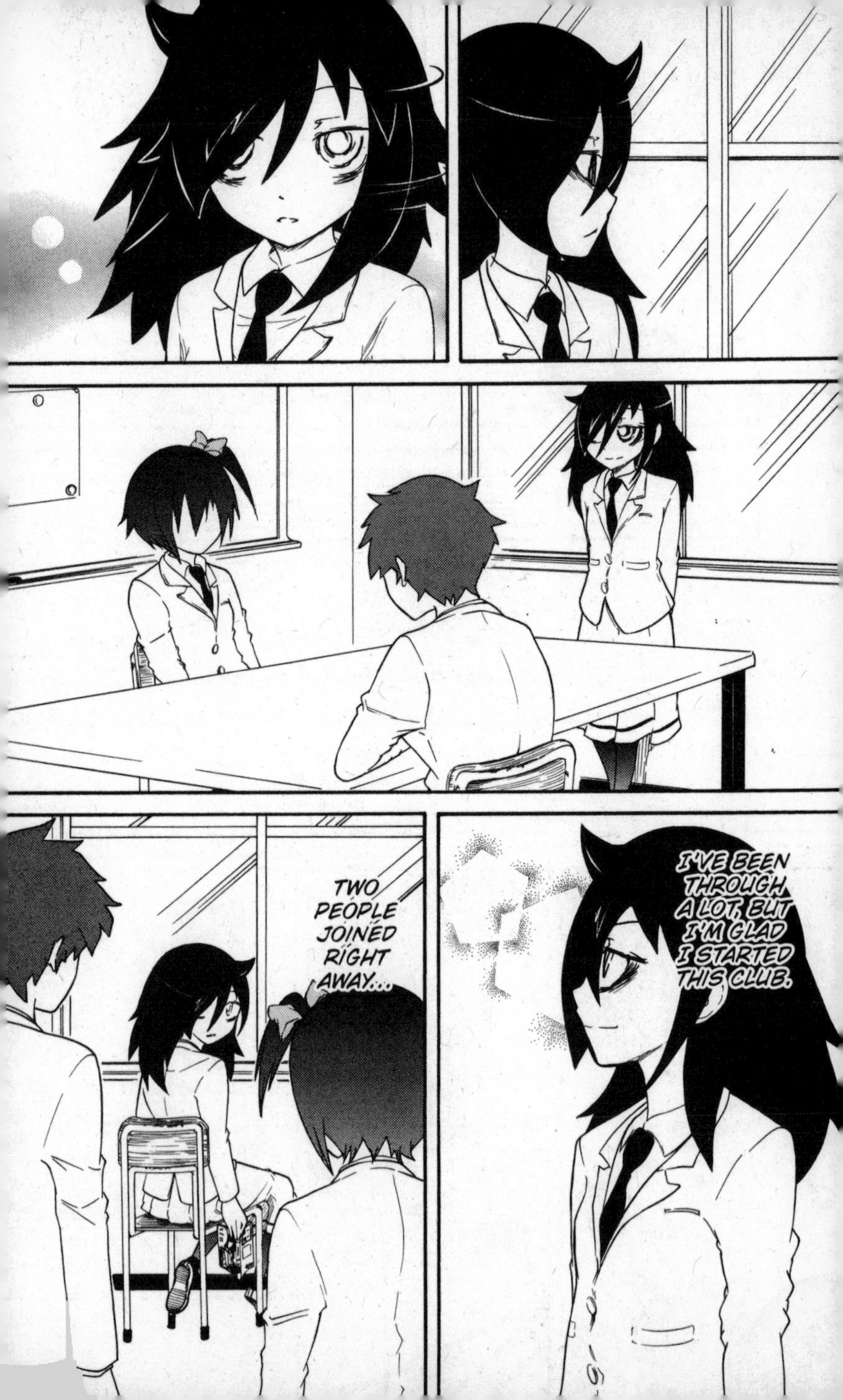
I'VE BEEN THROUGH A LOT, BUT I'M GLAD I STARTED THIS CLUB.
TWO PEOPLE JOINED RIGHT AWAY...

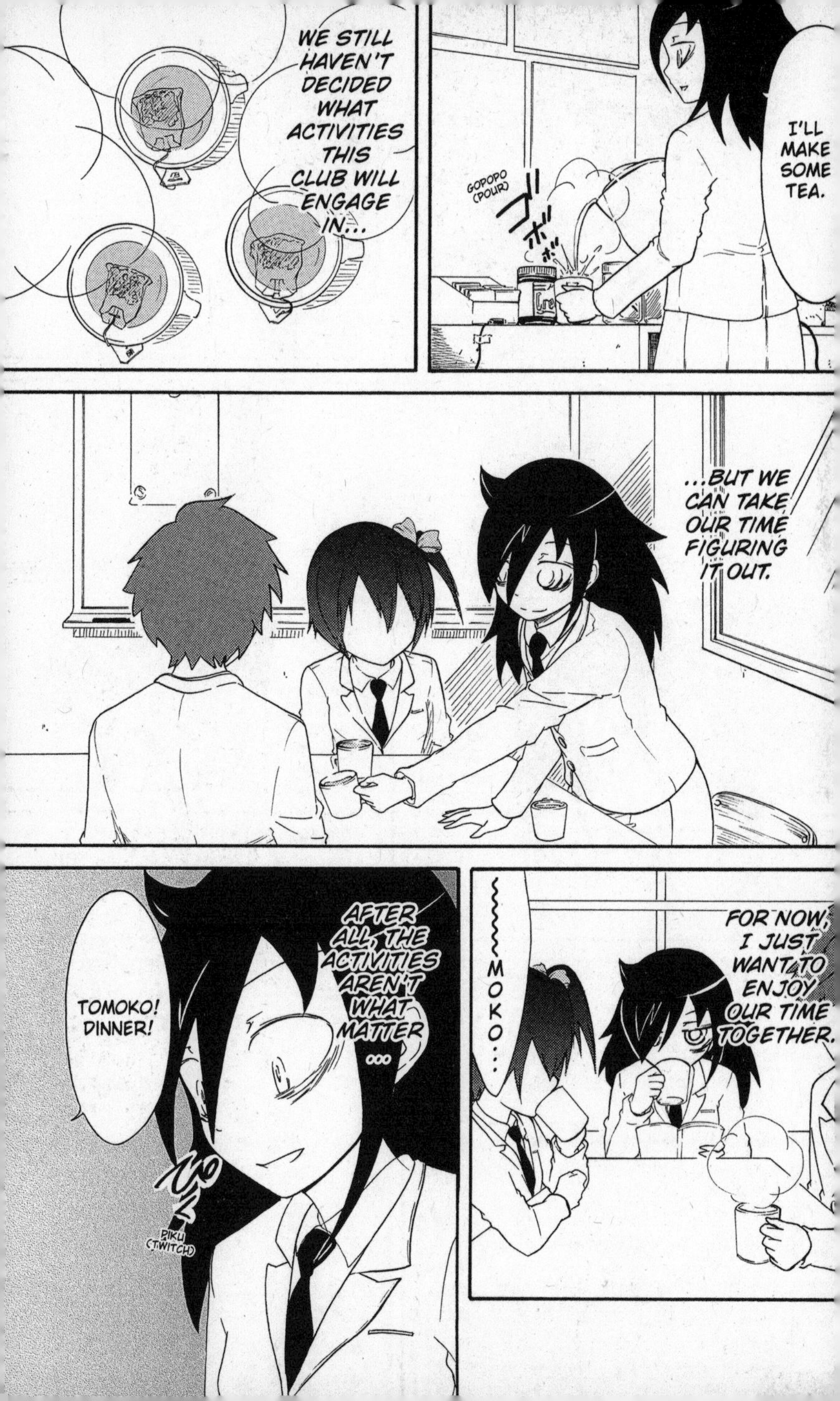
I'LL MAKE SOME TEA.
GOPOPO (POUR)
WE STILL HAVEN'T DECIDED WHAT ACTIVITIES THIS CLUB WILL ENGAGE IN...
...BUT WE CAN TAKE OUR TIME FIGURING IT OUT.
FOR NOW, I JUST WANT TO ENJOY OUR TIME TOGETHER.
~~~MOKO...
AFTER ALL, THE ACTIVITIES AREN'T WHAT MATTER...
TOMOKO! DINNER!
PIKU (TWITCH)
~~~

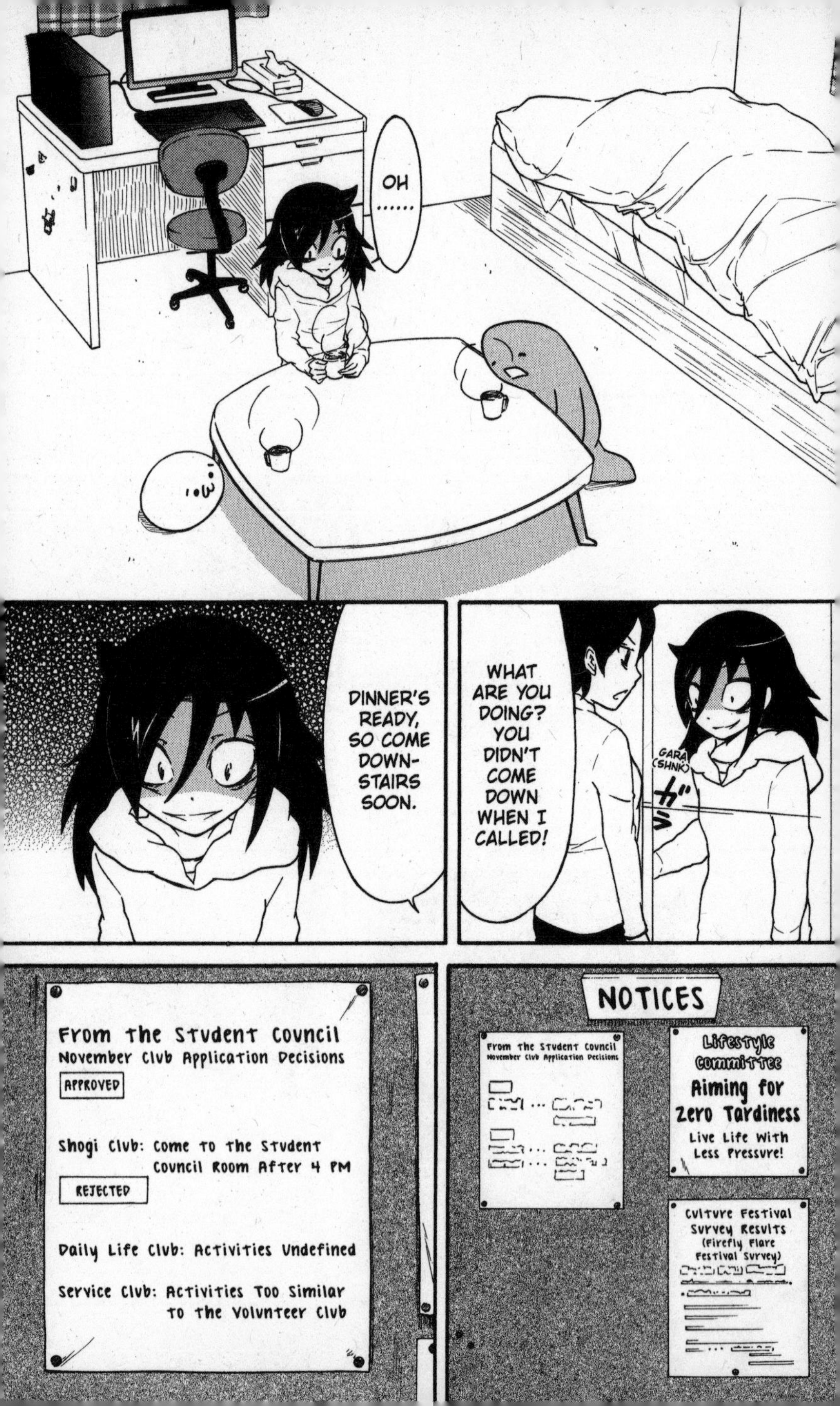
OH ......
GARA (SHNK)
WHAT ARE YOU DOING? YOU DIDN'T COME DOWN WHEN I CALLED!
DINNER'S READY, SO COME DOWN-STAIRS SOON.
NOTICES
Lifestyle Committee
Aiming for Zero Tardiness
Live Life with Less Pressure!
Culture Festival Survey Results (Firefly Flare Festival Survey)
From the Student Council
November Club Application Decisions
From the Student Council
November Club Application Decisions
APPROVED
Shogi Club: Come to the Student Council Room After 4 PM
REJECTED
Daily Life Club: Activities Undefined
Service Club: Activities Too Similar to the Volunteer Club

No Matter How I Look at It, It's You Guys' Fault I'm Not Popular!

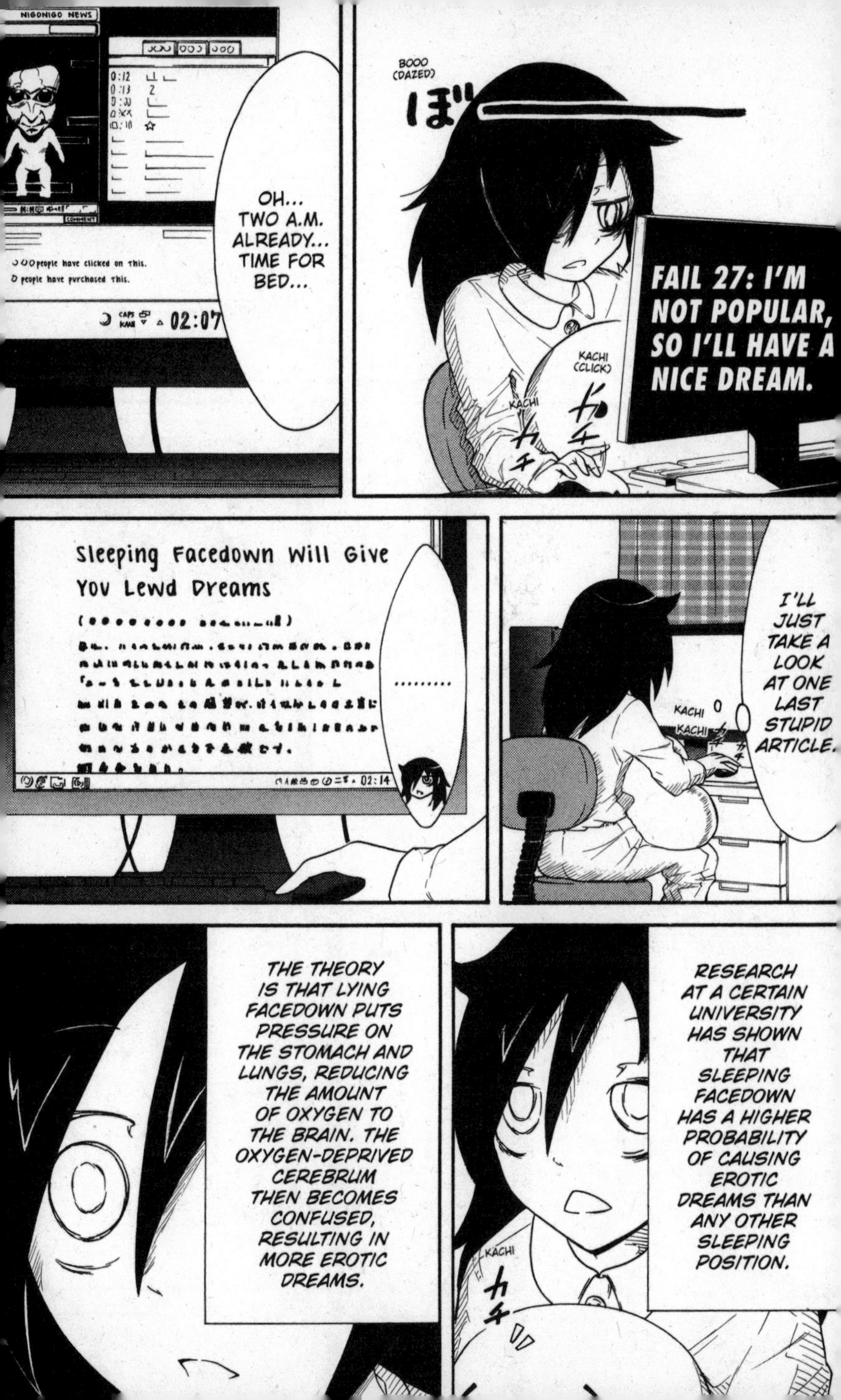
BOOO (DAZED)
ぼ
FAIL 27: I'M NOT POPULAR, SO I'LL HAVE A NICE DREAM.
KACHI (CLICK)
KACHI
NIGONIGO NEWS
COMMENT
people have clicked on this.
people have purchased this.
02:07
OH... TWO A.M. ALREADY... TIME FOR BED...
I'LL JUST TAKE A LOOK AT ONE LAST STUPID ARTICLE.
KACHI
KACHI
Sleeping Facedown Will Give You Lewd Dreams
02:14
....
RESEARCH AT A CERTAIN UNIVERSITY HAS SHOWN THAT SLEEPING FACEDOWN HAS A HIGHER PROBABILITY OF CAUSING EROTIC DREAMS THAN ANY OTHER SLEEPING POSITION.
KACHI
THE THEORY IS THAT LYING FACEDOWN PUTS PRESSURE ON THE STOMACH AND LUNGS, REDUCING THE AMOUNT OF OXYGEN TO THE BRAIN. THE OXYGEN-DEPRIVED CEREBRUM THEN BECOMES CONFUSED, RESULTING IN MORE EROTIC DREAMS.

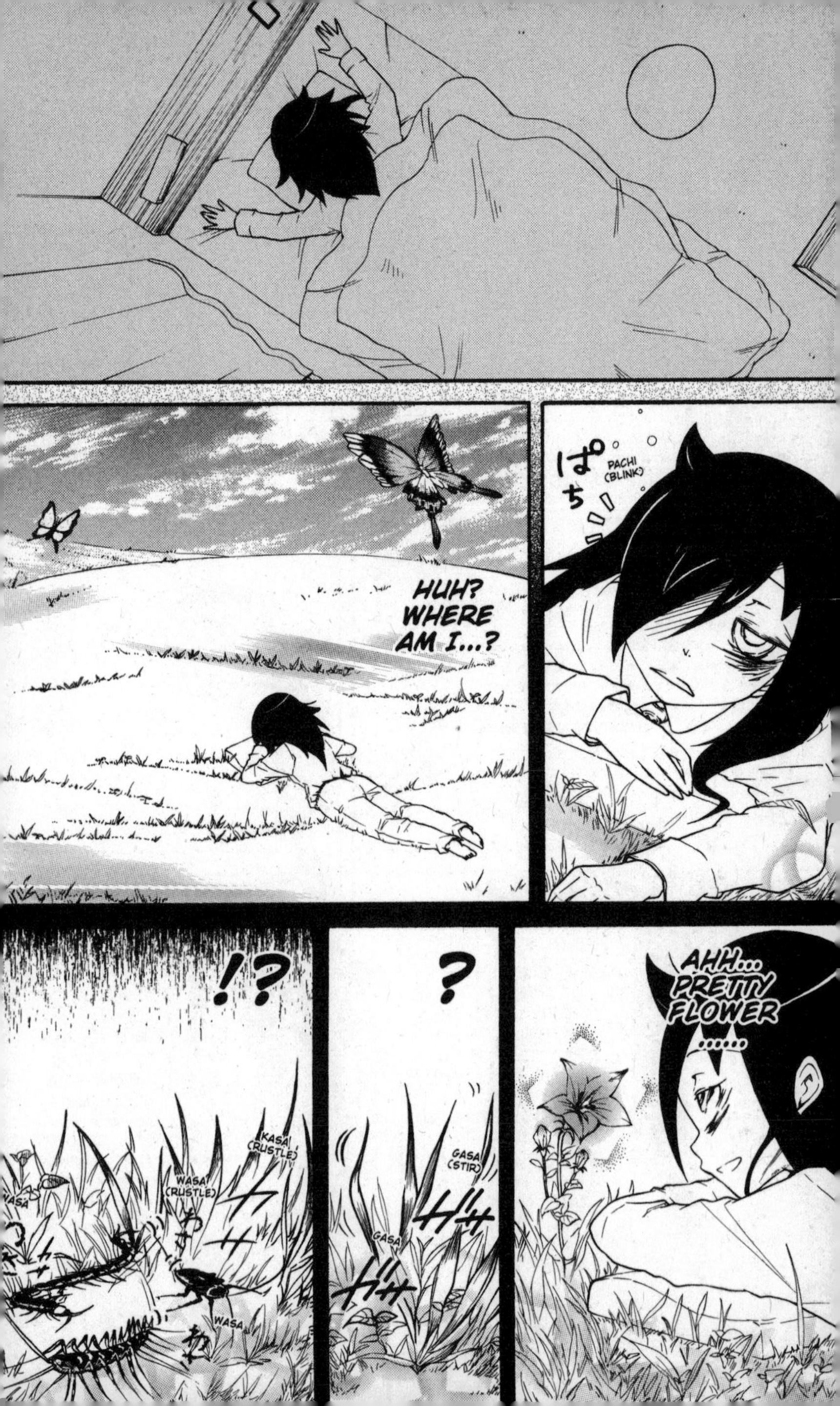

ぱち
PACHI (BLINK)
HUH? WHERE AM I...?
AHH... PRETTY FLOWER ......
?
GASA (STIR)
GASA
!?
KASA (RUSTLE)
WASA (RUSTLE)
WASA
WASA

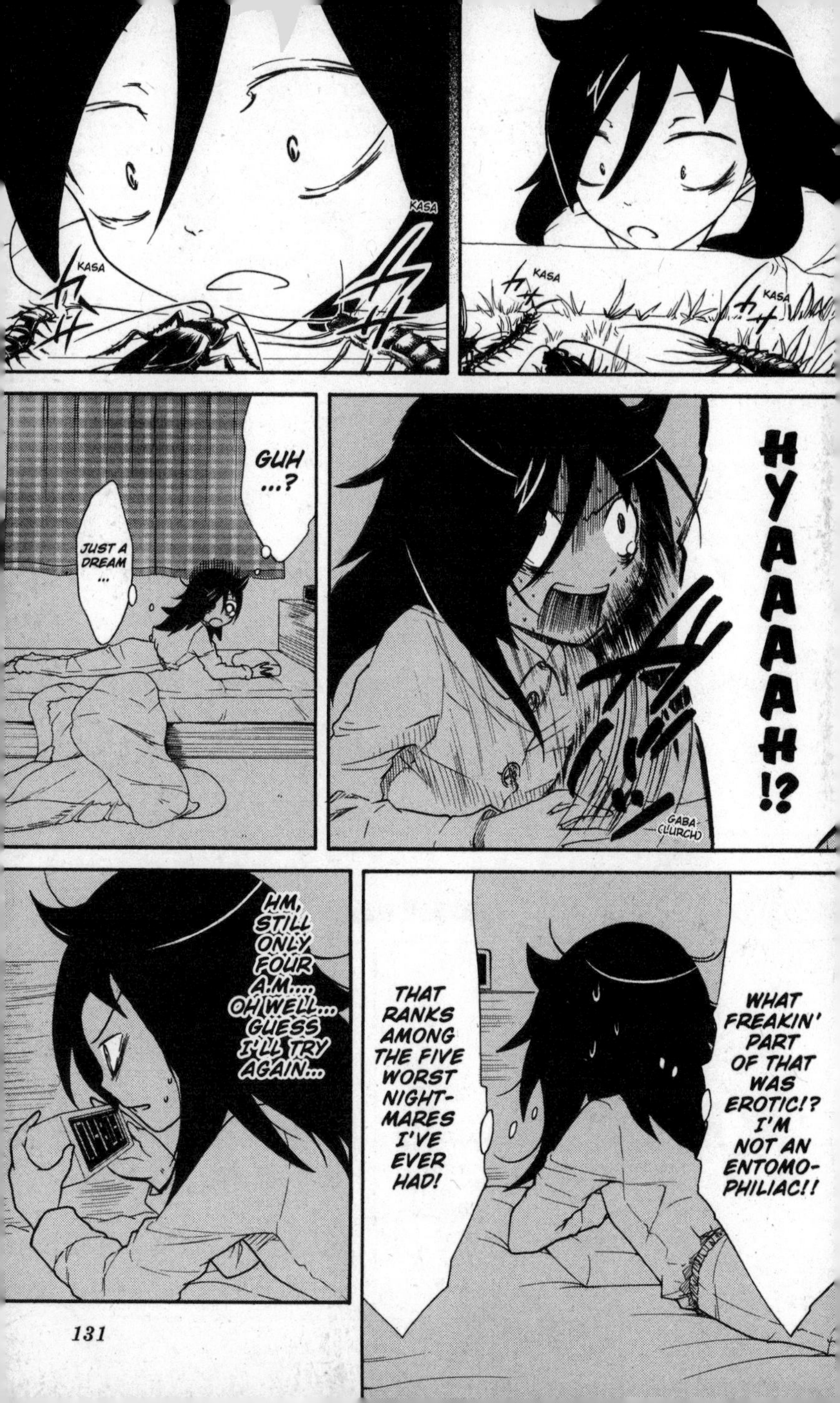
KASA
KASA
KASA
KASA
HYAAAAH!?
GABA (LURCH)
GUH ...?
JUST A DREAM ...
WHAT FREAKIN' PART OF THAT WAS EROTIC!? I'M NOT AN ENTOMOPHILIAC!!
THAT RANKS AMONG THE FIVE WORST NIGHTMARES I'VE EVER HAD!
HM, STILL ONLY FOUR A.M.... OH WELL... GUESS I'LL TRY AGAIN...

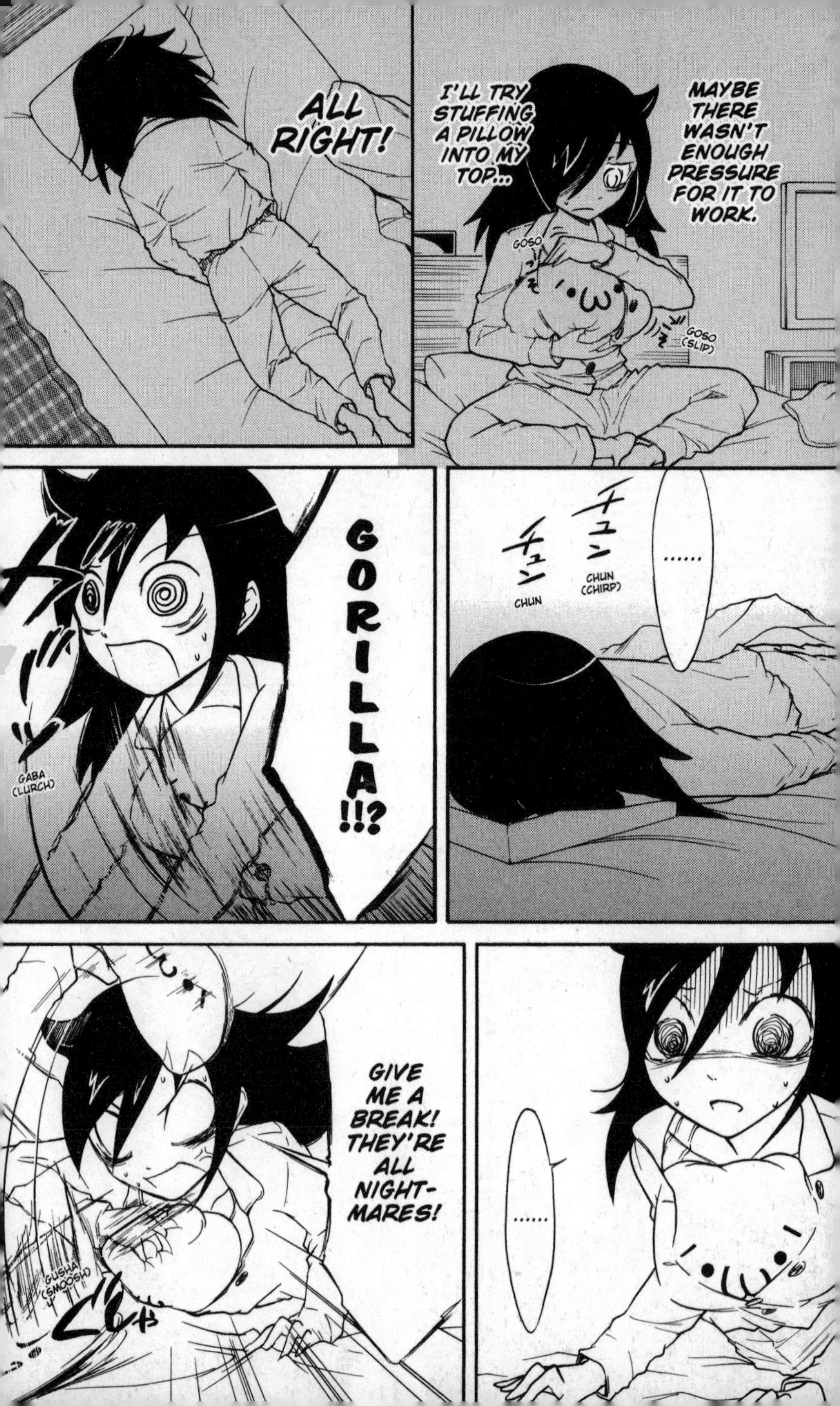
MAYBE THERE WASN'T ENOUGH PRESSURE FOR IT TO WORK.
I'LL TRY STUFFING A PILLOW INTO MY TOP...
GOSO
GOSO (SLIP)
ALL RIGHT!
チュン
CHUN (CHIRP)
チュン
CHUN
......
GORILLA!!?
GABA (LURCH)
......
GIVE ME A BREAK! THEY'RE ALL NIGHT-MARES!
GUSHA (SMOOSH)

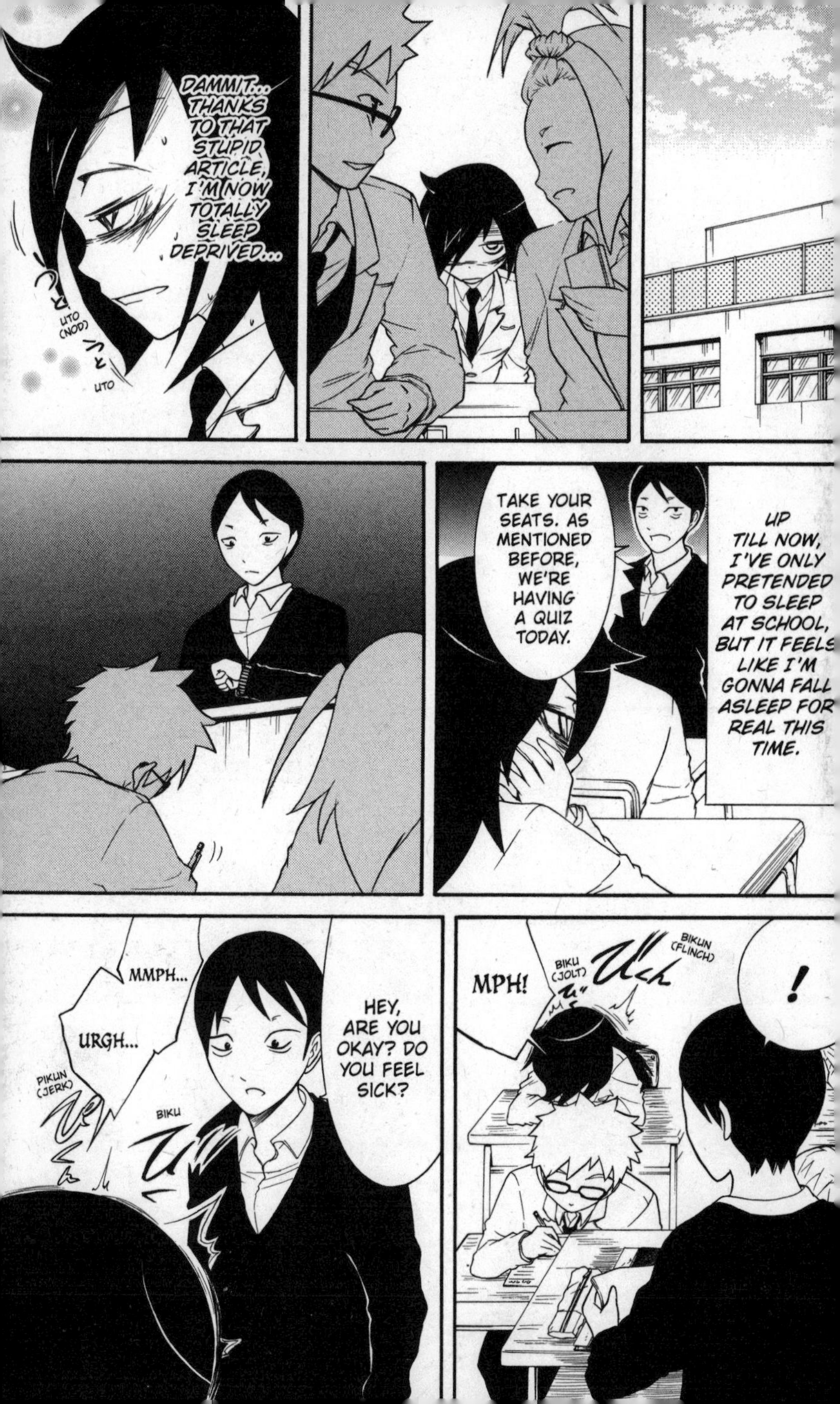
DAMMIT... THANKS TO THAT STUPID ARTICLE, I'M NOW TOTALLY SLEEP DEPRIVED...
UTO (NOD)
UTO
UP TILL NOW, I'VE ONLY PRETENDED TO SLEEP AT SCHOOL, BUT IT FEELS LIKE I'M GONNA FALL ASLEEP FOR REAL THIS TIME.
TAKE YOUR SEATS. AS MENTIONED BEFORE, WE'RE HAVING A QUIZ TODAY.
!
BIKUN (FLINCH)
BIKU (JOLT)
MPH!
HEY, ARE YOU OKAY? DO YOU FEEL SICK?
MMPH...
URGH...
PIKUN (JERK)
BIKU

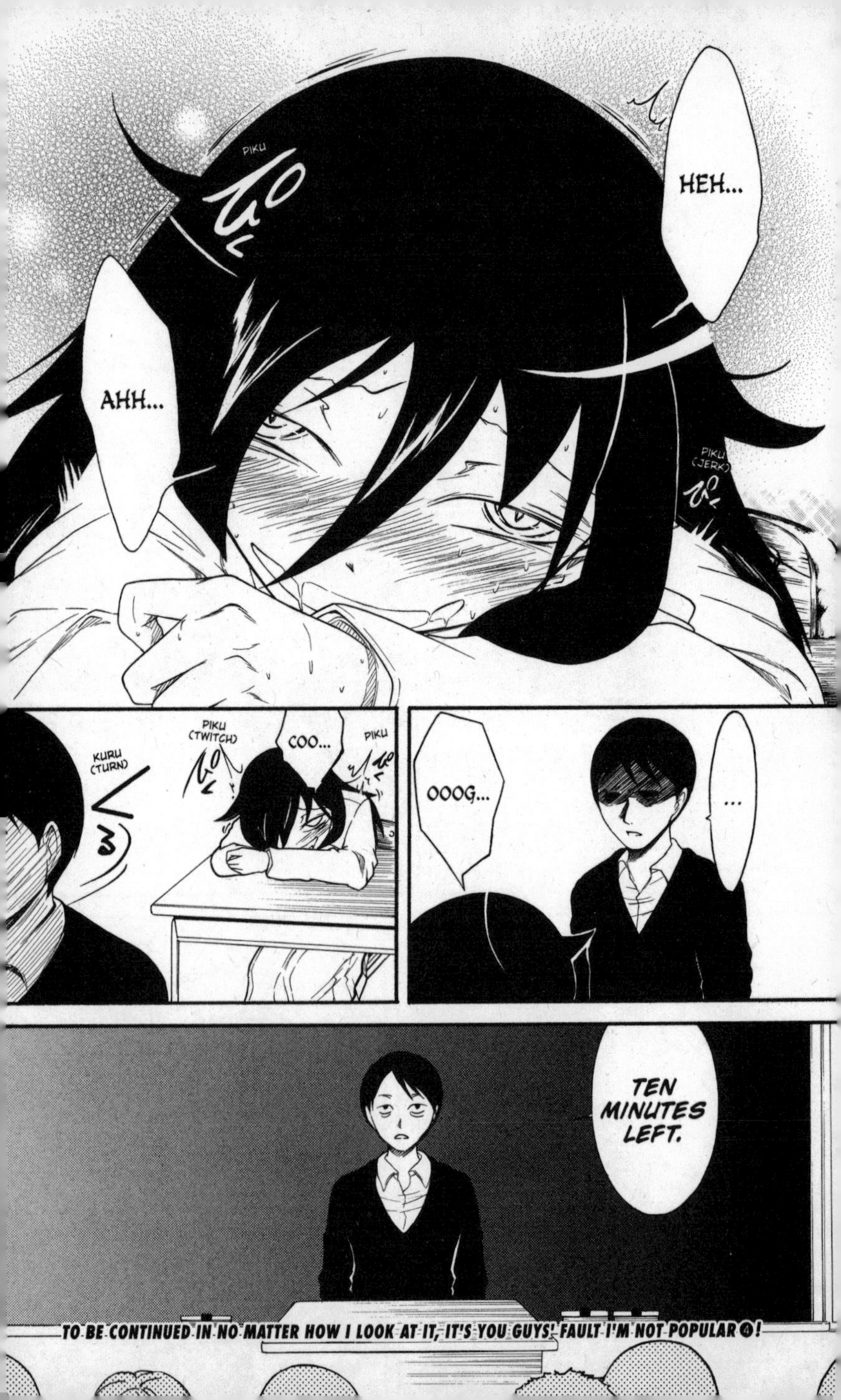
HEH...
PIKU
AHH...
PIKU (JERK)
...
OOOG...
PIKU
COO...
PIKU (TWITCH)
KURU (TURN)
TEN MINUTES LEFT.

TO BE CONTINUED IN NO MATTER HOW I LOOK AT IT, IT'S YOU GUYS' FAULT I'M NOT POPULAR 4!

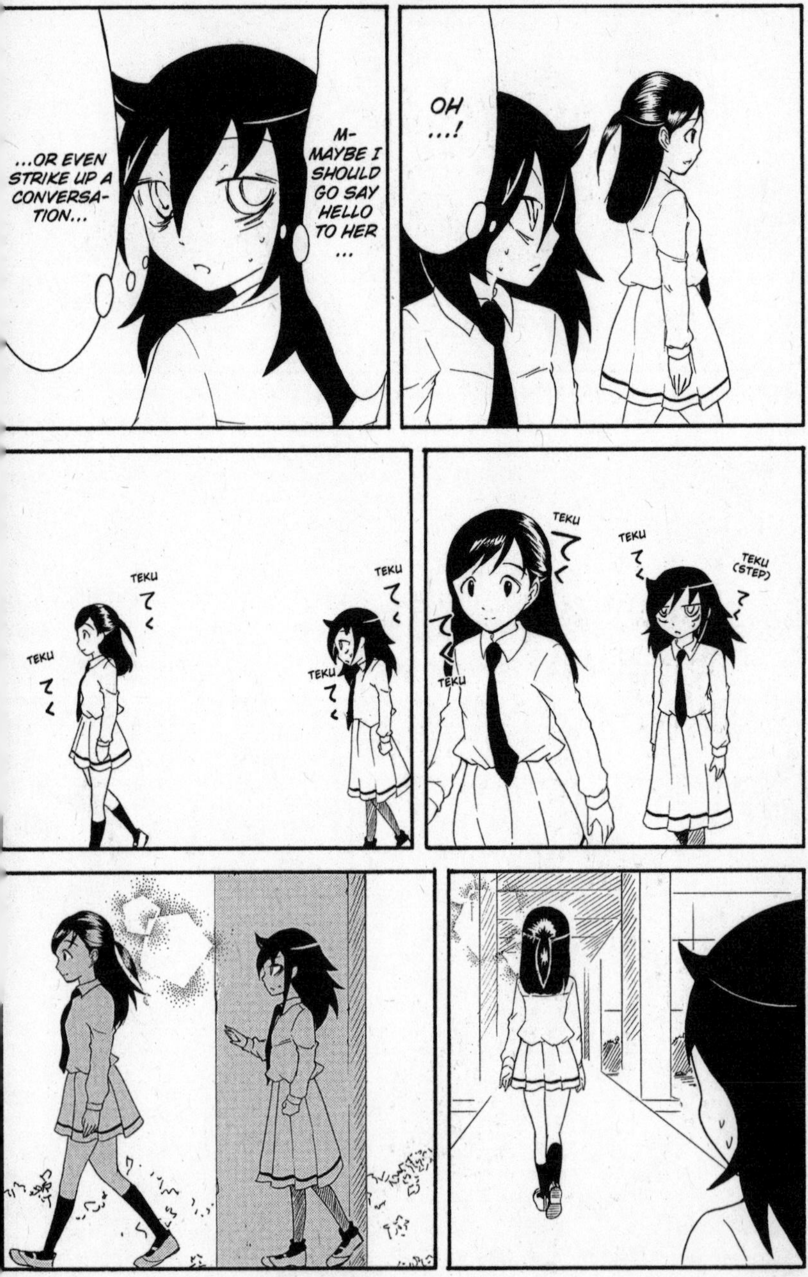
OH ...!
M- MAYBE I SHOULD GO SAY HELLO TO HER ...
...OR EVEN STRIKE UP A CONVERSATION...
TEKU (STEP)
TEKU
TEKU
TEKU
TEKU
TEKU
TEKU
TEKU

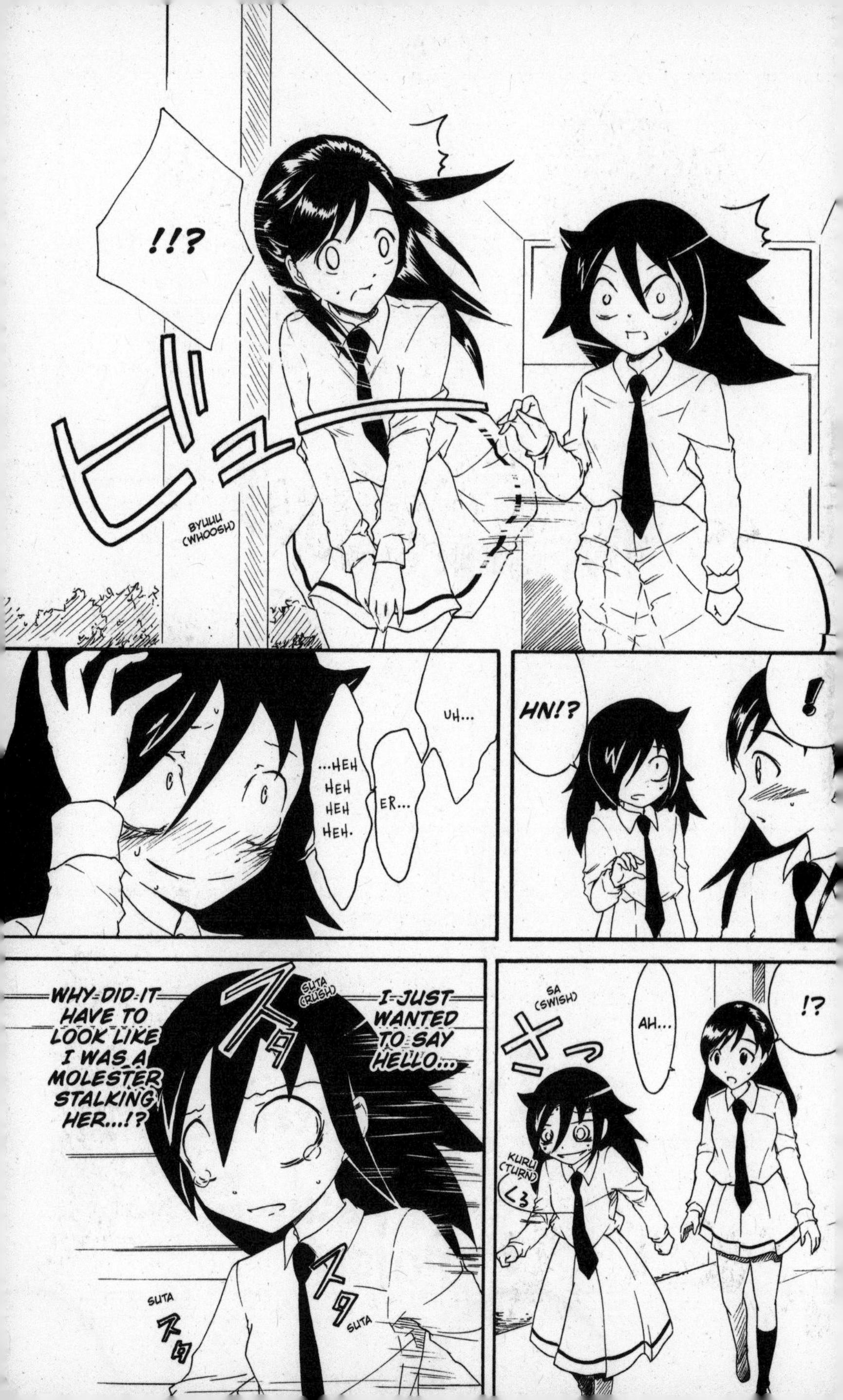
!!?
BYUUU (WHOOSH)
!
HN!?
UH...
ER...
...HEH HEH HEH HEH.
!?
AH...
SA (SWISH)
KURU (TURN)
I JUST WANTED TO SAY HELLO...
SUTA (RUSH)
WHY DID IT HAVE TO LOOK LIKE I WAS A MOLESTER STALKING HER...!?
SUTA
SUTA

No Matter How I Look at It, It's You Guys' Fault I'm Not Popular!

STATUS UPDATE

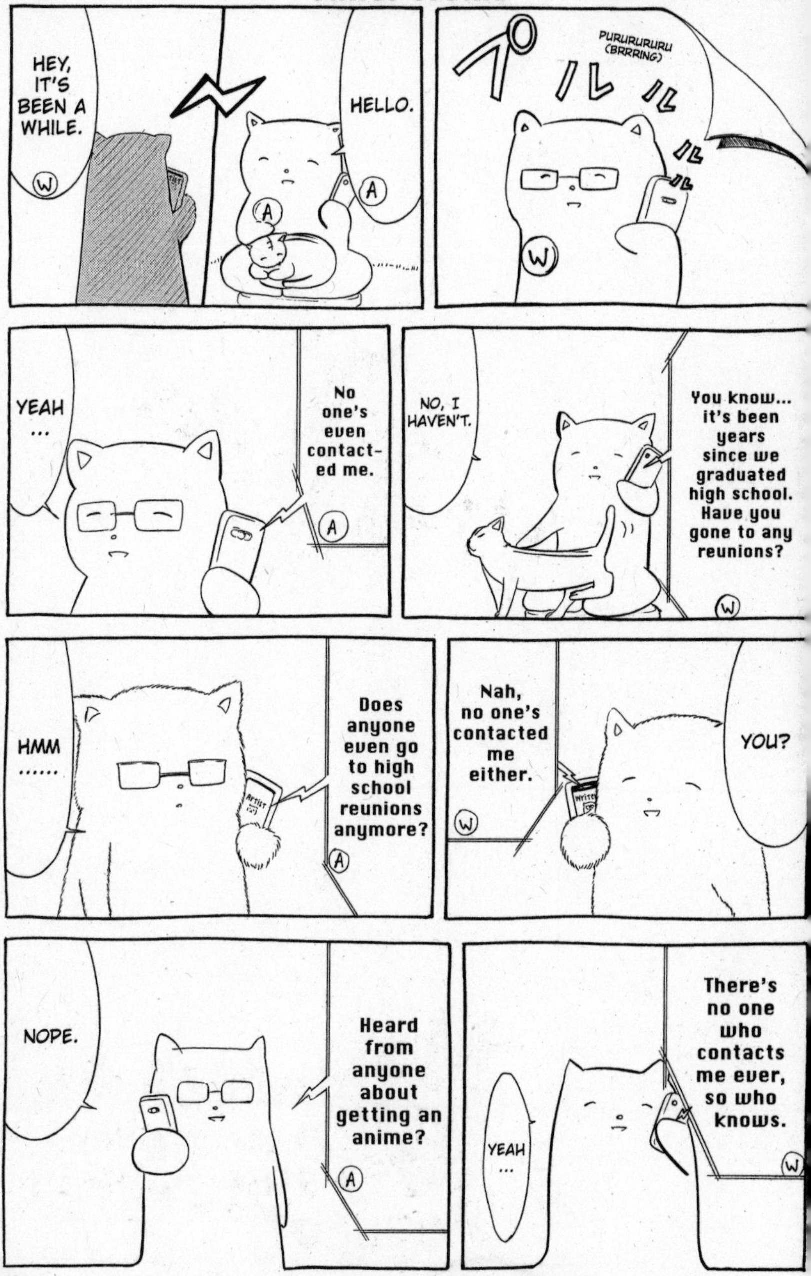
PURURURURU (BRRRING)
HELLO.
HEY, IT'S BEEN A WHILE.
You know... it's been years since we graduated high school. Have you gone to any reunions?
NO, I HAVEN'T.
No one's even contacted me.
YEAH ...
YOU?
Nah, no one's contacted me either.
Does anyone even go to high school reunions anymore?
HMM ......
There's no one who contacts me ever, so who knows.
YEAH ...
Heard from anyone about getting an anime?
NOPE.

☆☆ SPECIAL THANKS! ☆☆ YUUJI ASAKURA-SAN

PAGE 5

Battle R●yale is a famous 1999 novel by Koushun Takami, in which an entire middle school class is kidnapped and forced to kill each other until only one student remains in a government-sanctioned death match. Tomoko's planned strategy and choice of weapon is the same as that of the main female antagonist in the novel, the manipulative and ruthless killer Mitsuko Souma.

PAGE 9

Nigonigo Douga is a play on Niconico Douga, a Japanese site primarily known for free hosting of streaming videos, similar to YouTube.

PAGE 10

Culture festivals are held at Japanese schools, usually on a weekend close to the national holiday, Culture Day (November 3), as a way for students to show off their school and what they've learned to other students, parents, and the general public. Another purpose of these festivals is fostering teamwork and responsibility, especially in high school, as the students are expected to manage most aspects of preparing for and running the festivals themselves.

PAGE 11

Don Quin is a reference to the Japanese discount store chain Don Quijote, which is often referred to as Donki.

PAGE 11

Ochonan-san is a character from the ongoing anthology horror manga *Seeds of Unease* that appears on the cover of the first volume in the series. It is a humanoid monster with the eyes and mouth oddly rotated and rearranged with each other. Either Tomoko's drawing was not clear enough to be recognizable or the reference was too obscure at the time.

PAGE 11

Straw dolls, or *waraningyou*, are usually made from straw and used in a similar manner as voodoo dolls.

PAGE 28

The **bunny-girl guitarist** is a reference to the title character's performance at the school culture festival in *The Melancholy of Haruhi Suzumiya* light novel series by Nagaru Tanigawa.

PAGE 29

KEI-ON! is a reference to the popular slice-of-life manga and anime series *K-On!* Tomoko is imagining herself not quite fitting in with the rest, like the younger character Azusa (though for the opposite reason as Azusa...).

PAGE 33

The store where Tomoko buys her costume is **Don Qui-ohte**, another reference to the actual Don Quijote chain of discount stores.

PAGE 37

Yakisoba is a popular Japanese dish of noodles, pork, cabbage, and other vegetables stir-fried together with a sweet Worcestershire-style sauce. Despite the name, the noodles are generally regular wheat noodles instead of buckwheat (*soba*).

PAGE 37

Mochi is a soft rice cake, traditionally made by pounding glutinous rice to form a sticky paste that can be molded into shapes.

PAGE 38

The **"Class 7, Chocolate Bananas"** sign is a pun. One way to pronounce the number seven in Japanese is *nana*, so "BA7" can be read as "banana."

PAGE 39

Takoyaki is a popular Japanese dish made from pieces of octopus (*tako*) in a savory batter that are cooked in a special pan so they form small balls similar in size to donut holes.

PAGE 39

Yok●do is a reference to the popular Japanese general merchandise chain Ito-Yokado. It is in the same umbrella company as 7Eleven and sells groceries and clothing, similar to a Target or Walmart in the United States.

PAGE 49

You may recognize **Masa Shiba** as the likely pen name of Hatsushiba (a.k.a., Fatty) from Chapter 9 of Volume 1. The character even has his trademark generic girl face!

PAGE 55

Pur●kura refers to *purikura*, photo booths that make photo stickers, or the stickers themselves, which are extremely popular among young people in Japan and other Asian countries. The term is a shortened version of Purinto Kurabu ("Print Club"), the trademarked name for a brand of Japanese photo sticker booths that first came out in 1995.

PAGE 56

The real life equivalents of the **Soft Milky Face** machine are Funwari ("Soft") Milk Face and MiLK Beauty, a line of *purikura* machines that allow users to modify their photos with a variety of appearance adjustments and touch-ups.

TRANSLATION NOTES 2

PAGE 57

Tomoko is reading the July 2012 issue of *Dengeki Girl's Style*, a magazine aimed at fans of otome games.

PAGE 60

"Tee-hee! Silly me!" is a cute gesture of smiling with the tongue licking over the upper lip that is usually accompanied by a wink and meant to placate someone for having irritated them or for laughing away a mistake.

PAGE 61

The last step of making a *purikura* photo are the **fun touches**—drawing decorative pictures and words on the photo using a stylus and touch screen before printing it out. Tomoko is tired and skips that step entirely, so only the default decorations show up on hers.

PAGE 64

The **calendar labels** indicating a "Very Unlucky" day read *butsumetsu* in the original, which literally means "Buddha's Death." *Senpu*, the original label for "Maybe Bad," indicates a day that is unlucky in the morning but lucky in the afternoon, when it is best to avoid disputes or rash decisions.

PAGE 64

Kanto is the region of Japan comprising Tokyo and the immediate surrounding prefectures.

PAGE 70

In the original, **virgin for life** is written *doutei*, which can mean "Catholic nun" or "male virgin" but is here used as a more extreme word for "virgin."

PAGE 93

A **naginata** is a pole-weapon version of the Japanese sword. It was originally a staff with a long, curved sword blade on the end that was widely used in battle. However, after the introduction of firearms, it became a weapon used primarily by women, and in Japan it is still considered a martial arts weapon for girls and women with which to learn discipline and etiquette. The curve at the end can be used to hook an opponent, as the girl on the train unwittingly does to Tomoko.

PAGE 99

Kuroki's Basketball is a reference to the popular sports manga and anime series *Kuroko's Basketball*, in which protagonist Kuroko aids his team by using his tendency to be overlooked as a weapon on the basketball court.

PAGE 103

"Stay by your side" is a reference to a key scene in the visual novel and anime series *Angel Beats!*, although there it's a boy named Hinata saying it to a girl named Yui.

PAGE 108

Not only is the box and logo design mimicking that of Amazon.co.jp, but the *konozama* of **konozama.co.jp**, which means "Curse you!", is also used as Internet slang for ordering something from Amazon and having it get delayed long past the promised delivery date or never delivered at all.

PAGE 108

Sag●wa Express is a reference to the actual Japanese package delivery company Sagawa.

PAGE 118

Both **S●S Brigade** and **Ne●ghbors Club** are references to nontraditional clubs from Japanese light novel series—the SOS Brigade from *The Melancholy of Haruhi Suzumiya* and the Neighbors Club from *Haganai: I Don't Have Many Friends* (*Boku wa Tomodachi ga Sukunai*) by Yomi Hirasaka.

PAGE 118

Kazeh●ya-kun is a reference to Shouta Kazehaya, the popular boy who befriends the shy heroine Sawako in the popular *shoujo* manga series *Kimi ni Todoke: From Me to You* by Karuho Shiina.

PAGE 119

Dokra Mokra is a reference to *Dogra Magra*, a 1935 avant-garde science fiction novel by Yumeno Kyuusaku.

PAGE 121

"Find" Your "Want to Be!" is a paraphrase of the title of a popular Japanese career guide for students.

PAGE 123

The **Victim's Pain** poster is a slightly altered version of the 2010 poster for Victims of Crime Week.

PAGE 129

The **weird little man** in the video Tomoko is watching is Ao Oni ("Blue Demon"), the villain of a Japanese RPG-style puzzle game of the same name. A series of videos where two guys play the game (badly) became very popular on NicoNico Douga.

NO MATTER HOW I LOOK AT IT, IT'S YOU GUYS' FAULT I'M NOT POPULAR! ③

NICO TANIGAWA

Translation/Adaptation: Krista Shipley, Karie Shipley
Lettering: Lys Blakeslee

WATASHI GA MOTENAI NOWA DOU KANGAETEMO OMAERA GA WARUI! Volume 3 © 2012 Nico Tanigawa / SQUARE ENIX CO., LTD. First published in Japan in 2012 by SQUARE ENIX CO., LTD. English translation rights arranged with SQUARE ENIX CO., LTD. and Hachette Book Group through Tuttle-Mori Agency, Inc.

Translation © 2014 by SQUARE ENIX CO., LTD.

Yen Press
Hachette Book Group
237 Park Avenue, New York, NY 10017

www.HachetteBookGroup.com
www.YenPress.com

Yen Press is an imprint of Hachette Book Group, Inc. The Yen Press name and logo are trademarks of Hachette Book Group, Inc.

First Yen Press Edition: April 2014

ISBN: 978-0-316-32205-8

10 9 8 7 6 5 4 3 2 1

BVG

Printed in the United States of America